THE QUATTRO CENTO

FLORENCE AND VERONA

D1264093

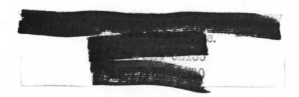

THE QUATTRO CENTO

A DIFFERENT CONCEPTION OF
THE ITALIAN RENAISSANCE

FLORENCE AND VERONA

AN ESSAY IN
ITALIAN FIFTEENTH-CENTURY
ARCHITECTURE AND SCULPTURE

ADRIAN STOKES

SCHOCKEN BOOKS · NEW YORK

First published in Great Britain in 1932

First SCHOCKEN edition 1968

Library of Congress Catalog Card No. 68-28902

Manufactured in the United States of America

TO
THE KNOWING LOVERS OF ART
IN ANY DISPUTE
WITH STILL MORE KNOWING HATERS OF ART
THIS BOOK IS DEDICATED

CONTENTS

PART I: THE ITALIAN SCENE

INTRODUCTORY NOTES TO *FLORENCE AND VERONA*

PART II: FLORENCE AND VERONA

vii

ILLUSTRATIONS

ix

xi

xiii

PART I

THE ITALIAN SCENE

INTRODUCTORY NOTES TO
FLORENCE AND VERONA

I. JESI

No sign of Frederick Hohenstaufen in the railway station at least. They say that his mother was delivered of him in the piazza San Giorgio, afterward named the piazza Federico. Jesi, to-day called the city of silk because there are silk factories outside the walled town, a city upon a hill with walls pushed half-way down the slope. A light afternoon rain has been prepared, falls upon the road from the station. Here, then, the town above the road that fumes into hovel doors. Before the gate there is a bridge over water that rushes to turn a mill. Inside the gate climbs old Jesi. At the moment three children under the age of six descend the steep cobbles under great eaves and long, shuttered buildings. Neither rain nor sunshine disturbs a corpse. But wait a minute! A siren yelling at the silk factories rattles every rickety shutter. Ruins are kindly; they have no shutters. They whisper through baked, uncovered lips. These buildings abound with an evil life. They are not ruins. Beneath the dust on this tin plate are the arms of Savoy. Somewhere at the back of this palazzo white-gloved, dirty-necked carabinieri are crowding in a guard-room, while somewhere on the other side of the street, a hopeless nib guided by a dry-of-mouth scrapes on sheaves of papers. Every room was long ago white-washed. Nothing ghostly about such palaces and buildings. Their floors lie too long and straight and empty down the street, much of their dirt is recent, their smell is borrowed from the roadway. Even a monastery here lives from outside, never replete, without a glow. Great *cancelli* close upon empty cellars, empty, perhaps, but for a basket of hay that seems to float above the gigantic floor, loosened from an overflow of wisps upon the tiles. Yet they live, these buildings, they serve a purpose not modern nor yet an ancient purpose as does the cathedral campanile. Forbidden to grow venerable, they sleep. Not the sleep that breaks with the light. They do not sleep in the dark. Theirs is the light but well-corded slumber of the afternoon. Without recess they are living from the outside, drawing in great breaths of air specked with noise, sound of a cough muffled by a bell, of a boy's scramble shot with the hoof of a standing cart-horse out upon the cobbles of the piazza; noises that give themselves upon the few loiterers who were not seen to move up and will not be seen to move away, noises woven into a dream of basket-firm somnolence.

Better be a beggar here than a loiterer; the beggar can position himself at dawn, watch the changing light, outsit the afternoon. But in a world already made horizontal by rain, the loiterer is put under the spell of this long, shallow sleep. Less evil in the end, if more frightening, is the life of Rococo palace and church in the south which a few basket balconies, each curved rusty railing an old rip, now suggest. Nothing dreary about the murderous southern life, a different existence of which Jesi also partakes, then, by right of balcony. With beautiful lines as if traced in a spill of cream by a jocular artist, with lines that cause to mount and curve a lipper of stucco, with awry masks and prehensile balconies, loops and twirls of iron and coloured paste, the Sette Cento nobles built their palaces in the pandemonium of southern cities. In its own day, too, the eighteenth century of the small towns must have been frightening, as are the bright-coloured Sicilian sweetmeats, harder than the cohorts of the sun, and the sugar Easter-lambs, nimble as a Sicilian landscape, creation of the people's carnival, tasting of bullock's blood. Heavily disguised, Punchinello travelled far north. Portentous England was most successfully deceived. Dickensian England is related to the grinning

4

Neapolitan slums. Hypocrisy and larded tarts, hot negus, great fires and coaches, are good disguise. But are not the courtyards of all the inns a-jingle, like the sun spangles on a southern balcony? Do not toby caps appear at upper windows and bob and mock, their bobbets then tossed between the curtains of the heavy beds, reprobate like the Rococo grotesques, old men with evil faces swollen with toothache? And what of the ferns, the cracked frames askew, the pots, those dusty aquariums and blood-red gold-fish, those thousand bird-cages, hopping canaries scattering bird-seed—how like the crowded, crazy balconies hanging with fern and damp linen, quaking with the quick, rickety children playing with flies in the flotsam spray! There is the same flitting bat-like quality about Victorian bric-a-brac and about the smirking coffin so dear to that age, the same terrible noon-day eruptive *jingle*, though one be beautiful, supremely beautiful, the other ugly, the same jingle as is to be heard in the mirror room at Bagheria. Less awful by far is the nocturnal restlessness of the ghost, a more natural noise the one that is given by the bell cap of the medieval fool. Something evil can come to birth and swarm in sunlight, garrulous sores that have power to inform the glumness and heavy comfort of the north, making even the cold sky chatter with a profusion of glass and fern, wax likeness and canary seed.

The *lazzaroni*, mouthing sly catches of the wicked macaroni song, took easy possession of these southern palaces. Perhaps these buildings are judged entirely by their new life. But probably the whiteness of the stucco was always a lazzar whiteness, the delicate lines of the stairways never averse to the slither of rats. The small churches have an even more terrible vitality. In Sicilian Ragusa, the stunted and multiple domes, red like *pizza*, sprouting with a green scum, elbow their way into the alleys, squat among the teeming houses, stifle the air, hasten on the charnel smoke, just as the dwarf immensities of Hindoo temples make loud and durable recesses of the bazaar. Here as in the East, the crooked street, as it approaches a religious edifice, bursts into brighter colours, becomes crowded with the pick of beggars and those diseased, leads on to a building that has relinquished its ancestry and throbs with an epochless, evil life in turn distributed to the neighbourhood. Here is a vitality that can beat the railway though the station be near. That is the attraction of the South. A volcano is always beautiful, and always fun if care be exercised. It is clever to borrow from the strength of a volcano; everything here is volcanic. The restlessness of the Rococo ornament is an hundred times augmented by the volcanic nature of the dirt that lies about and in the church. One feels the explosion, sees the explosion in the played-out washing that hangs between the houses. The lit candles in the churches are a million fuses, the wealth of rolling twisted pillars, the priceless marbles, inexhaustible loads of powder.

Yet the life of the convulsive noon-day is less harmful than depression diffused by the afternoon towns of north Italy, by the casermas of Pisa, the hotels of Vicenza, the arcades of Cesena, the perpetual road-mending of Florence and Modena. And the beauty of good Rococo is obvious. But one should pass through southern Italy quickly. Not that Rococo buildings do not wear. Why does one complain? Perhaps beauty ought to reassure. What of this Quattro Cento palace that one has come to see at Jesi? Will it wake the town, or will it capitulate to a time of the day as does Vicenza to the afternoon, Palermo to noon, Catania, Lima and Barcelona to the evening hum broad with cisterns of shadow, cities that carry their parks as caparisoned horses their plumes?

This piazza does not seem helpful. Rain falls on a fountain of imperturbable, spewing lions, like a torrent that pours off a good mackintosh, leaving the stuff wet, but no wetter than before. The fountain faces an enormous theatre. Pergolesi, as well as Frederick Hohenstaufen, was born in Jesi. What courage to build that theatre now, but even greater courage to open it and stage a soirée at Jesi! Sitting in the café del teatro—benches and wine of the country—one gets a good

Jesi: Francesco di Giorgio (*The door is later*): *Palazzo del Commune*

PLATE I. A QUATTRO CENTO MUNICIPAL BUILDING

Rimini : School of Francesco di Giorgio : *Window of palazzo Letimi.*

PLATE II. STONE-BLOSSOM, 'IMMEDIATE, WITHOUT RHYTHM, LIKE THE OPEN FACE OF THE ROSE'

view of the priest's room upon the topmost floor of the opposite building. He has the keys to the library and to the gallery with the Lorenzo Lotto pictures. Should one ring the bell, certainly a woman will lean out of a high window and in answer to the question whether the priest is at home, will say, either that he sleeps, or that he is in the church, or at the café, or out eating, or that he has been dead these three months, the *poveretto.* . . . .

So this is the building one has come to see, this square brick edifice that is in bloom. For the decrepit brick has given birth to straight stone window-frames beaded as with the pips of young fruit (*Plate I*). Wood litters the broken-down courtyard within. The stone arches are filled up. How stone hates wood, even this afflicted stone remembers that. Afflicted? No. The miracle begins to catch the heart, the miracle of Aaron's blossoming rod. That was a Quattro Cento effect, just as Moses' miracle of the splashing water from the mountain side is Baroque. But Aaron's rod is the greater wonder.

And now the East and North recede. Here is the southern effect scattering time and memories. For it is immediate, without rhythm, like the open face of the rose (*Plates II and III*).

I write of the South in contrast to North and East thus brought together; not the South of the eruptive noon-day which has relation to North and East, but the South in which life is outward, spread in space.

This southern stone is neither barren nor volcanic, but the repository for humanistic fantasies, particularly those symbolizing southern compulsion to throw life outward, to objectify. In the great period of the fifteenth century, Renaissance sculptors made stone to bloom.

Such effect in relation to stone, and other effects that will gradually reveal themselves, are referred to in this book by the symbol 'Quattro Cento', actually as one word the Italian chronological expression for fifteenth century. *I will not use it at all in this its proper sense.* The special content with which I am concerned, though neglected by writers on the period,

7

permeates the spirit and the art of the fifteenth century. But I call 'Quattro Cento' only the direct and manifest expression of this content.

And I hope in the end that my use of the term will become an idea inevitably associated with the naming of those hundred years.

I write of stone. Few Northerners and few Orientals love stone: to the majority it is a symbol of barrenness. London streets would be unbearable except for movement and noise and night. Is it not horrid, so much stone standing there in the two minutes' silence; and can you think of the endless pavements without the feet upon them? Yet stone inspired the development of the visual arts, that is the southern arts, so far as 'visual' refers to arts concerned with spatial, rather than with rhythmic or temporal, values. I want to show the highest effect of mass as unrelated to suggestions of rhythm or movement, as a supreme achievement, the only mirror of human aim. I exhibit stones the opposite of barren.

But I need to introduce you gradually to southern stone. The easiest images will at first be those Venice can inspire. There, even a Northerner must observe stone; for it is omnipresent. And he can bear this omnipresence because water, though silent, courses irresistibly, stemming for a time images of death that so much stone might shower on desperate lovers of green fields. Yet since the water runs slow, stone stands among it with the minimum of distraction, between water and sky. It is rare to see a stone building rise compact and white from soil: how much more solid when grown from water that bears a gondola brushing its hollowness against the lowest moulding.

II. VENICE

S o youth and Death are sharp in the Italy of which I write. Italian animalism, rasping unreserve, must grate sometimes on Northerners. There's no general escape, general shade, no perpetual autumn, nor the perpetual half-life-half-death miasma of the East. Life is stark, facile. Art, life and death must be close together; nowhere are they closer than in Venice. Death in the canals. But there must be no embrace of death, no retirement to green shades or sacred river where men are sobered by their guilt. Death must remain frightening right in the midst of life, not absorbed completely into life. Then the people will be poor and they will be dishonest and they will be artists. For they are not sobered. They will be beautiful in their youth. When death is mitigated, so too is life. When the desire for life wanes, so too does desire for death, as in the old who cling to life.

These things you may learn in Venice, stones mounted up on the sea. Venice is a creation of the Quattro Cento, as I will show in my third volume.

When with a rap, a groan of wood and a clatter, shutters are thrown wide (try the campo San Polo after a hot day at evening), unavoidably one looks up. For in such appearance at a window, in this heralded apparition, the heart recognizes its oldest wish for the dawn, the new day, the new unimagined sun at arching rise. And should the figure that appears after the flung-out shutters, appears from the gloom into the white-

9

specked even light, be old, then to this curious emotion of the dawn is added a thought of dying suns, the light to which we live and by which we die.

Pre-eminently symbols of birth are the distinct windows and doors of Italy. And when the chill frightens you, the stoniness of Venice where black against the very teeth of rats is the water at night, where only garbage dulls the echo of feet on those terra firmas or filled-in canals to which no sun can penetrate, so that they seem frozen dirt —remember that from similar hard stones Giorgione figured forth the rich softness of Venetian painting, from colours of these geologies drew out suffusion, that warmth of blue distance, of the earth without its many impurities, steeled by memorable summers.

With some days of sirocco Venice is a sea-monster on whose glassy tongue you are scaled. Now this, now that campanile is a sharp decaying tooth, minatory, while the oily sirens of ships are noises in the head of the monster who has caught you, rousing your envy of fish that squirm from between claws to depths of basalt rock.

But at twilight things lie horizontal among the bell-peals. Nothing mounts. So churches have their sway over the toppling water. Everything rests on the bobbing water, rests at ease or firm. The very smell of the boats which fought with whiffs from the *calli*, now are fresh out there on the lagoon, released ; while the churches float firm like swans, the water risen to its greatest fluidity in these motions of spread and relaxation.

People walk or glide in boats, ever passing junctures of stone. But should you fall there's no secrecy available. The sick must be carried through a holiday crowd to the hospital, on a stretcher. There are not four wheels in the whole of Venice. Anyone who is moved here on land recumbent ... one knows that a sick person comes from the swooping of the pedestrians about,a silence and a current of air that lifts the tail of a pigeon escaping between the marbles. You cannot fall by the kerb. There is no kerb. The piazza will serve up a stricken body as

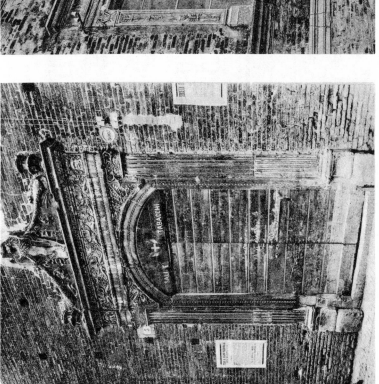

1. *Jesi*: Francesco di Giorgio: *Palazzo del Commune*:
Side-door.

2. *Ancona*: Francesco di Giorgio: *Palazzo degli Anziani*:
Windows.

PLATE III. INCRUSTATION EFFECT AND STONE-BLOSSOM

Siena, San Francesco. Urbano da Cortona : *Monument to Cristoforo Felici.*

PLATE IV. A QUATTRO CENTO SEPULCHRAL MONUMENT

on a plate. You must keep upright in Venice when on the move and not on the water, otherwise all the bipeds from the nearer tall stones and porticoes will be on you, released from chatter around the columns. Prisoners are moved at night so as not to excite the day. Nothing can be sunk here except in water, and then abysmally. One realizes, almost with horror, the impossibility of the earth opening to swallow you up. There is no earth. Beneath the stones more uprights, a forest of piles driven in sand, sodden some of them for a millennium.

Earth tremors we don't fear in Venice, and no doubt on the terrible last day it will be a tidal wave reared up on the shifted sands, come up over the lagoon from the Lido and higher than the Campanile, which will avenge sea's long intricate rebutment by the stone. Then the Ship of State will perish, stone holding down the wood.

The idea of Venice in many parts of Italy was an important element in fifteenth century art, or at any rate in Quattro Cento art as I shall attempt to show. Perhaps I should say in broader terms that the idea of the sea and of the elements in general were constantly expressed in terms of stone on which they have such sculptural effects in a bright climate. One of the secrets of Venice is the bleaching effect that sun and salt air has on exposed Istrian stone, while on unexposed surfaces lichen spreads.[1] Thus light and shade are magnified, every recess is potentially dramatic, each silhouette of statue salty white and black against the sky. The top storey of the Procuratie Nuove looks positively unreal, a stage setting, also the façade of the church which is now a cinema, at the back of San Salvador.

One could write at length of the interaction of the sea and of sea air on marble. For instance, a particular salt wind they have at Pisa causes strange incrustations to appear on the leaning tower. This is a poetic subject in view of the limestone origin of marble.

[1] The absence of soot in Venice and the greater percentage of lime in Istrian stone prevent me from making a parallel with the Portland stone of London.

Sea slaps the rocks of sea-girt Italy. Sands are the exception. Not only because of the wealth of marble nor only in provinces which have belonged to marine powers, does one continually scent the Mediterranean inland. Stoppani in 1874 found marine shells near Como among gravel deposits, thus demonstrating that not so long ago the sea was in contact with Alpine glaciers.

Sculptural incrustation effect, answering process to stone-blossom, reflection of sea-influence and of moon, as the other is of earth and sun, was a Quattro Cento motive. In both cases there is expression of vitality in the stone, of movement. Movement was the preoccupation of the Donatello school of sculptors and of the many Renaissance painters that followed him. Even in the sixteenth century painters loved stone.

Spend a day in Venice with eyes on the ground. It will teach you as well about Titian as about the sculptor Agostino di Duccio. You will note when you finally sink exhausted at Florian's that the second step of the Procuratie Nuove under whose portico you sit, is made of white Istrian alternating with Verona[1] marble . . . or is it reflection of the sunset, so faint are the salmon pink veins, just a glitter, a confused warning, or is it somebody to the right reading the pink *Gazzettino del Sport* which comes out at this hour? The edges of the steps of many bridges are lined with the same stone. For instance the Ponte del Vin. One can just trace the colour; for Verona in long ages tends to lose its calcium and lime, leaving the clay.[2] But here no lime at any rate has been lost. There are a few veins of pink in a moonlight white (this is the context for Agostino di Duccio who worked Verona stone at Rimini to the luminous

[1] There's an Istrian marble mottled and resembling Verona, of which the staircase in the Savoia Hotel at Trieste is made. I am not at all sure that this isn't the stone used so extensively in Venice for paving. A stone mason there tells me not. In any case I will go on using the name Verona to cover such stone.

[2] *Cf.* the panels at the base of the Campanile loggia where the old stone has been used in reconstruction. The seats, on the other hand, are red and polished.

effects of moonlight), while the bridge banisters of Istrian have gone an old ivory yellow. In paving below water this Verona becomes pallid, touched lightly by the moon; but sometimes the water gives back a yellow rusty stain as on steps in the Rio del Canonico.

I hesitate to refer to the colours of the marbles of St. Mark's. They are not so subtle, so consistent. Besides I attribute a specially stimulating power to Verona—examine the seats of this stone inside the vestibule of St. Mark's and also the pavement—because of its colour in which each sunset fire is apparent as well as the rich pinky flesh of succulent fishes, and also because of certain more strictly sculptural properties to which I will refer later. If you have wondered where the rich light comes from in those great barns the Frari and San Zanipolo, know then that it is faintly reflected from the floors, as is most of the light in Italy. The floors are Verona *diamante* alternating with Istrian. The walls of the Doges' palace are made up of an alternation of the same stones. The Verona flanks of the niches on the Porta della Carta attract the eye, so too the Verona bases and cable-ornamentation on San Zanipolo's entrance. For the live colours amid the blackening stone excite one orally. The same stone helps out the much admired Miracoli church. The lower panels on the outside walls have two Verona bars let into each of them in the shape of a cross. This gives the flesh tones, the original incentive to every tonal effect, stimulating our love both of colour suffusion in general and of Venetian colouring in particular.

These effects are not for England, where Verona marble looks ill as seen in the Holborn restaurant bar. In Venice one can transpose to interiors the outside light from which one has come. The light is uniform at evening. After dark the stone is watchful to catch the ensuing day.

An image of living process as an order in space depends entirely upon the medium of clear light which is yet not dazzling. Light and shade are large in Italy. One becomes conscious of light and opposes it to the lights of the northern day whose emphasis is upon the transitory or rhythmic nature of light-effects. The northern air is luminous. In the South the air is clarid and the stone luminous. 'Atmosphere' effect is solid, tonal. Does not marble reflect the light, enforce the tones? Or do you think tonal painting is an art that might have arisen unaided in a northern atmosphere? France belongs equally to South and North. All great French painters have had behind them the abstraction of spatial value which a southern climate induces, though many of them employed it, and employ it, to catch ruthlessly the non-pictorial or rhythmic northern subject and to achieve small, sharp design and to erect a morbid, staccato classicism. Thus they have always increased their power to 'make' pictures, pictures that owing to their discipline are 'better than they look'; that is to say, though mean from the emblematic standpoint,[1] the use of southern handling on the poorly or 'forceful' northern material has 'come off'. Here are pictures full of *relentless* pictorial value. To many of them are preferable those Italian pictures by lesser masters which are not so good as they look; that is to say, one sees at once they are not very good, but one sees also (and so becomes prejudiced in their favour) that they belong to a tradition in which spatial values have been projected without the relentless stress of making pictorial ends meet, without the fuss of classical sumptuous severity or of romantic omnipotence.

And so, should you remain in Venice, the marbles may afford you an image of living process, one that is complete because therein is employed the perfect objectivity that petrifaction or death alone can give. After seeking this and that while your experience along *calli* and of twists of canal and bridge was punctuated by the resounding circus of successive *campi* where full light showered down, you emerge as from the minotaur's labyrinth on to the vast piazza and the pinkish piazzetta that stops the sea and sky. You have emerged into a world

[1] *I.e.*, as symbols of living.

14

of space where the rigmarole you carry from the *calli* is now before you, not behind the eyes but before you, superb, immediate, gathered in white stone. Above is the sky—nowhere vaster than in Venice. But here sky is but the decor, the wide mode of arrangement under which the human process stands revealed. Stone is the greatest instrument of mass-effect, of instant revelation: non-rhythmic, for the flux of life has passed into objective forms.

Stone is solid, extensive and compact, yet reflects light preeminently. The process of living is an externalization, a turning outward into definite form of inner ferment. Hence the mirror to living which art is, hence the significance of art, and especially as the crown to other and preliminary arts, of the truly visual arts in which time is transposed into the forms of space as something instant and revealed. Hence a positive significance to man (as opposed to use) of stone, and of stone-building.

Succeeding to the centuries of spiritual torture and enhancement, Renaissance men discovered the concrete world to be satisfying. It is no longer a desire but a compulsion for them to throw life outwards, to make expression definite on the stone. I call Quattro Cento the art of the fifteenth century which expresses this compulsion without restraint. The highest achievement in architecture was a mass-effect in which every temporal or flux element was transformed into a spatial steadiness. Meanwhile in sculpture, all the fantasies of dynamic emergence, of birth and growth and physical grace had been projected within the stone. The stone is carved to flower, to bear infants, to give the fruit of land and sea. These emerge as a revelation or are encrusted there.[1]

[1] Nearly all Italian 15th-century decoration has this exuberant appearance, as a glance at the illustrations of such a book as Baum's *Baukunst und dekorative Plastik der Frührenaissance* will show. My aim is to distinguish the conventional or stylized modes in the expression of the underlying spirit, unstressed modes used sometimes to indicate even coldness of feeling, from expressions which are newly created or direct embodiments of that spirit. These latter alone I call Quattro Cento works.

At no other time have the materials that artists use been so significant in themselves. The materials were the actual objects of inspiration, the stocks for the deeper fantasies. Quattro Cento art is the one which displays this special attitude to material, but particularly and primarily to stone. Owing to the love of objects in that time, art could express life and individual aim without difficulty. In the following notes I argue that so direct an emblematic art could develop only in a southern climate, in that part of the South where light induces even a Northerner to contemplate things in their positional or spatial aspect, as objects revealed, as symbols of objective realization. The aim of this volume is to isolate that emblematic art both from the art of other periods and also from the contemporary and more famous Renaissance art, generally Florentine, in which ambitions foreign to my subject appear uppermost.

Quattro Cento art is the nucleus of the Renaissance. One can well imagine that at some time or another Italy was bound to achieve a period of art which expresses fully the most positive fantasies connected with stone. That the Renaissance occurred when it did is due to many causes, on the æsthetic side chiefly, I think, to a unique concurrence of developed art-forms amassed through centuries from almost world-wide sources, giving the technique and the wealth of themes that could stimulate for their treatment a general humanistic infusion, and for their finality, a concretion into mass-effect. I shall indicate some of these art-forms gathered from the past. The Renaissance was an intensification of all forms.

The political and economic reasons given to explain the Renaissance are well known. To these I should like to add the Black Death of the fourteenth century, a general disaster which, like the late war, brought to some survivors other values. But in this case death struck out the elder generation. Men rose from their knees. Such plagues do not finally result so much in disbelief as in hedonistic conviction, at any rate in Europe. Life stood opposite death again. And when life is seen opposite death the religious hierarchy falters.

Art is the symbol of all expression, of the turning of subject into object. The powers of artistic creation gained the deepest reverence of Quattro Cento heroes, not as a symbol of culture so much as a symbol of life. This is true of no other period. At that time the aims of life (not cultured life only) and of art were almost identified. All art has close relation to the life it mirrors, but at no other time could the emblematic significance of art be so personal, so individual, so particular. For the act of artistic creation was itself the specific symbol of release that men were feeling or desiring. Quattro Cento art, so to speak, is art twice over.

By 1500 art was no longer so emblematic, emblem of individual vitality. Architecture was æsthetically more comprehensive, better defined, but articulate of less emotion. In this power of emblem, implicit in all art, the Quattro Cento exceeded other styles: or, to put it in another way, the Quattro Cento themes and technique were perfectly adjusted for expressiveness.

Now if one needed to find another word for 'art' it would be 'emblem'. Preoccupation with æsthetic values[1] tends to blind one to this fact. Perhaps it is as well, since our own art lacks emblematic tension. This is no fault of artists. They are bound to reflect our lack of corporate emotion by lifting the structure of their art to a feasible distance. On the other hand I do not claim for the majority of Quattro Cento works the highest æsthetic value, nor even always the highest æsthetic value among works of their own age. I have dragged from obscurity several works confined there by critics. A Quattro Cento masterpiece, however, eludes the traps of æsthetic appraisal. These traps cannot govern emblematic momentum. To-day we cry out for emblem. The æsthetic sense cries out for emblem, an aspect of art that is a proper subject for literature.

[1] By 'æsthetic' values I mean those values in relation to a work of art which can be discussed—at any rate for a time—without referring to the connections of art and its period.

The true emblems of our age appear over-negative to give the complete reassurance we require of art. And so, should they exist, great would be the reassurance afforded to our time by emblems of our civilization so far as we inherit it. These emblems I claim to exist in Quattro Cento art, the emblems of Europe. Only to-day could we contemplate them. For only to-day are we rid of all the pseudo-medievalism which the Renaissance that is known to art-manuals perpetuated at the expense of the Quattro Cento spirit.

III. SOUTH OPPOSED TO
EAST AND NORTH

ATKINSON AND BAGENAL write in their book *Theory and Elements of Architecture*:[1] 'Now in both the Egyptian and Mediterranean cases one result of the bright light and of the excellence of the climate was that men had not only leisure to contemplate . . . but had also forms and colours worth contemplating. Men not only conducted affairs and lived largely out of doors in a physical sense . . . but also thought and mused out of doors. The "artists" and "thinkers" were able to grow old in the open air. They used their eyes and thought a great deal about what they saw, and thus they came to criticize buildings, as much from the outside on account of their shape and ornament as from inside on account of their convenience. This kind of criticism from outside in a manner leisurely yet acute, and the detachment of mind that it produces, suggests the origin of what we now call "the æsthetic attitude".'

And again, in northern climates, 'The hearth becomes the "focus" of the dreams which men substitute in long dark winters for direct sensuous enjoyment. . . . Also the fire upon the hearth—the substitute for the sun in Northern winters—must be visible. . . . But the greatest change is felt by the type of mind we call the "artist". He cannot so easily, in northern countries, contemplate shapes and colours in the open air, paint on

[1] Benn, 1926. In the course of the next few pages I lift several ideas from this book, to the authors of which I hereby make acknowledgment.

walls in the sun, or refine still further the shape of a shrine. Instead, in the intervals between more urgent activities, such as fighting or hunting, he sits in the firelight and carves the handle of a hunting knife or traces an ornament on a pot. Such objects come easily to hand, and on them he can spend his fancy. Thus in hard climates art and ornament tend to be connected directly and frequently with objects of utility. The utensil or the weapon rather than the shrine becomes the characteristic refined object, and the art expended on it has a constant reference to its use or its function. The logic and skill of the maker of beautiful weapons and utensils—the skill of the smith—suggests the origin of what is now termed craftsmanship and the craftsman's attitude to art.'

The southern detachment is more direct, perhaps originally more truly æsthetic,[1] even when hidden beneath a naturalistic style which it can easily govern. As for architecture, in the South the coherence of any stone wall is always worth contemplating. Here is the mass-effect that Mother Earth can never give us; while the apertures of a building are ultimate symbols for humans, being not only apertures, but 'reveals' that vivify the mass. We know that the Egyptians, and according to Penrose, the Greeks, oriented their temples so that a particular sun-ray or star should pierce the inner sanctuary as if it were a womb to be fertilized. (In the Quattro Cento the stone bears her sons.) The Egyptians personalized not only the complete building but each aperture and member. The effect they wanted of stone building was monolithic; joints were reduced to a minimum. But this was an imitation of mud construction, and one feels their use of stone was guided almost solely by its durability; they believed in 'salvation by masonry'. So they shut the dead in a stone womb with thousands of years in which to attain new birth.

[1] This detachment, though, since it is so facile, is very limited and has often led its devotees into most unæsthetic courses the remedy for which, as I shall show, is an introduction from North or East of a more circumscribed æsthetic.

The Greeks are largely explained by their marble. They understood how it stands clear, a surface, unlike wood or mud, with little absorption, a solid outwardness, then; and in this its character there lies the key to all humanism. Indeed, there exists a parallel between the Greek and Quattro Cento position.

As a rule the Greeks used plaster on their stone to obtain a smoother, more homogeneous and more reflecting surface. But the unique Pentelic marble of Athens could be made to show a surface brighter and more homogeneous than Poros or other stone treated with plaster. Thus the beauty of the Parthenon.[1] The courses are laid dry, and so finely ground are the joints that some of the stones have actually grown together. This does not suggest a relation to Egyptian mud design in stone because the Attic builders worked pre-eminently to magnify the tones of light reflected upward.

So great is the proportion of light reflected from the ground in the South that it is not uncommon to see the shadow above, and not below, a string-course. Now in the North, most of the light is shed vertically. Walls, soffits and undersides have no longer the same significance. Thus æsthetic as well as climatic necessities mean expenditure on roof. Gone is the wall-bulwark, posited and informed. Instead the roof as a spread bat, stuck in masonry and unable to fly off. Instead of apertures as distinct symbols agleam, myopic eyes and their flamboyant, minatory lenses, the dormer windows of France.

This perpetual 'looking-out' stimulates sense of guilt in the beholder. Sometimes the Gothic cathedral is a ship moored to a reedy bank. But northern Gothic is occasionally defiant of mass-effect, of all that stone means. Wherever possible a surface is pierced, originally for light. At worst the Gothic cathedral is a ship moored in dry dock. For it is only just balanced. That is the effect as well as the actuality where the weight of pinnacles alone secure the buttresses. In these cases, as in all

[1] Possibly, when new, the Pentelic marble was too bright and for this reason, contrary to the usual one, was toned with plaster.

Gothic altogether, there is bound to be an effect of sitting up and staring, a mean betwixt the desired effect of pinnacles soaring away upwards and the constructional fact that their weight in its downward thrust secures a dangerous balance. Though not disposed to advocate that a building should express the truth of its construction, I find disturbing so vertical a contrariety.

'Sitting up and staring' suggests the strange figures that recline on elbows above Etruscan tombs. For Florentine Gothic has a similar quality, whereas fifteenth century Gothic in other parts of Italy is often the vehicle of mass-effect freed from the northern necessity to pierce and probe and fret for light. Often what I call Quattro Cento is transparently Gothic; Gothic powers in treatment of emblem lavished on the nature of the stone. A wind-swept Gothic exuberance that forges intricate the corselets of the fierce German aristocrats, that hoods simply, classically, the eagles of the Apennines in sculpture, yet revels in the pleasant South; such Italian Gothic of the elephantine foliage and disky bosses inspired Quattro Cento carving.

As well as possible Etruscan affinities, the Florentines showed northern traits. Their masons were the best craftsmen in Italy. Except for some of their great sculptors whose masterpieces led the Quattro Cento ('great' partly because of revolt from their tradition), they were essentially craftsmen, I mean in the sense of a few pages back. They belonged to the North in so far as they were cold with their material for all their unique skill, I might say *because* of their great skill since, for the completely self-contained work of art, a major withdrawal, a slightly inhuman sternness is essential. The artificer whittling an ivory night after night before the hearth becomes a trifle abstracted. The pattern hangs in the void, isolate but for convention. A sobriety, then, borrowed from the complete objectivity of death; economy not of design nor of emotion but of emotional transparency, must be imposed, generally by means of convention.

All art must have Form, a trick of completeness. This sobriety that I mean is a further withdrawal and realizes Form narrowly. Creation is not so fresh though it be better defined. How vulgar to gild the lily when it may be frosted for the generations! Yet in some moods you feel but the narrowness of Chinese painting however varied the examples. It is an old Spanish custom, a way they have in the Highlands. Mode of contemplation is subtle, fixed. Naturally. In northern and eastern climates contemplation is less easy and more searching. The artist rescues beauty. He dilates or abstracts, for he is not incessantly stimulated, except he surround himself with refinement upon refinement. Yet where the light comes up from the ground the year through they needed but a grand order for their beauty.

The greatest regional distinction that can be made in art is between the naturalistic abandon toward which southern art tends to develop (not always to advantage as in the case of some Hellenistic sculpture), and the more conventionalized art proper to the North and the far-East. The abandon, rather than the naturalism, is the point; exuberance, so vastly different from luxuriance in northern and oriental art: not the later virtuoso exuberance of the Baroque but the exuberance that originates solely, as it were, in the stone itself because by its nature it is the only object from which all the primary fantasies connected with light can be made to emerge, all the fantasies, that is, underlying visual art as a whole. For this compact and direct exuberance only found in Quattro Cento work and in the Buddhist and early Hindoo sculpture of India and Khmer (to arrive at the conception Quattro Cento, I needed often to visit the Amaravati sculptures on the staircase of the British Museum), in which beauty is not rescued but discovered, taken together with a contemporary and crowning art[1] that treats the desire to make manifest as a desire fulfilled, I enter a

---

[1] This is a reference to such Quattro Cento artists as Luciano Laurana, Francesco Laurana, Piero della Francesca, Antonio Rizzo and Mauro Coducci.

special plea in this book. For though other art may be infinitely more 'perfect', that is to say, better defined, more 'eternal' in its values, that is to say, with a more withdrawn and therefore better selected objectivity, no other creative power is so tense and direct ; and in so far as all life is an attempt to transform subject into object, an outwardness of a complete not a withdrawn subject, southern art is the mirror of human aim.

A misunderstanding that I must immediately guard against when using such phrases as 'naturalistic abandon' in contrast to 'convention', is that I should seem to infer an absence of 'style' in the Quattro Cento. Actually the Quattro Cento would never have occurred if the inherent love of a grand style which underlies the Italian genius for magnitude[1] had not been excited by Roman studies, by rediscovery of classic forms, by reassertion of æsthetic order. This style is to-day still largely made up of Roman remembrance. Every trumpet note in Italy rings out against the embossed side of an old triumphal car not far drawn out in the close night of Italian time.

The triumphal side of the Renaissance has been written up. But we best catch the sense of it when reading of some festival celebration, probably in honour of Borso d'Este, lord of Ferrara, in which overloaded medieval allegories are manipulated as elements of a *trionfo*, the acclaimed entry of a man into his town. The idea of triumph is not primarily that of success, but, following the Roman model, that of victory over the barbarians. As the fillet about the conquering brow chastens the forehead, cleanses, distributes the hair, and is chastened, so man and his enemies, human and natural, after a conflict in which he has won by noble exertion of intellect and passionate desire, uncover in the event a wealth of sanity and emotional coherence that scatter the delicate agonies of man distraught and incapable.

The people of Italy in the fifteenth century were fully capable. Artisans, craftsmen of all kinds, were busy making trium-

---

[1] As much in evidence to-day as ever. For instance, the new Milan railway station.

phant objects for their free-living despot patrons—free-living because they had loved the near thing, perhaps in the first instance a stone wall.

Now the Quattro Cento was dependent for so general a manifestation on northern, and no less, as we shall see, on oriental exquisite craft, as well as on southern temperament. I have already indicated the importance of the Gothic spirit in the Quattro Cento. The movement is partly that of a northern people discovering the South, the light. At any rate the aristocracy were for the most part German stock whose fiefs had been granted by a German Holy Emperor. Gradually and increasingly old Rome and the Mediterranean had worked on German and Lombard blood and on imported oriental art-forms.

And here an attempted analogy between this Quattro Cento position and the Greek. 'It[1] is important to remember in Homer the special sense of beautiful and elaborate craftsmanship everywhere displayed, and the prominence of the god of the forge, Hephaestos or Vulcan, who is indeed the husband of Aphrodite. Beautiful craftsmanship existed at all times as a background to Greek art. Also in Homer, columns (on the exterior of a building) are mentioned rarely as compared with "high roofs", and a custom that is common to the Northern and many primitive cultures is found in Homer, namely that of covering a building with sheets of metal (*Odyssey VII*, 37, House of Alcinous). But the Dorian Greeks are generally believed to be a Nordic people come south; the impression given by Homer is of a people with a new and youthful relish for light and for brightness. The adjectives "bright", "shining" and "polished" are frequent: the sense of surface brightness is everywhere in the Odyssey and Iliad. The impression conveyed is of a race with a strong culture of its own but sharpened to a relish of surfaces and textures by new and brilliant climatic

[1] Atkinson and Bagenal, *op. cit.*, p. 22. The same analogy could be extended to India where Aryans, still faithful to Iranian pattern, developed the representational intricacies of Buddhist and Hindoo sculpture.

conditions—conditions which in the course of centuries were to modify original forms. The Homeric conception of Olympus, or the dwelling place of the gods, is the conception of a people who take conscious pleasure in light. It is explicitly described in the Odyssey thus :—"Not by winds is it (Olympus) shaken, nor ever wet with rain nor doth the snow come nigh thereto, but most clear air is spread about it cloudless and the white light floats over it" (*Odyssey VI*. Butcher and Lang, p. 93).'

My ignorance precludes my attempt to labour the Indian parallel. Early Indian sculpture in which there appears intensification of every manner, every borrowing as in fifteenth century Italy, resembles the Quattro Cento more than does Greek culture which was occupied with imposition of order. The same Greek *human* standard was also the objective of the Quattro Cento but not so much as a principle of order; since they could not unravel at once the medieval hotch-potch of order and theology. The immediate object of release would be anything solid and material. The stone is carved to express bond-breaking birth. This phrase suggests low relief and arabesques and other sculpture treated pictorially, which are the primary manifestations of the Quattro Cento. But that spirit was later capable of expression in severest architectural design.

However since Quattro Cento, and indeed Italian sculpture as a whole, can with few exceptions be condemned by a purist as 'pictorial'—that is to say, not essentially plastic —I must defend the low relief.

IV. PLASTIC AND MUSIC

I ADMIT THE charge: I admit that even much free-standing sculpture—even the work of Michael Angelo—is conceived from a front view, not, as by a good modern sculptor, wholly in three dimensions. Also I agree that only pseudo-sculptors will attempt the pictorial effect to-day. Because stone to-day cannot have the overwhelming significance that I have described; nothing bursts from the stone demanding perspective or emergent effect. Those of us who are artists rescue, but do not discover, beauty. Plastic conception must be strict in order to satisfy, to endure the modern hubbub. But in view of the attraction to the stone that underlies the whole Renaissance, it is absurd to attach to this sculpture the word 'pictorial' as a pejorative. Of course it is pictorial. Not only love of colour but sense of space derives from the tones of marble building. All the southern arts have this architectural foundation. Sculpture in the Renaissance is an extension of architectural fantasies, but, so far from aping pictorial art, sculpture led it: the sculptors fired the painters, taught them perspective, showed them space.

But when the perspective relief is used to describe a history —and by that I mean an incident that is in no way treated decoratively as, to some extent, it is when the subject reflects a major cultural theme—I cannot on these lines defend pictorial treatment, whether of bronze or stone. For such reliefs (generally crowded and complicate with figures) are in no sense an animation of structure, of architectural material. There is a big distinction from my point of view between Donatello's bronze *Miracle of the Ass* relief at Padua, and his more decorative bronze reliefs (though there be plenty of incident) upon the base of the Judith. The latter are a Quattro Cento expression. So too the reliefs of pagan deities under the guise of planets and the reliefs of the sciences in the Tempio Malatestiano. These articulate the emblematic intent of the building. So do the sculptures on Alfonso's arch at Naples. Again, Madonna reliefs and so on are not highly-organized incident. The distinction I am making is laborious. I might have simplified it into a distinction between carving and modelling, between the use of stone and of bronze, were it not for the fact that the bronze can well convey an emotion primarily imputed to the stone, while, on the other hand, stone can be carved, as it was by Lombard sculptors, to perpetuate a conception not only founded upon the model but inspired by modelling technique. However, it is safe to say that the convenient use of bronze led to an elaboration of pictorial relief beyond what love of stone demanded; and that thereafter, in some instances stone-cutters aped the effects of bronze.

Generally speaking, where the visual inspiration is common to them all, an interchange of forms among the visual arts is natural. But even in the South this ideal condition is apparent only in some Greek and Quattro Cento art. Even southern visual art has otherwise suffered the interpolation of temporal or rhythmic values. While in the North and East the common ground between visual arts has been not of spatial, but of musical, values. No wonder the modern devotee of plastic finds the reflective pauses of Dutch painting as distant from his own art as a symphonic poem. Yet his 'pure' plastic shape, no less than a T'ang piece, is eked out by rhythm.[1] On the other hand Dona-

[1] Such rhythm, of course, is bound to exist in an æsthetic appeal to the tactile sense, which is a 'gradual' or progressive sense. And architecture and painting, as well as sculpture, in fact all visual art, must make *some* appeal to tactile sense. The question is solely one of degree, or, rather, of

tello's Judith or an early Greek statue is an apparition. One's plastic sense is assaulted rather than wheedled for a circuit of exploration. And a Laurana bust, though built in cubes and cylinders, is a concretion rather than something withdrawn, generalized or abstract. It avoids the slow music.

But no truly northern nor eastern architecture, nor sculpture, nor painting, however abstract, is innocent of musical effect. Perhaps this is only another way of saying that these arts show the 'withdrawn', the craftsman's attitude, a withdrawal from the violent light where the visual arts flourished, to a shade nearer death, toward a more delicate, less confused, objectivity; and in such shadow the artist can rhythmically dilate upon chosen limitations, conventional or personal. And if the assault on one's plastic sense is less purely visual than in true southern art, yet it is more thorough, prolonged, and for the majority, more complete. Rhythm has allowed the artist to reinforce his abstractions and so to isolate, except from rhythm, his plastic conception.

A different purist, I put plastic in opposition not to painting but only to music. To my fellow purist, a true Northerner whose art is often ruined by a hopeless longing for the South, I would recommend Japanese *netsuke*, conceived perfectly in three dimensions and of miraculous texture. Let him be content with Chinese and Japanese[1] ceramics. They are the highest achievements of northern-oriental plastic, exhibiting so complete an attention (as distinct from love) to the nature of the material which is exalted always in Chinese ware, that shape and tone and texture fulfil one another and are combined with a function that helps out their continuity—the music

precedence. I consider that in painting and architecture, and even in sculpture, the appeal should be first and primarily to the eye; that is to say, the appeal should be such that the eye, with the assistance of previous tactile experience in materials and textures, would be able largely to synthesize the successive element in the tactile part of the appeal, and cause it to be something immediate as vision itself.

[1] The colour designs, though, of some Japanese pots and porcelain occasionally earn for that people the title of 'Italians of the East'.

so pleasant to 'live with'. And how easily are these joys examined, caressed! If you want something more 'expressive' you must turn to the South or to where the South has more forcibly intruded—it has intruded almost everywhere at some time or another—or to something primeval, or at any rate belonging to a civilization that worshipped light. Allow me the exaggeration since, of course, sculpture or painting will everywhere be more 'expressive' than ceramic utensils. But do you then value 'expressiveness' so highly?

In this barren age it is extremely difficult for us to realize, though we examine the products, of what tremendous degree of affirmation men have been capable. We have some of their most successful work, yes, but little sense as yet of the vast emotional sources upon which Quattro Cento men relied. I attempt to measure their affirmation in terms of what they attributed to stone. The bas-relief needed adjuncts, a pulpit or a panel. It was both dependent upon, and inspired by, a hundred other activities in visual art, which in turn were inspired by the stone.

V. ROMAN ARCHITECTURE AND
THE QUATTRO CENTO

I RETURN TO the fount of my arguments, love of stone. The coincidence that Italy and Greece are richest in marble among the countries of Europe has probably been noted. But consider also the adjacent civilizations. Egypt, herself rich in sandstone, limestone and granite, obtained as well from adjoining territories quantities of alabaster and hard stones such as diorites and porphyries. Byzantium was well served by the Ionian shores and islands and by the island of Proconnesus whose white marble gives the sea of Marmora its name. Here were made those *pulvini* or stone cushions marked with crosses, which were sent out to all parts of Christendom to be put upon and to convert the antique pillars used in construction of nave and apse. We shall see how one night in 1449 Sigismondo Malatesta repatriated pagan stones from San Apollinare in Classe, Ravenna.

The Romans were greedy for marble. It was the more exotically veined African stones which first attracted them. Macedonian Metellus[1] is said to have been the pioneer importer of stone, and not before 50 B.C.[2] was the Carrara used of which the Etruscans had built near-by Luni. Suetonius reveals how by the time of Augustus the raising of precious pillars in rivalry to invest their palace walls with marbles of tearing vein, was the principal passion of the rich. Beside those used in con-

---

[1] *See* Velleius Paterculus, *Hist.* lib. 1, cap. 11.

[2] *I Tesori Sotteranei dell' Italia.* Guglielmo Jervis. Florence, 1889.

struction, pillars just stood bearing no weight in the baths. Marble was admired when neither for building nor statuary but in the block.[1] So great the importation—Lanciani calculated that 450,000 columns alone were landed at Ostia—that the streets were cluttered up with lumbering transport.[2] Cicero affects not to know the names of artists and of their luxuries. But Pliny writes: 'A person of consular rank, who some years ago used to drink out of this cup (a Murrhine cup costing 70,000 sesterces), grew so passionately fond of it as to gnaw its edges even, an injury which only tended to enhance its value.'[3]

When funds dropped or the quarries of the world were obstinate, then composite materials and painting feigned marble sheetings[4] to the walls. No one who has visited Italy, who on his first visit needed to go up to a house to make certain whether that window and shutter and shadow were real or painted, will feel these cheap deceptions forlorn, belief in which is as strong now as in Roman times. Nor vulgar. The feigning is serious.[5] At a small cost the joys from the light of gaiety, tone and proportion can be, and must be, suggested. And this virtuous power of gay deception (all art is a trick) amounting often to deft resolutions to grandeur, a Roman tradition from which pomposity has been dropped with empire, explains that brio of Italian æsthetic which always remains whatever else is lost. And what an inducement to art is such uniform resolution to achieve an effect!

Doubtless in many directions the Romans were vulgar. One

[1] *See* Tibullus, *Epist.* 86.

[2] *See* Tibullus, lib. 3, *Eleg.* 3. In 1870 Baron Visconti discovered the Emporium near the Marmorata, and some docketed foreign blocks.

[3] *See* his natural history. Book 27, chap. 7.

[4] Another Roman process, the technique and intent of which has always survived in Italy, is ornamental stone inlay.

[5] It was therefore easier for them to counterfeit. Dramatic sense underlies all such deception, as in modern Italy.

is inclined to feel for this word when reading that on entry into Attica under the spell of the Greeks, they immediately dug the many highly coloured quarries which the Athenians had ignored.

Romans lacked the particular love for the stone I praise in this book. For them, marble was magnificent, a scenic display, though they gathered from it the warm splendours of tone. Some Roman painting anticipates the Venetian school. Of colour they had the highest sense. Yet their love of the scenic preserved their architecture, not from massiveness in which they were unrivalled, but from adulation of the plain smooth but tense surface (attracter of the deepest fantasies) which, had they loved, their sense of drama would have caused to bloom in Quattro Cento manner and to be encrusted with the life of both sea and shore, with saltiness and dry fertility. Roman chunkiness, however, was not so much emblem of human tensity as a powerful concatenation of rude dramatic landscape. Probably I overemphasize this point. Quattro Cento and other Renaissance arabesques, most Renaissance ornaments, are founded directly on Roman models. The very word 'Renaissance' is meant to indicate rebirth of pagan spirit and classical forms, though it is truer to say that the Renaissance is an intensification of all previous forms. More intimate to my purpose is that I must confess I find in some Roman decoratives a certain feeling for incrustation. A marble altar[1] unearthed at Cales near Volterra reminds me of Federighi's holy water basins in the cathedral at Siena. At any rate the Roman decoratives prompted Quattro Cento incrustation and provided themes.[2] The same is true of stone-blossom. I am not thinking of the swags and foliage of classical ornamentation but of the lovely arabesques on the local marble jambs of the Porta dei Borsari,

[1] See *Bollettino d'Arte*, 1925.

[2] *See* the bases of Federighi's entrance pillars to the San Giovanni chapel in the cathedral at Siena (*Plate XXXVII*, 2). They are in the form of a Roman altar with undisguised Roman decoratives, and so make a better analogy than the stoup to the Cales altar.

Verona. Those swags and foliage, also, were used in the Renaissance, though by Quattro Cento artists to an intensely emblematic effect. And this is the point, this personal emblematic effect; this the meaning of 'Quattro Cento' as I use it.

Thus, the Romans are not to be identified with the tension I would isolate, though their example and their forms were indispensable to Quattro Cento creation. Besides, I have referred to a Gothic element as belonging to that tensity, and under the label 'Gothic' I inferred many emotions that are essentially Christian and medieval. The clash of Pagan and Christian subscribes to that tensity, when Christian is the established and the Pagan is the new as well as the immeasurably old; in part a reversal, then, of the position in the Roman Empire.

But I do not wish to infer that scenic ambitions and the superb Roman sense of drama played no rôle in Quattro Cento æsthetic. Roman virtuosity was always enlarged upon in Italy, especially after its renewal at the Renaissance. But it was only when the Quattro Cento and the later 'Classical' movements had dropped away, that the Renaissance reached its paramount scenic effects in the Baroque. In Quattro Cento work the scenic is subject to the tension I have described. Yet dramatic effect is always evident. It is implicit, for example, in the sudden emergence from relief and arabesque of the Roman-derived winged cupid or putto shaking the marble dust from his eyes.

I have already mentioned Venetian painting, and I should add colour in general as interpretation of form, in relation to Roman painting. But, further, one must include the quality of Italian painting as a whole when contrasted with other European schools: I mean the preference for a dramatic subject and for the immediacy of effect which colour alone can afford. This quality is Roman heritage, a warmth that welcomed renewal from Christian sentiment to effects so fervid that in comparison, true classicism, the Greeks, seem cold.

But about the Quattro Cento there is as well something Greek to which Rome is foreign. The Romans developed a conception of mass far different from the Greek homogeneity of surface. This Roman mass is synonymous with a massiveness that employs rustications and projecting voussoirs. I fancy the Roman scenic conception of mass, as too of drama in general, belongs to their Etruscan heritage. To take an instance from masonry treatment alone, certainly *opus quadratum* is Etruscan in origin. It appears that a tendency to the Baroque had long existed in Italy. This different conception of mass derives from the different love of stone as scenic. Perhaps in the case of the Romans it was reinforced by that remarkable limestone, the rough and tawny travertine from Tivoli. Pozzolana, too, which made the finest cement with an enormous tensile strength, allowed the huge development of concrete arch and vault, of the majestic power in construction we associate with Romans. What proficiency for those without the magic pozzolana to emulate! Romanesque builders managed the Roman vault. And the Renaissance cannot be isolated from many previous centuries of Roman endeavour in Oriental-Christian styles.

Partly, no doubt, because they possessed to hand at Rome the strongest building materials, the Romans were the finest connoisseurs of stone. 'There does not exist a Roman building in which the stones are second-rate. If building stone is wanted in any country in which the Romans have left monuments, it is only necessary to seek out the Roman quarries'.[1]

Though lost to a great extent in engineering, the tradition of that connoisseurship survived in shelter among the precious marbles. There is a connection between the solitary pillars of great worth raised in Roman baths to stupefy, and the thousand tiny columns that cluster famous Byzantine churches within and without. Santa Sophia and St. Mark's are treasure-houses of rare and distant marbles. As such they were the pride of their cities.

But, for the Quattro Cento, though not for the rest of the Renaissance, the more tense mass obtains, that stolid bright-

[1] M. Viollet-le-Duc. *Dictionnaire Raisonné*. Cf. 'Pierre', Vol. IV, p. 126.

ness which stands without scenic emphasis; a new love of stone which, however, would not have arisen if the older Italian love had not survived. Coloured marbles will be used, of course, precious marbles because their worth points to their granular solidity, compactness; but stones of dark tone, stones with tearing, coiling veins will seem almost liquid compared with the distinctness, the large surface, the *nitidezza* of plainer marble. No doubt a comparative poverty made for this result. Luciano Laurana's courtyard at Urbino, which conveys to me more than any other building, effect of mass, is only stone as far as columns, arch and window mouldings and entablature go. The wall-spaces are brick. But never was stone so distinct, flowering, stolid there betwixt untraversable spaces. There is silence, *nitidezza*, a world of space alone.

In the essay itself I shall give reasons for thinking that when Luciano built his courtyard it was not without a definite defiance of the Florentines. The Florentine builders, in so far as they arrived at a conception of mass at all, had adopted the more scenic Roman variety. In the construction of palaces they employed rustication and invented some beautiful channelling. But by adherence to Brunelleschi's running lines that made continuous the members of their planes, they sacrificed the modicum of distinctness the Romans had always preserved.

I shall also give reasons to think that Florentine monumental endeavour which I shall trace back to the outset of the Renaissance, showed even in Ghiberti's time the beginnings of Baroque.

Scenic mass won the day. The Quattro Cento was very soon swamped in the Renaissance, the Renaissance as you find it written up in the hand-books; swamped, that is, in the historical centres, all except Venice. But in humble ways the Quattro Cento has persisted. And if not the emblematic Quattro Cento, then at any rate the Greek conception of mass is about to come into its own again with steel construction. The load is once more of the kind that pressed on the Greek lintel, concentrated; whereas rustication expresses a distributed load.

Rustication is absolutely meaningless in London streets, but screening a steel frame from the weather. The panel rather than the course is the unit of future construction, as Messrs. Atkinson and Bagenal remark.

Some aspects of the Renaissance I refer direct to Etruscan art, and not through the intermediary Roman. In the course of the essay I suggest that a certain kind of plastic was inherent in Tuscany, that, in some manner undefined, its influence remained powerful and was easily brought to consciousness in the Renaissance, the genius of which was the uncovering and consolidation of all that men in those regions had accomplished in art.

It was sufficient for the Florentines to awaken to their landscape. I have mentioned the figures that recline and stare upon Etruscan tombs. There are some aspects of Florentine sculpture and architecture to be detailed, in which I feel this very same steadfastness trimmed and lightened by renascent Christian sentimentality, a steadfastness made sprightly in a cold and calculating manner that I find repulsive. The expression of the Etruscan terra-cotta Apollo from Veii in the Villa Papa Giulio, Rome, will suggest to some the elusive smile that Leonardo exploited. In this statue there is movement expressing a psychological intensity utterly foreign to the Greeks with whom some periods of Etruscan art are too easily identified. Though less hieratic and planted, similar movement was the preoccupation of the Florentine sculptors and painters and of one branch of Quattro Cento sculpture that centres around Florentine Donatello. *Characterization, one feels, however far back one goes, will distinguish the Italic from the Dorian.* The Etruscan use of funeral vases in the shape of human figures favoured the rise from the eighth century B.C. of a vigorously modelled portraiture afterwards in favour at Rome and in the Italian Renaissance. Perhaps the fundamental distinction between Greeks and Etruscans in terms of what is hardly more than a metaphor, is as between carvers and modellers, and perhaps not until the intense Renaissance communing with stone is the race of modellers ready to do justice to the stone, and so infuse it with the psychological postures to which the modeller attends.

If suspense is eliminated from the Etruscan quality of staring, there results a firmness. The best Etruscan sculpture is noted for this compact firmness and ineradicable rootedness. Fifteenth-century Piero della Francesca lived at Borgo San Sepolcro in the Tiber Valley, on the borders of Tuscany and Umbria. His own roots were in the circumambient pasturage. Such Etruscan firmness he exalted into a mathematical religion of space, as did Luciano Laurana who no doubt pondered on Piero's pictures at Urbino. The process of externalization, of movement out of and into the stone, is now complete, and treated by their art as an immovable, exact objectivity. Beside the painter and the architect there are other architects and a school of sculpture which express this Quattro Cento finality imposed on Quattro Cento exuberance.

VI. GENOA

I HAVE WRITTEN that something Quattro Cento persisted in humble ways. I was thinking of Luciano Laurana's courtyard in two materials at Urbino, which called to mind many ordinary modern Italian houses and farmhouses of beautiful proportion. Their doors and windows, unornamented openings except for an articulation of shape by colouring, stand distinct in one colour on a differently coloured wall-surface, very often white on pink. Though some of the tenement buildings are lovely, even cheap construction in the towns is generally more ambitious and marred by inferior actual moulding, though the beautiful tone and proportion remain, the proportion of the block as a whole, of the long narrow windows and of their intervals. Still more ambitious construction, of course, will emulate the Baroque or Roman variety of mass. Yet the other tradition is strong, particularly in the clear and mathematic design of factories.

Stuccoing of all surfaces (the Romans nearly always plastered brick as well as tufa) and the picking out by one colour contrasting with the wall-surface, of apertures and other features should there be any, is, no doubt, a very ancient Mediterranean cliché. But especially strong in Italy. And Luciano at Urbino exalted that cliché to reveal his conception of mass as final objectivity. The windows of the courtyard in white stone are thin on the brick, absolutely distinct (*Plates XXXIII and XXXIV*).

How distinct, too, are the white frames of many modern villas, windows flush with the darker wall, how distinct they stand holding a deeper darkness, or shuttered with green that later will be thrown apart so that the inner cool and black may pass out to swell the night! How separate and easy those passages like sculptured nostrils that breathe in and out unsensitized!

If you can overlook the detail, the proportions and wall-surfaces of the high tenements in the North Italian towns are even more exciting. How beautiful the approaches to Milan by train, the enormous spaces with the taut rectangular tenements, their whiteness specked with the earth of the lumbering plains; how beautiful for such mood is the engine water-tower just outside the station. (Compare this shape with similar erections in France.) In modern Italy they use concrete to the homogeneous effect; and the light will give tone. The Fascist station has, of course, a Roman imperial aim. But if you are going on to Venice, look out of the window at the Lombard store-houses with their brick and tile grilles which the country Romans used. And the farm-houses with the unornamented noble arch that pierces a white wall for entrance to the courtyard. The light beats up from the ground on to the under-side of the arch, so that you feel the entry and the exit. No wonder whatever else goes in Italy, proportion, spaciousness and facile virtuoso power survive. Space, spaciousness are themselves keenly dramatic. The spaces outside the stations of even small towns have all the roominess of the architect's plan, keen space that in England, no matter what the architect intended or what his design shows, cannot be realized.

When you understand the Laurana and the Roman mass and how they mingle in Italy, you have made the approach to Italian genius. And since the traveller's first visit to that country is often a stay on the Riviera, I will indicate what fantasies Genoa herself, rather than her sights, may arouse. From the continuous noises of Genoa I can make another bridge to the South for the northern mind.

Up a pediment, up the red stucco slope I see a white dove strutting, and just beneath that inclined eave, over the harsh confusion of palaces, over clear and raucous harbours, black in the window two off-duty carabinieri swing locked in play.

The dove moves slowly up the long slope, easily through an air riddled with noises none of them composite. The air patched up in a moment is torn again by a pure sound. So buildings on different levels stand firm to inhabit the blue. No rococo fancy can live among these pure reports from steamer and electric train, parched as the cries of peacocks. Sunlight adamant, without garrulity, cleans the livid and dusty stone dry and fine like the dust cloud from the collapse of a house, each particle stinging the face: so that a heavy Baroque remain, the Porta Pila, isolated amid the weary new roads and the ponds of railway network, suggests the settling of overthrown houses and the material for new construction.

Horizontal movement thunders minute in the immense spaces about Brignoli where the new commercial house-blocks, terrace upon terrace of them, tip up the sky. Or else some dwarf wrinkled bit of Baroque holds up the traffic and menaces the latest lithe and russet stuccos. The Doria gardens, once of many degrees, now possess but the lowest level, the higher taken up by the Miramare Hotel. But behind the hotel, looking into fifth-floor bedrooms, is the gigantic statue of the Doria admiral as Neptune.

Dry, distinct, but incessant and distraught like the streaming of red hair, the hair of a mad and desiccated Elisabeth—such the general effect. But the rigidness of noise between tall buildings sustains you. Later, in other parts of Italy, you must learn to recognize the instantaneous concert pitch without the aid of noise. Genoa, though, is your best introduction to space, to the distant brought near. The very vacuity of the russet blocks in sunlight allows you, brought swift to your surface by peacock noise, to confront the city with what imagining you choose.

Extraordinary distinctness, the exciting soberness of sheer

drops from level to level, easy apprehension of the crowning, circumventing mountains, near, it seems, above the last range of houses; the lofty viaduct, say, Ponte di Carignano, that strides over tenements, others creeping thin up its sides to overlook the track, bare tenuous brick instead of ivy, or lower roofs rubbing an apex against the key-stone of an arch,—invite imagination to figure forth out of this crude space, especially a Roman sky-line, heaven populated with statuary, columnar sky-scrapers and their toga-ed figures contemplating the harsh cascade of baths and villas, marble parliaments and rose terraces, forum and temple, down to the dappled bay.

In Genova la Superba the images do not teem as at Naples, also a city of different levels upon the harbour. Rubbish is clean in upper Genoa, man makes his own earthquake as the broad electric trains thunder over the house-tops or crash into the wide embrace of white panicky tunnels; or as the trams of the via Garibaldi which push you into a Baroque orange court-yard fumigated with petrol from the street, make rattle against the stone hollow, without give, until after their passage crumbling yet immaculate specks of dust record the detonation like unrepentant tears their evocative.

And lest the reader should feel that I introduce some image of New York with so much insistence on height over horizontal movement, let me quickly add that the buildings are rectangular, rising to no peak but shouldering the sky, windows long and distributed on the side of the mountain—let me quickly add that the noise, the restlessness of Genoa are ancient as its Gothic tone, its hard finery; that the modern blocks are built previous to the streets which they determine, that they are looming with space between, themselves in conformation with the curves and steepness of the slopes, each building of municipal regulation height, seven storeys, so that this measure is seen a-jostle at all angles, blocks remarkable for their equality in perspective carried to great distance in the clear light, and for the dramatic spaces between them which dusk snatches tremulous, night forgotten but for its breeze that lifted the dark foliage of orange trees at basement and roof and public arbour—it must be quickly added that dusty Genoa is smokeless, gleaming, broken by country walls and scaleable piazze upon each of which sounds a different gong of peacock noise, that palms watered with sirocco spread over embankments upon railroads arid of smoke, shadow and light interminable as the trains run smoothly under and over the houses, so many rivulets of steel as to make their pond at Principe beneath the old lighthouse which searches the early morning trams, beneath the further Miramare, beneath again the Doria giant at the back, from the station platform seen above, naked in the cameo of his grotto, should you be able to arrest your eyes at the middle distance.

One image of Genoa is not at all arbitary. I have hinted that Italian reference to the sea is not direct but yet more profound than in northern countries, as if unconscious. Proud Genoa, historic emblem as much as Venice of sea-power in Italy, herself is the pattern of a vessel. I do not intend anything so farfetched as the shape of the town seen from an aeroplane. I am thinking of the old city by the harbour, gloomy, narrow, loaded and guttered like the hold of a ship; then the emergence into space about the main thoroughfares, and then above, reduplications of levels like poops and superstructure over the deck, and above, the long line of tall tenements which catch all the staccato noises like wireless upon the masts, washing and telegraph wires making the strands. Thus Genoa's pride is expressed by turmoil. Like a ship she is now hollow, now replete, constitutionally prepared for patching and mending and for the raucous vibration of engines. A ship has stateliness to its very bowels; distraught red hair was but the wind whistling past. Like a sailor to the rigging you will take to the pleasures of the house-tops and the different levels. You stumble over refuse, you have disappeared up alleys of towering painted walls that float in the gloom, to emerge on an open place of bright stucco, beggars and churches in the sun, light in which things stand. . . .

VII. REPRESENTATIONAL
AND NON-REPRESENTATIONAL ART

THE RENAISSANCE was an intensification of all known art-forms. From the preceding pages it might appear that that material was entirely western; which is far from being the case. And now that I have roughly indicated the manner of Italian genius, I can proceed to suggest with less fear of being identified with those who find the roots of the Renaissance in Byzantine or Mohammedan or even far-Eastern culture, the diverse heritage of linear treatment that the Quattro Cento concreted into mass-effects.

I am aware, then, that throughout the early Christian and medieval period, Italy was inundated with successive waves of oriental forms in art as in life from Syrian, Sassanian, Coptic, Byzantine and Islamic cultures. I am aware that near-Eastern workmen created the later Roman art. I am aware that all European art-forms have come to the West from the East except for what the Classical Greeks created out of their Semitic heritage and spread into the eastern world through Hellenistic art. Even that art, to express the authoritative psychology of Empire, be it Sassanian or Roman (*vide* Trajan's column with its Assyrian-like bands of commemorative procession), or to express the authority of a spiritual idea as that of Christ ruler of the world, tended to go back on its development and reveal at the touch of contemporary Semitism, the stylization or expression by symbol from which Hellenic naturalism had grown. For representation must be less objective, less realistic, more patently a symbol, to express a solely spiritual content or the forces of Nature in general or any generalized authority. The symbol or emblem must be formal, abstracted, lifted away from the particular and the individual, in short, an emblem less objective than in Quattro Cento art for instance. In the case of Semitic and, indeed, of most art, creation and re-creation of conventionalized but living symbol, *is* the creation of art. This is safe-guarded art, a safe and confined projection of symbol. Whereas for Quattro Cento art the process is reversed. The creative act itself, the turning of subject into concrete and particular and individual form, *is* the symbol, one that is universal and that cannot confine and direct artists except those inspired to the pitch of so universal a range, except those for whose period art itself is the living emblem.

Further from the Mediterranean where the distant can be made near and objective, beyond Semitic centres of the fertile valleys where representational art as we have it in Europe arose, the great and popular art of nomad peoples, whether Aryan, Semitic or Mongol, has flourished, the radical art of North and East, which, for purposes of antithesis, I simplified earlier on into terms of craftsmanship.

Strzygowski writes[1]: 'Non-representational[2] art is not more backward nor more primitive than representational; it is simply different. Instead of being proud of what we have done, we of the north ought rather to deplore our excessive surrender to the histrionic feeling of the south. To personify and to anthropomorphize all and everything is to attempt the opening of every door with the one master-key "Man", and to recede far indeed from great Nature and her secrets. It is clear enough that the present generation has deliberately turned against representation. . . . Christians were once as far removed from representation as were the Greeks originally.' And again:'In my

[1] *Origin of Christian Church Art*. Clarendon Press, 1923.

[2] This means an art that definitely avoids human representation. Animal forms are plentiful.

book *Altai-Iran und Völkerwanderung* I attempted to show that in the perfected style of Islam there still survives that non-representational northern and nomadic art known to us through the work of pre-historic times and that of the later Teutonic and Turkish tribes. In the period of the great migrations, both these races advanced towards the ancient forcing houses of culture, just as the Greeks, Celts, Persians, and Indians had done in pre-Christian times. Originally none of these peoples represented; they first learned this mode of artistic expression in the south. The student of art is inclined to think that the contrast between north and south may be explained by the transition to a higher stage of culture. In the south, man passed immediately from the culture of the earlier Stone Age into a social system which sought to cast a spell on the object by representation, as the primitive hunter attempted to do when he made pictures of his game. In the north, on the other hand, formative art developed out of the handicraft of the later Stone Age. It enclosed space in borders and filled it with ornament which for the most part followed from the nature of the material and the process adopted, ornament which was therefore geometrically designed for the purpose of pleasing the eye.'

I do not want to twist Strzygowski's translated words. But I must remark on the phrase 'ornament which for the most part followed from the nature of the material and the process adopted'. 'Follows', not *founded in* the nature of the material. The latter will be the case only when the artist projects into the material his own vitality by means of humanistic fantasies.

It is unnecessary for me to defend southern art against Strzygowski. I prefer it for the greater objectivity he admits. I can agree about the baleful influence of southern art on northern, though I feel that but for a classical element due to the Roman church, which kept Rome alive and made renascence possible, Gothic art could not have achieved so fine a sculpture. But to-day the North is dumb after centuries of Roman Church and of the Renaissance. Circumstances of the machine age (which so far from being the antithesis of the handicraft ages, is their logical outcome and final triumph), though they heighten sense of design, outstrip the arts still rooted in the handicrafts from which they arose. The South takes over the machine and will make something of it, just as formerly it has taken over crafts from North and East to compose elements of a great art.

Southern art, in the course of a development, will be identified with some conception of mass. I would identify decorative art, according to Strzygowski the original art of all Aryan peoples, with the manipulation of line. The substitution in the preceding sentence of the adjective 'decorative' for 'non-representational', is to my present purpose because I would thereby indicate as well as pattern, the flatness on which pattern is made. The third dimension in sculpture and painting must be connected with the representing of human form from which, again, is derived conception of mass; or rather, from contemplation of the warm stone into which compact humanistic fantasies are projected, there proceeds a conception of mass. Not that linear conception can be eliminated in any art. The virtue of a mass-effect is the immediacy on which I have expatiated, that absence of music, or if you prefer, of *arrière-pensée*. Such content is narrow. As symbol, manifold symbol, elastic line, spiritual line exists even amid the greatest triumphs of mass. Everything can be interpreted by linear conception save immediacy.

On the other hand, solid objects of any sort must have *some* connection with mass. You pass a building or enter it, you revolve around, while the building remains immediate. But whereas this immediacy was magnified in the South (surely the home of architecture, the abstract art nourishing all grand scale design), in the North it is slurred over: even more in the far-East where we miss a grand touch in design.

The building and the human figure are things immediate to the senses. Hence the representational art of the South in whose light building fructifies. When, as has been the case

47

with the visual arts of most cultures, architecture is not the parent art, there results an intrusion of music. On the other hand mass, pure mass, will convey no effects, even of human form, beyond those so abstract ones of immediacy; no subtly-woven fantasies, no philosophy beyond the humanistic one of space, of the worship of beauty, of the open staring face of the rose. Comparatively few motives are eligible for immediacy-treatment.[1] Southern art, then, will easily become sterile, as it is less charged with diverse emotional content than the art that is essentially, though not perhaps literally, non-representational (for some naturalism from the South has percolated almost everywhere, just as decorative conception has been carried south).

Non-representational art avoids the complete articulation prized in the South, in south Europe as in India. For the feeling that inspires non-representational art is more 'profound', while the means by which it is realized are severely disciplined by some form on whose symbolic significance æsthetic significance depends. And whereas this art, with an æsthetic so guarded, so sound, less easily becomes sterile, while it also achieves a greater subtlety of subject or content, yet the symbol thus denoted is too easily stylized, conventionalized, mechanized even, and the obligation for original effort by every artist is diminished. Non-representational art subsumed under the heading, 'withdrawn art', will never sink into the vulgarity of which southern art is capable. But, equally, artists of pronounced genius are shackled. It is an art, then, tribal at root or popular, less dependent upon individual genius the cult of which, as we know from the Renaissance, is both the cause and the result of humanism.

In decorative art, landscape will be directly symbolic: at highly civilized periods it is, foremost, the expression of a mood, of a poetic idea. Poetry is near to music. Thus the pictorial art of the far-East of which Sung 'philosophical landscape' is a

---

[1] That is, except when this treatment has been ordered by such great genius as inspired Piero della Francesca and Luciano Laurana.

major but typical achievement, a cunning elaboration of the written character. Whereas Cézanne's flowers, innocent of moods or modes, do not point beyond themselves toward anything of a different sphere to which direct reference is impossible. They expose, these flowers, the ordered world of light and space and colour.

VIII. ORIENTAL AND
NORTHERN ART IN ITALY

'E sotto un'alta quercia, humile e stanco,
Legato stava un gentile alepardo;'[1]

I HAVE REFERRED to the subject of non-representational and Semitic art because I want to indicate the immense education in line and in the soundest or safest æsthetic that Italy gained from the oriental and Gothic culture of the middle ages. I would now stress the prominence in Italy of Semitic forms, because, apart from their importation throughout the middle ages as embodied to varying degrees in Byzantine, Persian, Syrian, Egyptian and Coptic cultures, there subsisted on Italian soil an ancient Semitic culture which had been far less properly hellenized than in Greece. For I believe the Etruscans were Semitic or Hittite by race. Certainly one attributes to them, besides their power of modelling and antecedent to it, the particularly *graphic* mode of Semitic, but especially Hittite, representation; also sadistic propensities in general, brutalities of a kind that we have always associated with the East. This vague suggestion will supply a theme when I examine Florentine art. For the moment I wish but to suggest an oriental substratum in Italy, which of itself explains both how easily oriental influences were taken up and how vital could be their transmutation into humanism.

One can too easily overlook the origins of Rome. Roman art, no less than Roman religion, in the first place is Etruscan. Roman love for the Greek has a coherent aspect if we imagine

[1] Luca Pulci. *Ciriffo Calvaneo—con la giostra del Magnifico Lorenzo dei Medici*. Giunta, Florence, 1572.

with what darker lore and fiercer characterization these Latins felt imbued before the shining Greek idealism. It was an Etruscan Italy the Romans conquered bit by bit, Etruscan but for the Greek south and the fierce Picenes of Romagna and the races of the Veneto. These natives, be it said, had kept their Aryan non-representational art.

A vast difference between Romans and Etruscans springs to the eye in political organization. Whereas the Roman nucleus spreads compact, spreads in empire over the Ancient World, Etruscan temper prefers the loosest of confederacies, non-colonial and based upon the brilliant unit of true (not public school) aristocracy. So Rome could conquer Etruria bit by bit. Veii need not have fallen if the twelve cities had helped. Even her nearest neighbours, Caere, Tarquinia and Vulci, remained unmoved. Historians tell the same story about Italy at the close of the fifteenth century. Not the Romans but the vulgar French, the Spaniards, the Germans and the Swiss, reimburse themselves from Italy. But before this, as well as the lust for Roman power, the cities, the twelve cities, the hundred cities at this time of renascence intensify their separate character from peak and on the plain, large in peace and in the Condottieri warfare that crowns the less intricate struggles of medieval Italy.

Of medievalism I will not attempt a detailed recipe. But in the third volume I shall show how medieval, how oriental, Italian literary pretensions during the fifteenth century still were. In spite of the humanists' and their patrons' enthusiasm for the antique and for the revival of antique studies, little really western thought appears before the neo-Aristotelian movement in Venice that inspired Giorgione at the beginning of the sixteenth century.

Popular imagination drew upon the East in the Renaissance. I take as an instance the illuminations[1] of the Florentine fifteenth-century Aeneid in the Biblioteca Laurenziana. In one

[1] Reproduced and commented upon in similar fashion by Soulier. *Les influences orientales dans la peinture toscane.* Laurens, Paris, 1923.

miniature we see the Trojans in Byzantine costume shooting arrows back to back at deer. Ducks swim the foreground. Both huntsmen and hunted posture decoratively. Another miniature shows Juno dressed like the Queen of Sheba, while the mitred Jove is no western pontiff.

As I have said, the Renaissance is an intensification of all forms; not least of the oriental. Witness the fifteenth-century cassone panels. This painting was a popular art; those rich processional scenes based on the festal cavalcades with which great nobles entertained the people, are decked out not only with oriental stuffs, but with oriental types from which the people created their fantasies, even those of religion. Eastern bestiaries supply many a detail and incident, symbols such as the Assyrian one of flying birds so loved of Pinturicchio[1] were used in fourteenth-and fifteenth-century painting, decoratively and with a gusto.

Manifold symbols of oriental religions find a place, particularly in the Siennese painting. This art, put in grand movement by the freedom of Giotto, sums up a whole era that has gathered colour and design from oriental textiles. Berenson[2] remarked in 1909 that no other European school is nearer to the painting of the far-East. He considers that the influence of the mystics made for this character. An art with something in common with the far-East was adapted to express spiritual content with a grace that classical precepts, though the church clung to them for grandeur, could not emulate. At Siena one is reminded of Indo-Persian painting.

Soulier[3] writes of the Siennese school in the early Renaissance: 'Les caractères d'Extrême-Orient, qui paraissent parfois moins accusés vers la fin du 14ᵉ siècle, reprennent une

---

[1] So loved too of Soulier from whom I take this point (*vide op. cit.*). He makes too much of it, while omitting to mention the oriental carpets so often reproduced in fifteenth-century pictures.

[2] *A Siennese painter of the Franciscan legend.* Dent, London, 1909, pp. 17-18.

[3] *Op. cit.*, p. 352.

insistance nouvelle jusqu'au plein milieu du 15ᵉ et au-delà: chez Giovanni di Paolo, chez Sassetta, Francesco di Giorgio, Matteo di Giovanni, Sano di Pietro, et chez Neroccio Landi qui pousse peut-être à son paroxysme le parti pris de la grâce artificielle et de la délicate afféterie. . . . On a voulu voir chez ces peintres un mouvement d'archaïsme: en vérité, il y a re-crudescence d'influences extrême-orientales, ce qui veut dire que les causes persistent et que les apports se renouvellent.' With that I agree in general. Consider the case of Francesco di Giorgio. It bears out the formula for the Renaissance: 'intensi-fication of all forms'. Francesco di Giorgio Martini was the great Quattro Cento architect, inheritor of Luciano Laurana, the model engineer who built, or was in charge of, 136 castles for Federico di Montefeltro; Francesco whom Leonardo and Bramante summoned to their aid because they couldn't put the dome on Pavia cathedral, who wrote his treatise on archi-tecture praising Vitruvius and the human form as the mean of proportion, who built at Cortona Madonna di Calcinajo which vies in monumental completeness with the works of Vignola and Palladio; Francesco di Giorgio of the delicate perspective drawings: yet he painted Siennese 'primitives'.

Intensification of all forms, but to the purposes of human-ism. Hence the importance of the antique, the worship of the classical world which the ignorant could but deck out with oriental finery. If I have kept the balance in these notes, it is now unnecessary for me to stress the pagan intent of the Quat-tro Cento or the introduction of classical architectural mem-bers, or the copying of antique bronzes, or the influence of the church in the middle ages, propagating the idea of Rome. Nor do I feel it necessary to expatiate upon the 'proto-Renaissance' of Giotto and the Pisani, an example previous to the Quattro Cento of charged and simple Gothic line caught to the South where that purity excites a grandness of style still Roman. But the time is not yet for line to be concreted into mass. The dis-tant still is distant, sacrosanct.

These influences are better known than the oriental. I need

more, then, to emphasize the fact that in the fifteenth century all this orientalizing was material for the expression of humanistic exuberance; the delicate and sensitive line, for instance, of Siennese and Umbrian painting, line which is both Gothic or Giottesque, Byzantine and Persian; as well as the rich zoning of colour won from long apprenticeship with oriental textiles—these were now modes of a western, new joy. Taken up with what Monsieur Soulier might call this paroxysm, Man was referred back to the materials from which love of colour still came and by which, more than by contemplation of art, it renews itself. But whereas in the glaring East these materials are preferably precious stones and plumage, in the light of Italy marbles of all kinds are loved, marble that is vast and tonal as well as brilliant; so that there arises, principally in Venice, the western art of tonal painting. But first those answering blocks of colour on cassone panels and the zonal treatment of colour by Siennese painters as a whole, had helped the greatest of all painters, the Quattro Cento figure, Piero della Francesca, to articulation of form by colour.

Upon education in line and in the unlimited content that line can express austerely, the humanistic impulse superseding, there follow the greatest achievements of mass-effect.

To reinforce this dictum which, in my opinion, more than any other single statement indicates the coincident circumstances necessary to produce so great an art triumph as the Renaissance, I must consider Gothic contribution to line. Gothic line is as important to the development of Renaissance sculpture as Gothic, far-Eastern and Byzantine influences are to the development of Renaissance painting. Therefore of far greater importance to the Renaissance as a whole. For the painters, if you remember, depend largely upon the sculptors and upon their love of stone.

Of Gothic art Strzygowski writes[1]: 'Northern art renounced its proper character in so far as it conceded to the human figure in architecture a place only equalled for importance in

[1] *Origin of Christian Church Art*, p. 97.

India. A distinction must, however, be made. In India the suggestion came not from the art of the immigrant peoples in the north of the country, but from that of the older population in the south, just as further west it came from Egypt to the Greek art of Southern Europe. In Northern Europe, in Gothic art, however, the essential lies not, as in India and Greece, in the human figure itself, but in the draped figure—not in the body, but in the covering given to the body by art. The figure is subordinated to form, as in East Asia; natural shapes become merely the vehicles of rhythmical line. Moreover, these Northern figures are in organic unity with the body of the structure. The consciousness that the various parts of the organism are thus naturally enlivened leads, independently of the human figure, to a luxuriant overgrowth of vegetable and animal forms unequalled in any other art, even in the South.'

In the North one will expect constant reminder in construction as in detail, of wood and thicket and their tall percolating light. Gothic constructional exuberance was the art-form of a religious pæan which gave in the manner of hymns and psalms the allegory of natural force. Similarly the centralized but spacious plan of an early Armenian church such as the cathedral at Ani which, though a purer expression of Aryan art-form, may be said to anticipate Gothic[1]; for it expresses doctrine. In spite of the compactness, in spite of economic planning which calls to mind the civilized Romanesque of Aquitaine, a style itself derived from Armenia, I cannot discover from these sources a true mass-effect. Such building is conceived as a whole, it is true, and compared with this planning, the columnar styles of early Roman churches seem so scrappy that one regrets with Strzygowski the triumph of the long nave in Christian art at the behest of ecclesiastics. But though you hold the plan to your eye, you cannot feel space or instantaneity. Spaciousness, yes, constructional certainty, but these were induced to foster particular emotions, Christian aspects.

[1] The buildings by the Armenian architect Trdat in the last quarter of the tenth century, have pointed arches as well as clustered shafts.

True mass-effect is itself an expression of worship, the worship of space, of things set in space which are destroyed by any mingling with afterthought. The clustered shafts of Thalish and Ani soar, blind arcades run, they have an aim. But mass-effect pushes out time or succession in favour of a thing complete, immutable, and so, innocent of direction. Fine architectural planning, then, economic and centralized, does not necessarily mean the kind of tension I call mass.

As for the immense constructional expressiveness of Gothic, come south it stimulated, even in large part created, the humanistic fantasy to have the stone alive. And how easily the Gothic riot of figure and vegetation, upon an access of paramount love for stone itself, became stone-blossom. A thousand years of expressiveness in line sought tense fixation in mass-effect. Gothic itself, the late Burgundian Gothic of Claus Sluter and his followers, sought compression of shape, sought to concrete rich lines into mass with the finality of a fierce and dramatic naturalism, though not based, as it was soon to be in Italy, on anatomy and the antique. So Burgundian sculpture is sometimes eccentric. For the antique imposes a sanity, a clearness by light of which each excess can be successfully perpetrated. Over Donatello's most heated excesses there presides a canon which is yet in no sense a restraint.

The Avesta tells of the power 'Hvareneh' which governs birth and sprouting, which makes the waters run. Wherever Aryan decorative art penetrated through symbolic animal, symbolic landscape and vegetation, Hvareneh images were expressed, though sunk into other religions. Strzygowski gives so diverse instances as scenes from the chase constant in Persian art, the steadfast animals cut on the façade of Spoleto's cathedral, the mosaic of river landscape in the apse of San Apollinare in Classe. Vine-scroll, even though mixed with acanthus by the Romans, kept an old significance. Principally from Gothic, forces of Hvareneh were collected by the Quattro Cento, and then attributed to the stone. Hence the parallel to Indian sculpture in which Iranian decoratives such as are to be found slightly modified by Indian flora on Sarnath stupa, obtain from coalition with Dravidian forms *representational* efflorescence, particularly in the Sunga sculpture at Bharhut and in the early Andhra sculpture at Sanchi.

This subject I must defer indefinitely. I believe a case could be made out to show that Quattro Cento art alone has expressed fully the symbols of the oldest Aryan cult in history, Mazdaism.

I conclude these introductory notes with a description of a Quattro Cento masterpiece, Verrocchio's *lavabo* in the small room adjoining the Old Sacristy of San Lorenzo, Florence. For thus, before embarking on the essay, I hope the better to give the meaning of stone-blossom and incrustation and emblematic tensity. Moreover I write of this *lavabo* (a basin for priests to wash their hands and vessels) at a length which would hold up the argument in the body of the essay, where it really belongs.

IX. VERROCCHIO'S LAVABO

INASMUCH AS Verrocchio and Pollaiuolo and the other great Florentines were principally concerned with stress and strain,—with movement,—it is obvious that composition will deviate more and more from simple correspondence; for movement must be balanced by movement corresponding *in power*; with the result that one resolute gesture may compensate a repeated directional stress. This extremely *qualitative* nature of the objects of balance when the main purpose is of stresses and strains, is also true, of course, of all objects of composition be they represented as animate or inanimate, in motion or at rest; but in the case of stresses and strains an ever increasing complication in correspondence is necessary to avoid their cancelling each other out, instead of enhancing one another. The sum must be a synthetic movement, generally circular, which keeps the whole process going.

Verrocchio was a great master of design. I say it contemplating the *lavabo* (*Plates V* and *VI*). This greatness, in itself, does not cause the *lavabo* to be the masterpiece of the Quattro Cento. Raphael was a great designer. His compositions are 'dynamic'; nevertheless he owed too much to the compass. Raphael's hardness can never be put in relation to the Quattro Cento. Raphael sailed very close to the wind. No one else has so nearly succeeded in reducing art to formulæ. We have paid dearly for this copy-book talent. To-day we have reckoned the cost of the Superb, the High Renaissance.

Florence, San Lorenzo : Old sacristy : Verrocchio's lavabo.

PLATE V. STONE-BLOSSOM AND INCRUSTATION IN
DYNAMIC DESIGN

Verrocchio's *lavabo*. (*See also Plate V.*)

PLATE VI.

This *lavabo* is Quattro Cento because here manipulation by design is much more directly the proof of an exuberant clarity. It glistens, ascended from an imaginative fund whence strong roots have shot up in unexampled profusion, necessitous thongs and twines bound for the light from stirred under-consciousness. But, to meet the day with felicitous acclamation, emergence has recognized marks, Piero de' Medici's signet emblazoned with diamond, his falcon balanced by spread wings as from the dawn; and to oppose all vestige of the night, not up, but down, not out only, but overlaying from crowded heavens shall the most distant progeny of earth and sea emerge with age-old abandon into the new life. So the falcon is spread upon the background, recognized mark nearest the depleted caves of under-consciousness, now shut with marmolite with which revolves a band of oak leaves and acorns. In front, coming clear of this wall an urn, a cup and bath, one inside the other; these upon their slopes and incrustations receive the large and slow rain of beasts more primitive than to act prehensile,[1] as scales drop inch by inch, wet thorny tissues caught by the sun as irridescent mud upon the vessels grazed to warmth and wet. The hooded beast-rain is perpendicular: any other that struck oblique would over-balance the stoppered urn set in the precious cup standing in the bath. Instantaneous, two enlarging drops, not to shrink in diffusion like water, clap the urn; arrested: then slide down the neck of the urn, now sliding soft, they slip and gradually slide longer again, till friction gathers them on the major curve. Thereon permeation begins within matter and life so primitive. Urn shall have living tissues so that there can be no roll or topple when thus held inside the cup. So beneath the lip of the cup where scorchings, water sifting and rime have long been encrusted, as if left to golden communion with the love-chalice after the banquet has been drained and the guests are drunk, boars' heads drop from the cup's pierced sides. But they are

[1] This phrase, which—I am told—is more than usually obscure, was constructed by analogy to the vulgarism, 'to act funny.'

not detached, they belong to the scaly bodies and bats' wings adhesive to the urn. This gradual falling had inevitable momentum, snouts trickling through beneath the lip of the solid cup. But the glissade of monster-rain is caught, and only condensation of the boars' breath will damp the bath below where two dolphins rear up behind the fluted stem of the cup, panting. The glissade is over, and living ropes rage about the neck of the urn to catch the ring. They are the tails of these boars'-head dragons. Contiguous the background, where wind revolves the heavily-garlanded marmolite free from sediment; and on the face of the bath below, a lion's mask looks out, while at the sides are griffins with women's heads and tails that intercoil to hoist dead weight of bath, rich cup and urn. The smooth rivets of these tails show by contrast how corrugated with flapping spines are the monsters of precious dropping above them. Marine splendours have *descended* upon the urn and crested cup, scorning the bath where priests wash their hands; marble embraced to remembrance of primeval beginnings in lime dropped by countless animals. White upon white stone, these symbols, these gradual amphibian progenitors; while the delicate mouth of the urn passed over, unencumbered, comes free from the background. There, oak in a huge wreath emblazons the green and slimy disc, setting off the architecture of the laden vessels. Ribbons stream on the wind; and where above the falcon sets on the day with his armour of plumage, the wind blows him back tense.

The monster-rain (blight to all but marble), and a tensity, incrustation and stone-blossom—how come they to be grandiose, mass *in excelsis?* First of all, there is the use of coloured stone, the porphyry arch framing the whole, and the serpentine central disc; also the dark colours of the huge lip of the cup. These make the white marble luminous, and lead the eye to the shadows at the junction of surfaces, to where, for instance, the bat wings, ribbed and ending in claws like an umbrella, cling to the urn. Hence the feeling of incrustation, surface into surface, and also of growth from within (witness the oak wreath) —of stone-blossom.

The intensive movements to which I have pointed are the outcome of subtleties in the design that merit a full-length exposition. Still more so, inasmuch as this monument finds little favour with the critics. Ever since Vasari they have attributed it as the work, not of one, but of two masters, largely independent of, or at any rate successive to, one another. And yet I can think of no monument of such complication with so compelling a unity. Here are some aspects of the design in terms of stress and strain.[1]

The falcon at the top with outspread wings faces left, and his left wing he thrusts up higher than the right. This upward and leftward stress has no simple counterpart as it would have in an ordinary 'symmetrical' design. Verrocchio used this same stress to realize the downward fall of the dragons on the urn. The transition is wonderfully carried off by the spiral patterned stopper on the urn, spiralling up from left through right to left. Beneath, on the urn's side, the right-hand dragon's wing continues the sloping line of the eagle's body, as a downward movement to the right. For this wing reaches higher up the urn than does the wing of the other dragon, and the tail of this first dragon shears off to the right at the urn's neck, so as to leave uninterrupted the line with the eagle's body, a line helped out by the spiral of the stopper. While on the subject of the dragons' wings, I would note the extreme subtlety of their inter-arrangement. I have said why the right-hand one must reach higher than the left, but inasmuch as the right one, as well as making the connection with the eagle's left-upward stress, is the means of carrying on that stress in a right-downward form, it must also reach down lower than the left-hand wing. The

[1] Left and right in this description are from the point of view of the spectator facing the monument. As outside wings of the dragons do not appear, 'left wing' is right-hand wing of left dragon and 'right wing' is left-hand wing of right dragon. The creatures on the urn with boars' heads are dragons, while the creatures with female faces beneath the bath are griffins.

claws of the wings fit into each other's spaces—the bottom claw of the right-hand wing being the lowest—and when the top of this wing is reached a space has been gained, so that it is higher than the left-hand wing. How is this: is the right-hand wing larger than the left? No, but they are in different positions. The right wing is spread out to a shape suitable to carry the downward stress, while the left wing is folded and therefore shorter. These shapes have other purposes to serve beside this trick, as I shall describe. For it is the attribute of so ideal a design that every line serves to carry at least one stress and one strain with perfect harmony. The diagonal stress movement—upwards to the left, downwards to the right—is now carried round the bottom of the bath by the griffins. Were they symmetrical, these snaky bodies doubling on themselves and diminishing in tails would turn inwards or outwards both together; but the left one coils inwards, the right one outwards, and so, taken up with the knot of these tails beneath the lion's head—left goes under right—the eye seizes upon a series of coils moving round to the left griffin's head. Thus, the right diagonal stress rounds the bottom of the monument and comes through to the left. But such a rotation is not a sufficient guardian of eternal living held to the instant, not in itself the means of a perennial source of vitality expected from the greatest art. And indeed, it is at this very point, where the tails knot below the lion's mouth, that the mystery resurges, the strain in answer to the stress is here distributed to the formal circles of infinity. The right-hand griffin allowed the stress to pass along her body and be carried off to the left. But she is pulling out to the right all the same, and the part of her body that pulls against the stream is stronger, more rigid, tauter, less mobile. Another prop or break resisting the stress, is the wing of the left dragon, thin and spiky, obstinate, pointing upwards and to the right. The angle of the falcon's body, too, though making the left-upward movement of the diagonal stress, betokens a wind that blows the bird back, so that the right-upward strain of the left dragon's wing, as well as the stress, is upheld by him. All the same, the diagonal stress in its upward and to-the-left division, is still far too strong, heightened as it is because the space on the left of the falcon with his uplifted claw on the ring is more crowded than the space on the right of him. Also the knotting of the tail of the left-hand dragon about the urn is more elaborate than in the case of his fellow, and adds considerably to the weight of the left-hand side. Against this left-upward thrust both the downward-right diagonal stress and the upward-right diagonal strain, are combined. But they are not enough, not if the pre-eminent movement of the whole is to be the slow downward-right of the right dragon's wing on the urn. To perpetuate a solution (one puts it that way) Verrocchio hit upon an invention as bold as any I know.

Without counteracting his stresses and strains, he achieves a supreme balance by (*a*) deliberately placing the centre of the cup marked by Piero's emblems to the right of the main centre which passes down the middle of the urn, and beneath the cup, down the middle of the lion's head upon the bath. The cup has been turned on its axis slightly to the right. The dragons' heads are in the conspiracy. They are equidistant from the centre of the cup, but *not* from the centre of the whole design. The left head has been brought forward, the right pushed back. Again, the left head is bulkier[1] than the right, and so makes up for the space relinquished by the cup as it was turned from the background plane. These heads were the handles by which the cup was turned. We are back in the realm of masks. On a former occasion they were the heads of primeval monsters set on a serious function. Here is interplay of the formal and the dynamic.

(*b*) (The second way the right side is emphasized so as to achieve balance without confusing a pre-existent movement.) The key to this is Piero's crest with its ribbons on the cup. Again an emphasis on the emblem which has provoked all this

[1] The right head has lost part of its snout, but the left was obviously always the bigger.

creation, and which was shifted from the centre for the previous most spectacular feat of balance. These ribbons are agitated by a wind that blows from left to right, the same wind that blows back the falcon on top and the ribbons about his claws. The flutterings, in accordance with the left origin of the wind, are very faithfully produced. But the climax in this extraordinary feat of compensation is clockwise movement of the wreathed marmolite disc, running from the top left-hand ribbon attached to the wreath, round through the right to the bottom left-hand corner. This time, then, the wind is a rotary movement: look at the different ways the ribbons double. They are not agitated indiscriminately, but to a vital purpose.[1] But finally, this movement is equivocal, neutral; for of the clockwise motion, three-quarters of a circle are completed, and the wind drops at the bottom left-hand corner—see how the ribbon there curls back on itself. So, the rotation has supplied as well the left *down* diagonal stress which the left-hand dragon's wing now echoes. This second function of the clockwise moving wreath makes it the complement to the movement of intercoiled spinous tails where the original stress was softened and rounded.

So, what with the eagle pressing to the left and driven to the right; what with the wreath moving to the right, stopping on the left; what with the diagonal stress cut out of a circle, a circular stress and the resurgence of strains from a knotted tail; what with both dragons' wings moving up and moving down, to left and to right independent of each serving far more intricate correspondences—yet they are a pair, so are the griffins, so are the wings of the falcon, so too the independent ribbons are pairs—were ever shapes more plain yet intricate, movings so simple, inevitable, yet subtle to run on for ever, to run on without compensation: when from another angle it

[1] 'It is true that the oak-leaves of the garland and the fluttering ribbons are somewhat mechanically arranged and lifeless in execution, and it is probable that these are the work of some assistant.' From Maud Crutwell's *Verrocchio*.

all is compensatory, though headed off by layer upon layer of redistribution, the sources hidden; when five or six emphases, all different, are clear and do not contradict one another, when the whole is a mass, whole, shaped, striking the eye, a manifestation of completeness and of resurgence . . . surely it is a unit representative of all art, which, breaking from the ideal marbles, becomes circumfluent and gives back to life the spirit of life redoubled.

Should it appear that a disproportionate space has been given to this monument, I plead not only that it is a great and neglected work, but also that it is the masterpiece in sculpture of the Quattro Cento spirit. And this helps out a definition. For here and in the sculpture at Rimini one witnesses culmination in the humanizing of the elemental, one witnesses common release humanized, articulated by the voracity of emblem, of one individual's actuate *virtu*. In comparison with the *lavabo*, the Colleoni as emblem is but a memorial, the *virtu* concentrated, pointed, cut free to flaunt the campo, not a contagion in the stone seen and unseen, but a quality, a public reputation, not the almost anonymous inner and personal life transfigured in accomplishment of solidity, the marble consumed. And after Colleoni, the vital Quattro Cento spark was extinguished, and art engages to figure forth the *flow* and *rhythm* of unexcelled vitality. Thus the Baroque. In the Quattro Cento that very flow was the genius that sprung to be solidified, to be turned to instantaneousness in the strong marble core.

Man never lived so deep in other ages, so uninhibited. Externalization has been more facile or crooked, and in art the near taken to the distant, not the distant to the near. Formal living has meant not only formal art with attitudes of discreet mistiness, but also for such chinkless spreading of externalization, has meant arts which magnify the successive, which manipulate various music; arts hostile to mass, to permeation of the solid requiring the full sap. While Romantics, excusably roaring, dissipate the horizon and glean random prophecies from the clouds.

Classical and Romantic, all of it is abstraction, not infusion. Where since the Quattro Cento has the whole spirit rushed to inhabit, rather than to generalize, particularize?

And that the *lavabo* should display such liberty, such a flow of design, yet fulfil itself solely as a tense concretion, makes it the point of convergence between the grandest emotional triumph and the greatest subtlety in artistic perpetuation, coincidents that uniquely glorify the capturing alive of the life-flux by traps of tangible stone; a glory, be it said, synonymous with civilization. For what else is civilization but a converting of formless power to organized show, to outwardness? More, to toss the deep to the surface, the contriving of outwardness, is the labour of all humanity, but the joy of humanism and of art. Death is the name for complete objectivization; the subject to be converted has been eliminated. Timelessness is complete. Detached thought is near death, is death's instrument, turning life to stone. It is more profoundly evincive to turn stone to life. Primitive man and the poet are more profound than Buddha. Every subjective attitude, however naïve, is preferable to objectivization achieved by the wholesale denial of that to be objectivized. There is a revelation of life and a revelation of death. Both are needed, they imply each other. Both are needed for untrammelled living. (The Quattro Cento sometimes struck perfect balance.) Revelation of life made possible by that of death, gives us consciousness; we feel living: and revelation of death made possible by that of life leads us to conceive the world, objects, to make ourselves manifest, to objectify, to concrete the flow of living into personality so there be passions and passionate intellect to the purpose of their expression. Spirit generally suffers thin, and death in season, out of season, employs his endless suction. Life becomes too sublimate. Deep life has not come up, but escapes unfledged to hunger in the void. No concretion, but inhumanly to abstract is now the deadly showing. Whereas showing should be victory over death thus 'used' by life and thus compelled to serve life, to give eternity to content, to quality, to feeling experienced in the present. Death is the end; that finality should be won to life as self-expression. Beyond this, as that which defines life and bounds it, as that which moulds life and destroys it, as that which determines the process of satisfaction and the end or final satisfaction, death should have no other significance for man. When triumphant, death is vile. Complete objectivity is horrible when life is conquered though not drained. The purity of death is easily come by, so too is the grasp of Nirvana when life is pale, when what is to be expressed is not at all lively. Such preoccupation is childish, impudent, cheating. But further, death itself pales if not fed by any blood of life; and as there is nought but life and death, since when one is in part denied so must be the other, a brood of sunken alivers proclaiming but the lively dead as they pass through the wheels of re-incarnation—some such shallowness can prevent all values.

But whether consciousness, the gift of death to life, has any right to stand aloof from life, whether, after all, death brings to life just a little that is beyond the life-death relationship, it is not our place to wonder, not till we have surpassed the Quattro Cento in self-expression and 'used' death to the uttermost for the purposes of living.

PART II
FLORENCE AND VERONA

CHAPTER ONE

FLORENCE AND VERONA

VERONA IS foil to Florence, the red marble to the grey and blue sandy stones of Fiesole. In no other sense. I give the essay this title to prolong the image of the excitements gained from Verona marble. For I hope the reader will persist in a desire for ebullient, even elephantine, shapes while I treat of the ashen stones of Florence and of the more dainty marbles there.

Pietra morta, 'dead stone', they call round Pisa way the various livid Florentine sandstones and arenaceous limestones. Strictly speaking *pietra morta* is only one of the group, the one impervious to fire because unquickened by any lime; but that is a good title for the whole lot, deficient as they are in grain and fibre, unreflective of light. So I shall use the expression *pietra morta* as a generic term, one that is no more inaccurate, and far more apposite, than the usual expression *pietra serena*.[1]

You may examine a lot of fifteenth-century *pietra morta* at the Victoria and Albert Museum, and nearby some lusty Verona marble. The crumbling sandstone fountain next to the Ambron altar arch, in so imperfect a condition is, perhaps, an unfair example of *pietra morta*, usually hard enough, too hard; for see

[1] I suspect this title has been used generically owing to a confusion in Vasari's essay on technique (a prefix to his *Lives of the Painters*), where he describes two quite different sandstones but calls them both *pietra serena*. Cellini confines *pietra serena* to a light grey sandstone only good for interior work. See *Vasari on technique*, translated by Louisa MacLehose, with notes by Prof. Baldwin Brown. Dent, 1907. Note, p. 57.

how 'stuck-on' and pointed, though crumbling, are the floral arabesques on the *pietra morta* doorways from Gubbio. Exhibit No. 5895, a doorway, also shows the acute deadness of this material treated for decoration. Relief is cut to a sharp edge; otherwise you could barely distinguish it on a stone so dull. Even then there is no light and shade. A sharpness that appears detachable, and therefore 'stuck on', is the sole articulation of ornament (*Plate XIII*, 1). For this stone cannot be seen as welling up gradually, as indicating some core within.

On the other hand tawny Verona, owing to vagaries of grain and to pockets of clay, can rarely be cut to a sharp edge. In addition, the colour needs to be coaxed by polishing; so rounded forms eventuate. Even the nimbus about the head of the infant in the Verona Madonna and child relief[1] is chunky; an eatable rather than a metal. Notice the power in reflection of the darkish stone, the suffusion of lights and textures, in effect, the growing and inspissating that makes a flower bloom. A similar suggestion of formidable powers in auto-plastic occasionally results from modelling in chocolate where light is reflected luminous. How much more luminous from the stalwart stone that is hacked and pushed with emery! You won't get such luminosity from sculptor's preferred stone, from the white Carrara whose crystals glitter or are polished into an almost tile-like smoothness. Whereas the eruptive smoothness of good polished Verona—I say *good* Verona because there are some ugly pieces of this stone in the Victoria and Albert, such as the lions that support the Malaspina monument—coheres by means of the very 'faults' that preclude employment of this kind of Verona for small shapes; a contrast, then, to the white pall upon polished statuary marble, which would hide the disconcerting *pointillisme* of its crystals.

For my eyes Verona has the most compact structure of all stones except porphyries and granites, and their kindred looking obdurate. Geologically, Verona is not a breccia as often

---

[1] On the entrance wall to the left, upstairs at the Victoria and Albert. This is a beautiful relief of the thirteenth century.

stated, but a fossiliferous amalgam compact with clay. And if you would have in cameo the impression of Verona paving in Venice as I have described it,[1] leading one by salmon fleshly beckon over bridges till the time of perfect suffusion at sunset, notice the uncatalogued panel of Verona stone on the end wall downstairs at the Victoria and Albert, adjacent, that is, to the *pietra morta* capella Maggiore from Santa Chiara. For this panel is one stone, and the rope-shape encirclement is, in colour, ivory-hinting; yet by subtle strands of pink, coheres with the openly red under-surface within.

Verona marble is the stone preferred by me for Quattro Cento effect of stone-blossom. Nature of the stone dictates that any conception of emergent and pictorial effect will be treated large, fruitfully. A nimbus will be a disk, a solid wheel, plumed helmet will be charged with the portentousness of an elephant's head under his waving bossy trunk; tendrils will twirl as thick as your thumb, not sharp but slabbed in relief. Given the Quattro Cento constriction to make manifest, effect will be truly sculptural. The well-head[2] engraved with the armorials of the Concoreggio family shows all these qualities (*Plate VII*). Notice the head which appears beside a fruit tree like one of the fruit. The workmanship will no doubt be stigmatized as 'provincial'. Certainly, native Veronese sculpture in the fifteenth century *was* provincial. Remember, though, it evolved from a local Gothic school that revealed similar predilection for oak-strong foliage, a school from which Pisanello learned so much shape; also that Matteo de' Pasti brought these shapes afresh from Verona to Rimini and engraved at the behest of Sigismondo Malatesta, the famous Tempio all about with the elephantine Malatesta rose.

Upon the well-head putti or infant cupids are at their stations; for so is the new heraldry, so the emblems of release, of a bursting from bonds. Turn now from the well-head to evidences around you of *pietra morta*. I don't wish to go the length

[1] *See* pp. 12 and 13.
[2] Victoria and Albert Museum. Catalogue No. A9.

of suggesting that the unresponsive nature of this stone determines Florentine reserve and coldness. I am about to find some echo of the reserve, gentle as well as cold, among the dells of Florentine landscape. I would, though, submit that the character of *pietra morta* is at any rate relevant to analysis of this reserve, particularly in connection with fifteenth-century ornamentals. How could the Florentine masons love their dead stone? And the architects and sculptors to attain Quattro Cento effect, will need an organizing of a supreme technical ability, a monumental aim that 'uses' Quattro Cento tensity of representation. The Florentine artists were equipped for the effort. It will be agreed that from their very reserve Florentines had evolved already before the fifteenth century, the soundest aesthetic and the most comprehensive craft in Italy. The new impetus at once entailed monumental discoveries in technique.

I shall trace the development of the Baroque in terms of a struggle at Florence away from the psychology of cold, if perfect, craftsmanship toward the perfectly constructed monumental: a struggle marked by the rise of great individuals such as Donatello, men who from their wider knowledge and their larger effort, gave to Italy technical means and fierce models of concentrated humanistic expression. But first my theme is the Florentine reserve which Donatello spurned.

CHAPTER TWO

FLORENTINE RESERVE

I. The Atmosphere

S O W H E N the Florentines carved a *pietra morta* arabesque on a door jamb, whatever the design it appeared formal compared with the teeming shapes Verona marble induced.

Formal, calm, yet busy. No fierceness occurs of itself in the sweet vales of northern Tuscany. Florentine landscape is secluded, sequestered, the atmosphere sprightly. This is the home of the statuesque, and immanent here, as if steadied by reclining watchers on Etruscan tombs, the strongest of all European art schools flourished, breathing in beat with the nimble thunder of dexterity from goldsmiths' shops. We must imagine the narrow streets of Florence ringing with the blows of deft hammers. And when nimble thunder of dexterity brushes the Roman hills once grand? Florentine artists will be capable, of course, in devoting their great, active skill to emulate this grandeur with reasoned and minutely wrought monuments. These artists possess the reserve of power that belongs to the psychology of industrious craft. Hence their fundamental affinity with the North and the East. The Florentines were teachers of Italy: pioneers of the Renaissance, not its embodiment.

I had originally intended to attribute a 'Japanese sprightliness' to the Florentine landscape. And now I feel I can thus record this obscure phrase, having read of the Etruscans in Randall Maciver,[1] 'A Japanese quickness of adaptation'. I think

[1] *The Etruscans*, Clarendon Press, 1927.

the north Tuscan landscape, the easy slopes straight with cypress, impel facility. To me it is sinister that facility, an exquisite gentleness of manner even, should in any way be *impelled*. What darkness does this compulsion hide, what the need for over-compensation in Tokio as in Florence?

The Etruscans, of course, were not a gentle race. Far from it. Their unabashed cruelties are perhaps the key to over-compensation with gentleness in the art of the Florentine, Luca della Robbia, as well as the key to the monumental full-bloodedness of Castagno and Donatello. But at any rate the Etruscans were expeditious craftsmen. Their superior working of bronze was admitted by the Greeks. As early as the seventh century B.C. large cauldrons cast at Vetulonia[1] were thought worthy of dedication at Olympia. Moreover the Etruscans, like their inheritors the Florentines, and like the Japanese, had a quickness to adopt foreign forms. They borrowed from Phoenician and Greek to such an extent, that it is difficult to isolate the purely Etruscan quality though all the time one knows it exists, and exists forcibly. A sign of it is their refusal to admit the Doric order in architecture, their clinging to the Tuscan column. Again, though permeation by Greek forms is continual, yet at no time are they weaker than in the Pheidias and Praxiteles periods.

To whom shall we compare the Etruscans? For there must be other races to put one in mind of individuals so constantly met, who, while being competent to welcome the play of many influences on the choicest of which they hope to depend, remain unobtrusively, even hopelessly, the same.

A reserve of power (hence facility) is the almost constant factor both in Etruscan and in Florentine art. Occasionally reserve is broken, with a result, as we shall see, so forcible, that a peculiar native genius cannot be doubted, though it be still hard to isolate.

However, I admit without shame that of the Medici, insti-

[1]The site of this Etruscan city has now been discovered near Grosseto. See *Storia dell 'arte etrusca* by Pericle Ducati. Florence, 1927.

gators and witnesses of Florentine fifteenth-century art, I have nothing to say in this book. The early Medici, in the act of creating it, stand outside their age; thus reflecting, it is true, the Florentine reserve I investigate. But they were special men. For though contriving to circumnavigate their epoch, yet they relished the epoch apart from their manœuvre and, rightly enjoying and improving upon their good discrimination, they decided to be foreigners to all times and places beyond Florence of the fifteenth century. Cosimo and Lorenzo *understood*, not to the point of coldness, for which events did not ever call (and the Medici, too, were Italians), but so as to appreciate their luck and so as sensibly to widen their appreciations. Such power of arrangement caused sympathy with the creative act, induced a rare acceptiveness. To be successful bankers they must stand outside. The Medici were not so much supremely fitted for life as for any of life's civilized eras. Commercialism taught them far-sight and cosmopolitan restraint, but also, by means of contrast, the values of luxury, youth, and the intellectual pleasures of being pleased.

And so the Medici built their summer palaces. 'Quale visto di ogni canto', this is the phrase used of the villa at Careggi by Galeazzo Maria Sforza in a letter to his father. But how different this sweet nightingale song changing its crotchets for those of a higher key like the cypresses that stand out expressed upon their different levels, how different from the enfolding lyric of Giorgione, how different from the dank and indelicate *villeggiatura* of the ancient Romans.

Cosimo de' Medici created archetypes for the 'pleasaunce' that figures so widely in the Renaissance as a whole. In Italy the aesthetic Medici were copied. But whereas for Tuscany the conception of the country villa was delicious, craze for it attending more Gothic families engineered the formidable country house, dominant social outcome of the Renaissance, an outcome which supplies a theme for the second volume.

Thus, both as pioneers and as patrons, the Medici assisted the new civilization that grows from the Renaissance. The heart of it, the Quattro Cento, was overruled. And though an aspect of the Quattro Cento spirit as expressed by the low relief survives in sixteenth-century painting, as well as Giorgione the generations inherited the eclecticism of Raphael and the universal fury of Michael Angelo who was impelled by the cross-tendencies of the Quattro Cento and Florentine.

The initial debt to Florence does not weaken the isolation of the Quattro Cento. The tragedy of Sigismondo[1] is to be lamented the same, and the highest exaltation of European art, in art as in living, with less attention to intrinsic achievement, is to be discovered and even invented, must be proclaimed for our deliverance from the toll of subsequent centuries. In delivering Sigismondo from lies we deliver ourselves from the primary mistakes of our condition.

'Quale visto di ogni canto' . . . like yachts that ride stillness, Brunellesque[2] villas, a convention in good building that proceeds from Brunelleschi through four centuries, remind from every gentle peak that age is of no account in reckoning their sway. But how can such seclusion, such judicious domination as of the wiry fish beneath the pool, how can such delicacy, such limpidity, be the heart of overwhelming movement? Verona is the setting for Shakespeare: the Florentine *villeggiatura* a refinement, an adornment of the Quattro Cento, the Venus of Botticelli an eternity of delight, but Diana at Rimini the portent.[3]

II. *Early Florentine Architecture*

Perhaps the reader, calling suddenly to mind the virilities of Masaccio or Pollaiuolo, will have already tired of my argu-

[1]Sigismondo Malatesta, lord of Rimini. He is the protagonist of the second volume.

[2]'Brunellesque': adjective formed from the name of the architect, Brunelleschi. I know the formation is unwarranted, but I cannot handle throughout the unwieldy word 'Brunelleschian'.

[3]A reference to a relief of Diana as one of the planets by Agostino di Duccio, in the Tempio Malatestiano.

ment. I would have him remember I can make my point clear only by enumerating aspects of Florentine art. This point about the rather cold delicacy of the Florentine tradition and of the underlying habit in calculated neatness, sends me back for the moment to the earliest Florentine architecture.

The neat Baptistery probably dates from the fifth century. I take Mr. Anthony's view[1] that this building emulates a late-Roman style. But no building could be more sleek. One is reminded by the black[2] and white marble revetment, more of a young man impeccably 'turned out' (rather disgusting in a 1500 year old building), than of the similarly striped zebra about which there remains something exotic, variable, if only because the sagging of stripes upon his legs suggest stockings that require to be hitched up. You forget zebras when you contemplate the black and white stripes of the Baptistery, of San Miniato, or of the Collegiata at Empoli. Arrangement is entirely geometric, revealing an enlightened care for spacing but no love of space: since surfaces, nearly always, are as flat or sheer as possible; and decorations, except they be imitated from oriental textiles as in the case of San Miniato's floor, rarely suggest a third dimension or even an intensity, a sphere of influence. They are just black and white patterns, non-intense even geometrically. In this matter, and in architecture and sculpture as a whole, a sharp distinction exists beween the Pisano-Luccan style and the Florentine.

Of Florentine Romanesque sculpture Mr. Anthony writes[3] —and who shall contradict him: 'We are struck by the small amount of the material, and the inferiority of the material in comparison with the other Romanesque schools. With the exception of the figure from the pulpit of San Miniato, and the

[1]See *Early Florentine Architecture and Decoration* by F. W. Anthony. Harvard Univ. Press, 1927. The reader will find enumerated in this volume the various arguments of experts on the date of the Baptistery.

[2]Strictly speaking the colour is dark green, the dark green stone from Prato.

[3] *Op. cit.*, p. 68.

reliefs[1] of San Leonardo, we have no works which are worthy to rank with the better products of other schools, even including the Pisan, and moreover, in the two examples we have mentioned, the chief value is decorative, and there is less of that striving for expression which we find in other medieval sculpture. During the proto-Renaissance, Florence was entirely absorbed by her own peculiar type of decoration in which the human figure played no part, and she remained almost immune from foreign influences in sculpture.' Perhaps this isolation helps to explain how Etruscan influence survived here more strongly than in other parts of Tuscany.

One feels the Florentines avoided a primitive expression, as if to avoid representation, to persevere in their geometrical, civilized neatness until such time as circumstances would allow a more vital style which yet was not rude. Direct Byzantine, and then Gothic, influences in the thirteenth century, were thought worthy of the Florentine discipline. Cimabue, Arnolfo di Cambio and Giotto spring up to enlarge their native crystalline measure by employing it upon great themes.

III. *The Statuesque*

Tuscany is poor in Roman remains. Not so seemingly fallen the Florentines, then, in the dark ages; never so medieval. They fought back hard the medieval world in which they found themselves. They alone were prepared, intelligent. Undoubtedly Dante and Giotto were spokesmen of Italy. Florentine Giotto alone in the thirteenth century could assume what Mr. Roger Fry[2] has called in this connection 'the urbanity of a great style'. I will call the style 'statuesque'. Neither Greeks nor Romans conceived of the statuesque. Only the mind remembering the solid Roman world and inheriting deep consciousness of stretch, of uneasy movement rife with pageant, as well as native artistry making for stillness, would conceive

[1] These are on the pulpit formerly in the church of S. Pier Scheraggio. —A. S.

[2] See *Vision and Design* by Roger Fry. Chatto and Windus.

the statuesque. Stately, crystalline, statuesque, a substitution of sheer purity of line for heavy ordinances of mass remembered from the distant past, Giotto's bright Gothic tower presided and presides in Florence.

This statuesque is one aspect of Gothic art, possibly the one sublime. But in the two succeeding centuries, the fourteenth and fifteenth, how could the Florentines share the psychology of Gothic exuberant, when they had trained their own Gothic to be crystalline and stately, to be like the threaded music that informs the visions of eyes half-closed to sunlight? (*Plate VIII*, 1). They could not, nor could they want to much. They felt exuberance as inventiveness, as movement, which confined them to their heritage of line. And when under pagan forms Gothic zest fired the other Italians in the fifteenth century, the Florentines kept their lead by creation of the monumental, a sometimes ill-assorted development of the statuesque ideal. From the previous fourteenth-century work, we gain an impression that once the controlled yet fervid spirituality of Giotto recedes into the past, how unfortunate is reduction of Gothic soaring style to terms of the statuesque. Precision, a cold precision is now the showing, an inhuman treatment of pointed shapes. An instance is the back view of the Baroncelli tomb[1] (1327) in Santa Croce (*Plate VIII*, 1). As for the acanthus crockets on the arch of the Bardi monument opposite, I should like to confront their tidied thinness (so false in late Gothic) with any example of the Venetian flapping variety, those, for instance, on the pinnacles of St. Mark's, which Giuseppe Fiocco[2] and others will insist were executed by purely Florentine artists.

The sculptured prophets of the Bardi tomb, in the treatment of which a rhythm can be felt warding off anything *emphatic*, foretell Ghiberti's style. Ghiberti's predecessor at the Baptistery, Andrea Pisano who made the first bronze doors,

[1]Reproduced in an article '*I Monumenti dei Baroncelli e dei Bardi*', by Heinrich Bodmer. *Dedalo*, 1929.

[2]See *Dedalo*, 1927.

shows a similar restraint, in his case unobjectionable. At the same time, curiously enough, some fourteenth-century buildings in Florence show affinities to the Gothic verve general in Italy in the next century, but which, by then, was difficult to the Florentines. Witness the robust Porta di San Frediano built in the fourteenth century, also the strong loggia de' Lanzi. Their effect edges on the Quattro Cento. I suppose that when narrow shapes succoured the ambitions of the rest of Italy, Florence, as too Siena, could expostulate a difference by such massive spaces. Perhaps the cry for the monumental was already abroad. For the monumental is the reply of those civilized ones who must compete with the outlandish intensity of the less civilized. Certainly the Gothic of Orcagna in whose workshops every kind of smith dexterity was gathering precious thunder, sometimes has a slow magnificence and tentative contortion as in the winding branch forms on the base of the Or San Michele tabernacle, which pre-figure[1] Donatello's balustrade to the altar in the sacristy of San Lorenzo (*Plate XLVI*, 2). At the same time the gradualness of the mixtiline arch,[2] a shape that appears in 1408 for Or San Michele's doorway, aggravates impression of queer and steady frigidity in Florentine Gothic. The mixtiline entrance of the Fraternita dei Laici at Arezzo by Bernardo Rossellino, horrifies with its gradualness. On the other hand this need not be. Michelozzo's use of mixtiline form at Sant' Agostino, Montepulciano, is not disturbing, nor Bon's at Venice nor Giorgio di Sebenico's at Ancona.

IV. *Fifteenth-Century Gothic in the rest of Italy*

So, in Florence, Italian Gothic forms were on the whole tinctured with the reserve of the native aesthetic. Naturally Gothic was never supreme here. Throughout the fourteenth century and before, Romanesque persists, sometimes comitant with Gothic, sometimes pure, if also changed from pre-

[1]*See* Adolfo Venturi. *Storia dell' Arte italiana.* Vol. VIII, p. 13.
[2]*See* Marcel Reymond. *L'arc mixtiline*, Rivista d'Arte, 1904.

London, Victoria and Albert Museum : Verona marble well-head from Verona.

PLATE VII. VERONA MARBLE

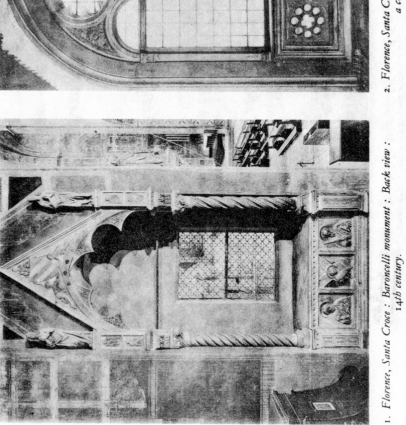

1. *Florence, Santa Croce : Baroncelli monument : Back view :*
14th century.

2. *Florence, Santa Croce.   Attrib. Michelozzo : Window in*
a corridor : 15th century.

PLATE VIII. FLORENTINE GOTHIC AND FLORENTINE NEO-GOTHIC

vious Romanesque. In the Renaissance which is foremost an intensification of Gothic spirit, Brunelleschi contrived a formula without reference to actual Gothic shapes. He caused a faster Gothic line to serve both Romanesque[1] spacing as well as the new classical forms he introduced.

Gothic itself, and the relation of classical forms to Gothic, were different in the rest of Italy. When I stressed the prevalence of Gothic spirit in Quattro Cento work which is classical in form and in aim, for the sake of clearness I omitted to add that complete Quattro Cento expression is occasionally found in Gothic construction and ornament having no classical pretence at all (*Plate VII*). The power, though, thus to articulate emblem, derives from the contemporary humanism. The traveller who has learned to date the Renaissance in art from Brunelleschi's visit to Rome in 1402, or from Masaccio's frescoes at the Carmine, will be surprised to discover that in Italy as a whole the majority of buildings of the fifteenth century are Gothic with little or no classical reference. The explanation is not simply that the Renaissance penetrated slowly. For these buildings are the crop of an enormous outburst in building, very often of the general substitution of stone for brick which was the most obvious mark of the new loveliness, and even noted as such by contemporary travellers.[2] In fact Gothic buildings of the fifteenth century in Italy must outnumber those of the recognized Gothic centuries by at least two to one. And whereas in the more outlandish parts from the Renaissance point of view, in Piedmont and the whole of the Peninsula south of Rome, in the Abruzzi and the lower Marches, there are few Renaissance buildings of the fifteenth century, in this sense of buildings which show renewal of Roman ambitions; yet intensification touched those parts to the flowering of late Gothic architecture. Even in the north, Gothic predominates, in Lombardy and even in Venice. Milan Cathedral be-

[1] Brunelleschi and Michelozzo did not need to adjust their style to complete the fourteenth-century Romanesque palazzo di Parte Guelpha.

[2] See, for instance, *Travels of Pero Tafur*. Broadway Travellers' Series.

longs largely to the first decades of the century, so too most of the exterior ornamentation of the Doges' Palace at Venice, the greater part of the Certosa at Pavia, the cathedral and San Domenico at Bologna, these among the largest structures of the land. But quite apart from such well-known buildings, and the equally well-known late Gothic of Venice, apart from Giorgio di Sebenico, chief exponent of Quattro Cento Gothic, apart from all transitional work, purely flamboyant Gothic of the fifteenth century can be found in any part, which to the attentive eye reflects, if it does not embody, the spirit of the Quattro Cento. I will instance such diverse structures as the terracotta-faced palazzo dei Mercanti at Mantua, the open side door of the palazzo Corvaja, Taormina, the casa Tabassi, Sulmona, from which the development is to the lovely palazzo dell' Annunziata also at Sulmona, this being an entirely Quattro Cento work, in style transitional from flamboyant Gothic.

Naples is rich in fifteenth-century Gothic suggestive of the Quattro Cento.[1] Used here as at Palermo in the Angevin period, the bent-blade arch[2] convention calls to mind the wrought and delicate tensity of Francesco di Giorgio's doorways. An

[1] I don't refer to the French Cistercian Gothic deriving from the Badia di Casamare, of which there are many examples at Naples, the best known being the doorway of the cathedral and of the capella Pappacoda and the Penna tomb in Santa Chiara.

[2] Aldo di Rinaldis (see *Forme tipiche dell'Architettura Napolitana nella prima metà del Quattrocento. Bollettino d'Arte*, 1924) does not think that this kind of broad arch, pressed down within a rectangle shape that dates here in Naples as a separate form from the Durazzan period, is a *ribassimento* of a Gothic arch, but a development of Romanesque. This may be, but the tension is Gothic. Incidentally, Naples gives good example of the Renaissance as intensification of all forms. For instance, the campanile (*circa* 1415) of the capella Pappacoda is early French Romanesque revival. When Alfonso of Aragon took the Angevins' place in 1447, there comes an influx of excited Catalan Gothic, superb in the great hall of Castel Novo built by the Spaniard known as Guglielmo Sagrera. Here you may see a depressed arch of a more violent if less tense kind, a Gothic arch turned inside-out so that the point falls down between two little rounded arches thus made.

instance is a doorway of the palazzo Penna,[1] a Gothic palace encrusted with deep emblem, and at Carinola, the Casa Novelli the windows of which, like those of the Penna, have the 'balance' cornice. The mouldings of such windows were deeply incised so that to the elasticity of their tensive shapes should be added the durance of reverberating iron.

Gothic prolixity, whether flamboyant work of the Lombardy masons, or these tense doors and windows of the south, is the root of which the greater Quattro Cento achievements are the flower; their season following rebirth of classical forms facilitated by Brunelleschi. Late Gothic was already discovering mass, but by substitution for the narrower Gothic shapes and mouldings of more ample, more regular, less perpendicular design, mass could win an instantaneous impression from the beholder, enormous.

V. Ghiberti and Elegance

The argument now centres on the use of perspective, and grows complex. For this science, indispensable to the Quattro Cento emergent effect of stone-blossom, to the boisterous rout from stone at the hands of Donatello or Agostino di Duccio, as also to the final religion of objects positioned untraversably in a timeless world,[2] was nevertheless perfected, and, indeed, perhaps only could have been perfected, from processes of cold and facile synthesis arranged to satisfy Florentine reserve. For it was tame Ghiberti, rather than Masaccio and Brunelleschi, who with graceful pictorial relief showed what *fluency* perspective allows. And this same fluency in the hands of others, made marble open, and controlled upon a broad surface the rush of exuberant Quattro Cento forms.

I exaggerate. For the Quattro Cento was well advanced by

[1]Built by Antonio Penna, secretary to the Angevin king Ladislaus.

[2]A reference principally to the painting of Piero della Francesca and to the architecture of Luciano Laurana.

the time Ghiberti had spent twenty-seven years in devising with perspective the fluent bronze reliefs of his second Baptistery doors, 'the gates of Paradise'. Moreover the reliefs of his first Baptistery doors are not distinguished for their use of perspective, and, indeed, but for an elegance, an 'effortless' (he was working on these bronzes for twenty-one years), 'natural' elegance, pair well with Andrea Pisano's earlier doors. However this elegance or grace, measured, smooth, informal, could be advanced still further only by exploitation of perspective. And such elegance, rather than a love of space (as opposed to spacing), of pure spatial effect, of mass, underlies Florentine perspective science.

First of all, then, we must understand what kind of elegance is this; since there are many kinds. One can say at once it is a fluency of form in direct contrast with the thin and formalized elegance of the East and North. This fluency of form, in turn, was connected with 'naturalism', with study of the antique, both as cause and effect. Just such fluency, such natural, free, almost purposeless grace, sums up Ghiberti's reaction to antique sculpture. And we must realize, not only in relation to Ghiberti, but to the early Renaissance as a whole, that fawning imitation of nature, imitation which, when practised to-day, is not pervaded by any necessity, was at that time an expression of new love for material and for natural objects, for aspects to which men had been blind, that is, to casual grace where life is most ardent. Naturalism in the Renaissance was primarily homage to fluent yet evanescent grace in flower or foliage, in animals,[1] but particularly in the young nude. And grace was identified with nobility itself, the ancient, and therefore to Renaissance eyes, the original nobility, and with good manners. Devotion to an unactuated elegance required studies, life-like rep-

[1] In the representation of animals, the novel fluent grace meets and joins with the more decorative or withdrawn grace of those oriental arts which had found their highest expression in animal motives. For an instance of such fusion of different types of animal elegance, see Pisanello's 'St. Eustace' in the National Gallery.

resentation, entailed perspective science for reliefs as for painting, in order to measure distance from the rigid formulae that dispense authority large from the backgrounds of primitive painting. In the Renaissance, measurement itself is measure, science an art.

So such elegance, such grace needed perspective. But with its employment a wider feeling gained full expression. I refer to the Italian love of drama and of the scenic, and also to *genre*. In what other mode can the 'big' pictorial conception ripe in glorious fires of drama be put, with all the needed fluent urgency? Could Persian Bihzad have covered a huge ceiling with one composition as could Tiepolo? And as for *genre*, consider, for instance, such a painting as the Turkish *concert*[1] *in a garden* at the Louvre. Here you see, though tinged with European influence, the oriental non-fluent elegance hostile to perspective. Ladies stand embowered in blossom, attendants represented minute (as befits their station) kneel in front. The music and, indeed, the afternoon, slip by.

Now an Italian artist is more independent, his respect for hierarchy, as a decor to life, far less: because of his love for fluency, he could never have tolerated attendants just befitting their station. He would have wanted one of them to fondle a dog.

But Italian *genre* expresses not so much an intimacy as a warmth. It won't distract, still less snatch away idea of the immediate purpose of a picture. In the North, of course, perspective and *genre* were used to enlarge the effects (thus atrophied) that the Turkish artist wanted. The *genre* of most Dutch and English pictures is a slow music, or else in the hands of academicians, an actual substitution for speech or description. One would be back with the Chinese written character were it not that the symbol has been horribly perverted: for seduced from pure formality by the technique of the fluent, plausible South, the symbol is no longer conceived as primarily decora-

[1]Reproduced on p. 277 English translation of René Grosset's *The Civilisations of the East*, Vol. I. Hamish Hamilton, 1931.

tive.[1] If academicians must go south, let them go further south. They make better Hottentots[2] than Greeks.

This is perhaps the proper context in which to refer to the academic discussion about Ghiberti and the low relief. On the technical side, be it said, Ghiberti developed perspective in making reliefs of many surfaces. The reliefs of his first bronze doors which lack perspective effects, nevertheless show a greater complication of planes than do those of Andrea Pisano. Hereafter perspective comes to organize surfaces even yet more complicated, with buildings introduced for the background (*Plate IX*, 2). But in the first place, for his first doors Ghiberti employed confluent planes to make his Gothic line resilient and to establish the elegance and taste he had at heart. The Quattro Cento emergent effect, also, appearing in every kind of ornamental, depended on the seething multisurface. When the fervour inspiring this mode died down, surfaces became more simple. Contrasted with Quattro Cento work, ornamentals of the sixteenth century look 'stuck on'. Instead of flowering from the stone, they seem to adhere for your very special occasion. The change, however, is justified by the demands of severely classical construction, and looks ill only when associated with exuberant fifteenth-century feeling as in *Plates XIII*, 1, *XVII*, 1 and *LVI*, 1-2. This justification, if you agree about it, side-tracks the whole academic discussion which dragged on through the eighteenth and nineteenth centuries about whether low relief should be 'pictorial', that is, of many planes, or whether following the Greek model, planes should be as simple as possible. The answer is that the demands of architecture determine the case. Multi-planed or perspective reliefs on the metopes of a Greek temple would obstruct the simple (in effect super-imposed) planes of the building. Whereas when Gothic spirit inspires, even though

[1] It is, of course, the independent and democratic spirit of the North, in this respect unfortunate, that has caused northern artists to relish the anti-hierarchic fluency of the South.

[2] *Cf.* the savagery introduced to brighten up things in the 1931 Academy.

many forms be classical, the modes of Gothic perforation and of excrescence will duly be expressed by multi-planed, and thereon perspective, relief. Thus it is that renascence of the antique in a Gothic age entailed large and more exact uses of perspective than were discovered by the ancient world. Moreover the capture of a science in technique redoubles the influences which led up to it, redoubles both classical measurement and the fervours of exuberance moving out of the stone, a process itself measured and celebrated by perspective.

Of this treatment Ghiberti admittedly was a pioneer, even when he made his first doors. However, it was not to the ends of such Quattro Cento exuberance that Ghiberti chose involved surfaces and, later, perspective, to order them. He wanted only an elegance that he identified with good taste. Ghiberti had his northern affinities; he was cold. He embodied the Florentine reserve. And so the argument is bound to be involved. For every achievement of this reserved aesthetic, makes possible Quattro Cento exuberance, sometimes in Florence itself, as we shall see; more often on the Adriatic coast. While, on the other hand, every achievement of Florentine reserve, after fructifying for a period in Italy, entailed, as well as these triumphs, calamities in the whole of art.

VI. Ghiberti and 'Finish'

The coldest temperaments are the most gracious. A general mounting of the pulse in that age upon more intense realization of beauty in the human form, was not to be satisfied with bare representation of grace. After all, you cannot interpret the Renaissance as a mere release from the old authoritative tension. Release at once created a new and stronger tension. While Ghiberti toiled with his elegant yet natural shapes, Donatello was winding tighter and tighter the Quattro Cento tensity not of representation only, but of *manifestation*—of life come through the surface of the stone. No doubt first, Ghiberti's temperament was essential to obtain measure for the attitudes of this excitement. I would not under-estimate the Quattro Cento debt to Florence and to the cold Florentine aesthetic. So I am aware that it is ungracious to find Ghiberti's aesthetic repulsive. Besides, his bronze gates are beautiful. But if one knows the failures, the inhumanity of the failures[1] that issue from the Florentine cold exploitation of Gothic and Roman forms, the successes, though beautiful, appear tainted.

I can think of no art more difficult to describe than Ghiberti's. You attempt analysis of his bronze, and it seems impossible the constituents could make a work of art. That Ghiberti was able to 'use' diverse tendencies and achieve serenity without imposition of anything but 'good taste', is the supreme proof of the power in Florence, the cold power to make adjustments, to succeed that way. It amounts to genius succeeding that way; which is difficult for us to understand when we meet persons who would (if they could) conceive art to be identified with the pretty or elegant. Ghiberti's success is at the root of this behaviour. Elegance, 'good taste', a spiritual serenity which is nothing more positive than a lack of emphasis amid moving scenes, these were the aims of his art, these the imprint of his personality. I have explained what a different value unassuming grace possessed in Ghiberti's time. But to appreciate intellectually how his work could be art, one must understand, besides, the strength of Florentine reserve, itself a principle of synthesis, powerful to 'use' rather than 'enter into' emotions.

The point is that Ghiberti avoided the Quattro Cento. Though he was the wrapt discoverer of a marble hermaphrodite among the Roman ruins, though *impelled* by the new fervour, *he exerted every human faculty so that he might blend it with the statuesque to which his bones held him*. He sought to counter tumultuous feeling with a non-stop elegance. Ghiberti made the running, but really he wanted to block the race.

And yet the treatment of the Baptistery reliefs has been admired as 'classic'. This adjective is meant to refer to the way

[1]To be described principally in Chapter III, Section III.

Ghiberti has prevented anything psychologically immoderate obtruding on to his crowded scenes, so that the reliefs individually and collectively can be harmonious in the ancient manner. But the word 'classic' in this connection may conceal a fallacy, or at any rate lead to a confusion, since artists with a more impressive concern for 'the classical', in the sense of the antique, Masaccio, Donatello, are not distinguished by the repose they put upon movement. These other pioneers threw up monumental and disturbing conceptions. Movement or action possessed them. While on the other hand, as Lionello Venturi pointed out[1] in this connection, more 'primitive', slightly reactionary artists such as Fra Angelico or Gentile da Fabriano, are distinguished for their calm unsullied handling of the new detail, of the new grace. Ghiberti is nearer to these Gothic painters than to Donatello or Brunelleschi.

Now I would seem to have overshot the mark in identifying with an ebullience of spirit the fifteenth-century Gothic in order to judge inapposite the Florentine statuesque Gothic. For Gothic as a whole undoubtedly has its repose or serenity. Perhaps no other art has equalled Gothic in charged sublimity expressed through sculptured figures. That is one aspect of Gothic carving, but one which belongs essentially to the North and to France in particular; one which, however, has far less reference to Gothic sculpture in Italy, and none at all to early Quattro Cento[2] apart from its dependence on the Florentine. Further, even if Giotto took of this sublimity to create the statuesque, I cannot think such sublimity may be identified with statuesque conception thereafter in Florence, the tale of which goes back far beyond Gothic times, and is based on a theme of more *deliberate* coldness and reserve than the North could invent. Gothic serenity has warmth, which is not expressed in the neat and cold Gothic architecture I have con-

[1] See *L'Arte*, 1923. *Lorenzo Ghiberti* by Lionello Venturi.

[2] There is a 'static' Quattro Cento sculpture connected with this kind of Gothic. But it is a later development under circumstances entirely different. *See* Part III, Section V.

demned at Florence. Besides, Gothic architectural plan in general, so far as one may isolate it from the accompanying sculpture, as a rule expresses a very different aspect of this Gothic spirit; and I cannot recall another building beside Giotto's tower in which this warm, sculptural sublimity appears in the construction alone. In this case the sublime joins with the statuesque beneath the warm sun. It is unique in architecture.

But as far as painters are concerned, the 'primitive' painters of the fifteenth century I mean, it is no cause for surprise that for their so decorative purpose they enlarged upon colourful repose, simplicity and charm. Sculpture in the Renaissance could avow no such formal purpose. The stone of late Gothic was massing all over Europe. Ghiberti, too, is eager for the new vitality, at any rate as a new elegance. We have seen that for this purpose he needed to make Gothic line extraordinarily resilient and to multiply the planes of the relief. Yet in his commentaries one discovers beside the conventional admiration for the Greeks whose sculpture he never knew, the greatest reverence for the fourteenth-century painters, for that sublime and simple Gothic repose which he attributed also to the Greeks. And so, it was Ghiberti's Gothic, his Florentine Gothic feeling, that led him to project into the antique this idea of gentle grace, and thereby to draw it out altered to a grace more fluent. Niccolo and Giovanni Pisano of the Giottesque Proto-Renaissance in the thirteenth century, attempted this same synthesis. Ghiberti is the true inheritor of their sculptural art. That he helped on the ebullient Renaissance was not his fault, but that he perpetuated the Proto-Renaissance was of his choosing.

How did he do it: when he, in common with the rest of the sculptors in Florence, was straining every nerve to accomplish naturalistic perfection, to be the spokesman of new and learned enthusiasm, how did he manage to inform reliefs of many surfaces, of engaging complexity of figures and of action, with serenity? I will describe how, partly because of the awful consequences in later arts, and partly because such perfect and final manipulation by one man shows how reserved and obstinate was the Florentine artistry, treating even the greatest enthusiasm that swept the modern world, right at the magnificent dawn of that enthusiasm, treating it as something perfectly estimated.

I do not deny the success nor the beauty of Ghiberti's first door. The reliefs are fitted into Gothic frames on Andrea Pisano's model. Andrea's Gothic line has been accentuated to suit the modes of more civilized expressiveness. Ghiberti, we can take it, vanquished Jacopo della Quercia, Brunelleschi, and Donatello among others, in the competition[1] for the contract which inaugurates the century. His victory does not surprise us. His workmanship was fine, his treatment traditional as well as modern. Ghiberti gave his judges exactly what all later judges of similar competitions have looked for in vain.

But when he began to make his second doors some twenty-five years later, the situation was completely altered. Ghiberti had been left behind. Monumental endeavour was now the sign of leadership. Donatello and Brunelleschi reigned unchallenged. Ghiberti must have hated Donatello's forceful art. He writes after 1450: 'Few things of beauty are made nowadays in Florence which aren't my work or under my direction (*cose . . . disegnate et ordinate di mia mano*.)' Meanwhile for twenty-seven years he had worked at his second doors, and brought it off (*Plate X*). The contract, no doubt, he had undertaken with trepidation. Somehow he must manage to incorporate the liveliness, the monumental distinction even, which was already so popular; yet preserve elegance to such supernal effect that the jeers of Donatello won't hurt. Perspective will give the means. In any case, he, Ghiberti, is admittedly the finest technician in

[1]According to the *Anonimo*, Brunelleschi's competition relief also won, and it was proposed that he should share the job with Ghiberti. Whereupon—the *Anonimo* goes on to state—Brunelleschi surrendered his share out of pique. Even if this is true, the fact that Brunelleschi couldn't force Ghiberti to withdraw, probably shows who was the stronger winner. The reliefs of the sacrifice of Isaac submitted by them to the judges, are now in the Bargello at Florence.

bronze casting. And perfection of technique is recognized as the beginning and the end of art. So the Donatello craze cannot go on. Besides, he will outdo the younger men, show them a rhythm more modern than the Donatello clangour, a rhythm that will endure, linked up as it is with the exquisite statuesque of the Florentine past.

Now to reproduce that feeling alone without the piety of a Giotto, would be difficult. And Ghiberti was not a pious artist. Long since in sculpture, unemphasized piety had become 'natural' beauty, ambient in fitful scenes. But to impute that sweet restfulness to the crowded and grandiloquent, sounds impossible. How could Ghiberti avoid emphasis that destroys good taste?

The case goes hard with Ghiberti when you analyze these perfectly-wrought reliefs. D'Agincourt and Lionello Venturi[1] have pointed out that the compositions have no inner necessity. Thus, foreground figures are almost free-standing statuettes and without an *urgent* relationship to the deeper surfaces. Every bit of Ghiberti's knowledge of the antique is crowded in without any *extreme* relevance. Ghiberti has nothing to put over, nothing to say; no inner necessity compels these forms. 'The spirit of Ghiberti', wrote L. Venturi, 'never loses itself, but is sure of itself, commanding a fixed and artificial intention. Ghiberti lacks vision. He has been blamed for lacking unity of action. This is a mistaken approach. Also Masaccio's "Tribute" lacks unity of action, but where will one find greater unity of vision? Ghiberti, on the other hand, is wanting in the unity of vision, a loss that amounts to aesthetic imperfection, because a lack of stylistic unity is a lack of synthesis.'[2] So here he places a page, here a dog, here a divine apparition, all interesting and all delicate, all impeccable as well as composed together, but corresponding to no *other* homogeneous necessity (*Plate IX*, 2).

To my mind, though, that impeccability, that mere good taste *is* a homogeneous necessity, though a sinister one, and in

[1]*Cf. op. cit.*   [2]*Cf. op. cit.*

1. *Florence, S. M. Novella.* Benedetto da Majano: *Detail of monument to Filippo Strozzi.*

2. *Florence, Baptistery : Meeting of Solomon and Queen of Sheba. A relief of Ghiberti's second bronze doors.*

PLATE IX. 'RECKLESS TAMENESS' AND 'PERFECT FINISH'

Florence, Baptistery. Ghiberti's *second bronze doors.*

PLATE X. 'UNASTOUNDING BEAUTY'

view of the fight to get art understood, impossible to defend. Ghiberti invented a quality to make the gentle, if obstinate, virtuosities of these reliefs cohere. Rather than impeccability I call the quality 'finish'.

I imagine the common conception, 'finish', derives from an acknowledgment of an attribute of Florentine sculpture that dates from Ghiberti's second doors, an attribute which some would wish irrelevantly perpetuated. For 'finish' does not popularly refer to the perfect objectivization of any aesthetic idea, but rather to the final result of a particular painstaking realistic treatment only. This is as it should be; for the conception 'finish' is the prime quality, the final aesthetic triumph of that fluent grace—in wider terms—that fluent realism, which we found to demand perspective treatment. Otherwise the concept 'finish' would never have occurred. It is always irrelevant when applied to other than a *fluent, unemphasized, realistic* treatment. One may find a fifteenth-century Persian painting had not been finished, but not that it lacks 'finish'. And because more educated people insist on introducing the concept where it does not apply, they talk nonsense about art, and think nonsense.[1] There are other reasons.

But there is plenty of excuse for the muddle in question. Few post-Ghiberti artists in Europe—and neither Michael Angelo nor Leonardo are among them—have escaped the problem of 'finish', just because 'finish' has been identified with the final state of *all* realistic treatment.[2] So they envy Ghiberti and his like for the equally-distributed rhythm of their works,

[1] I shall, however, keep 'finish', as I use it, in inverted commas to avoid possible confusion.

[2] That this should have occurred shows how immense has been the attraction in Europe, since the Renaissance, of a fluent realism. To-day, for the first time, we are far enough away from the Renaissance to examine it and to uncover the Quattro Cento, which, though underlying the Renaissance, was swamped by it. We would no longer identify the whole Renaissance with European values. And so I search out the Quattro Cento values, back to which the modern world directs us. For we have worked through the Renaissance as it actually developed.

gained by 'finish', while they themselves want to express, in addition, a definite emphasis. Now Ghiberti invented 'finish' in order to avoid any emphatic treatment.

I would suggest that this problem which needed always to be solved afresh with each work, has been the spur to the greatest and to the worst art in the history of man. To-day we tire of it; it is an obstruction. So back we should go to Ghiberti to analyze it and to rid ourselves.

I find myself inferring that these Ghibertian attitudes were deliberate, whereas actually they were largely unconscious. Perhaps one can only write in coherent prose of deeper motives as if they were deliberated. Purely on the surface, though, it is evident that whereas some Florentine artists arrived in Rome with enthusiasm for the big and monumental, others like Ghiberti were drawn there, not primarily from a general mounting of the pulse in that generation, but from increased interest, assiduity. Their keen intellects were real enough, and their eager civilization.

That Ghiberti was working twenty-seven years on the bronzes for his second doors, throws some light on the quality 'finish'. I shall remark later on Florentine affinities with the kaleidoscopic art of the North, which helped Ghiberti to formulate his 'finish'. Somehow the beasts among the foliage on the bronze jambs recall the convention of Flemish miniatures. The flowers themselves are 'posed' (rather than positioned), as if for photography or for a still-life class. They are unexceptional in their perfection of unassuming naturalism. This lack of assumption underlying 'finish' needed years of careful cultivating. Some of the leaves, besides, were undoubtedly cast from nature. Yet, unlike the narrowly intimate art of the North, the whole pulsates with rhythm. Every marking of the veins of leaves, every carefully articulated tuft of hair in the figures of the ten outside reliefs, every angle of the statuettes of prophets and sybils, convey the rhythm and the freedom of the whole. Remember how engrained was the Florentine aesthetic of the statuesque, remember the same as threatened by the new Italian ferment of which, too, the Florentines partook; remember Brunelleschi's invention of speed of line in architecture. Ghiberti invented for sculpture a similar speed, so as to sublimate to the ends of Florentine aesthetic the deep Italian dramatic sense. Movement is everywhere in these reliefs. Only thus can repose be saved. Repose must have no beginning and no end because it must appear in the guise of movement, continuous movement, a flow without emphasis. Conservation by division of strength. There must be no central emphasis, but a general rhythm. Therefore every detail must have its perfect rhythm and yet, at the same time, be *without emphasis*. Such unemphasized perfection of detail is 'finish', which could be attained only by fluent realistic treatment. For any other treatment that articulates by generalization, is too direct, too arresting. For this purpose the 'primitive' realism of the Giottesque would be inadequate, violent, clumsy. Perspective is the means of Ghiberti's movement. A pictorial treatment of low relief embodying perspective, guarantees the flow, while laborious naturalism both makes each detail safe from emphasis (which an economic, direct articulation would not do) and keeps each detail distinct, a miniature of potential actuality. And so this general yet precise flux achieves the Florentine clarid measure.

What a great artistic achievement is this, when the tricks of abstraction used in every art-period throughout the world are sacrificed! No wonder Ghiberti's success has been a stumbling block to many a normal artist. (If you contemplate art as a whole, you will see Ghiberti as eccentric.) Donatello, on the other hand, endowed his reliefs with an inner organization, apparent in their first composing. He had no need of perfect 'finish'. So far from avoiding emphasis, Donatello magnified it; for his planes are never divorced from one another, though interrupting and interrupted.

Ghiberti did not want any such intense composition. Writing in commentary of his second doors, he says: 'I have tried in every way to imitate nature exactly in these reliefs . . . the

97

nearer figures appear larger, the more remote smaller.' 'Imitation', of course, is never an exact term. Cultural values determine what is considered to be imitation. But the words quoted bring to my mind these reliefs ('the nearer figures appear larger, the more remote smaller') in which expressiveness is subordinate to an unastounding beauty, and every contour is left soft and rhythmic. In these doors, sculpture is certainly betrayed by pictorial treatment. Ghiberti describes himself as foremost a painter. But one cannot conclude that when painting he conceived in terms of colour, of tone. That is not the way to make a picture look as if it isn't there at all, however effectual in relief.

So, 'unastounding beauty', 'unemphasized rhythm', 'finish' and 'good taste' which so often, in part, expresses a desire to have things looking as if they weren't there at all—are in many ways synonymous. Introduced to the North, 'finish' was bound to lead to trouble. For bad artists have never realized that the whole point of 'finish' is the equal rhythm it enables. And who can feel an *equal* rhythm in a northern climate? Except it be bright in the sun, equal rhythm is monotonous. In our rains the porticoes of Greece and Rome loom long-suffering.

VII. *Bronze Statuettes and Clays*

Bode[1] and Planiscig[2] are agreed that whereas bronze statuette and group were evolved by the followers of Donatello, Ghiberti gave the original model in the figures that are niched on the centre and the edges of his second doors. It shows how wedded to architecture was the sculptor of that age, that Donatello's Judith and Holofernes should be the first entirely free-standing group.

Ghiberti's figures, we know, offer 'finish' as a substitute for

[1] *Italian Bronze Statuettes of the Renaissance*, transl. W. B. and Murray Marks. 3 vols., London, 1907-12.

[2] *Die italienische Bronzestatuette der Renaissance*, Kunsthistorisches Museum, Sammlungen, I. Vienna, 1925.

'style'. (It would be better, though, in the future if 'finish' were accounted a style, just one of many.) Donatello's bronzes have an opposite, a dynamic quality, but some of his followers eschewed both this intensity and Pollaiuolo's truculence. They preferred Ghiberti's equal rhythm, particularly in the reproduction or elaboration of an antique motive. And so, in some of the works of Riccio one can recognize that quality of inoffensiveness produced by 'finish', which is powerful to make the agitation of a Donatello figure harmless; thus a bad bronze may finally appear so undistinguishable in suitable surroundings, yet distinguished, as to be welcome to the sideboards of industrialists. The preferred group will be hazardously balanced following the model, perhaps, of Rustici's mounted negro in conflict with a lion.[1] The subject should be so worked in conformance with the aesthetic of 'finish', that there is conveyed to the spectator a non-intense feeling of violent movement and hazardous situation. These were occurrences of aeons and aeons ago; and the spectator is surprised (ever so mildly) that they are recalled fluently, just as he would be to hear a sound-wave from the golden age. No violent sympathy is enlisted.

I must now qualify in an important respect the assertion that the early Renaissance sculpture was rarely separate from its architecture. Sculpture in the strict sense, perhaps, but not modelling. For the production of cheap religious figures or groups in Florence was enormous. The more purposeful glazes of the della Robbia enhanced the business into a fine export trade. But before that, as far back as 1401, the churches of Florence were so congested with votive images, that the Signoria issued a decree to restrain these deposits. I suggest that that decree, issued in the second year of the fifteenth century, gives a better date to the Renaissance than any other single event. It is more significant than the date 1400 when the Baptistery doors competition took place, or the date 1402 when Brunelleschi travelled to Rome. For the Signoria's de-

[1]Foulc collection, Paris. For the attribution, *see* Planiscig, *op. cit.*

cree shows how vast already had been the practice of modelling, and how general the desire for the naturalistic image. Here is the datum for an extensive school from which great sculpture, as it seems to us, arose so suddenly.

On the other hand, the Signoria's decree shows that there existed in Florence a bourgeois demand for the tame realistic image as a fetish. Making allowance for the fact that these objects were cheap and would at all times appeal to popular taste, and that they provided the school in which representational modelling achieved its enormous advance, there remains a discrepancy.

The origin of these clays belongs to the native Florentine facility which is so oriental and which the great artists countered by projects that needed to become increasingly immense. And this adroitness in the ant-like workshops of the handling of charm, is inappropriate when put beside the investment of brick by stone that excited the traveller in Italy a little later, when put beside the far from domestic outburst in Rimini and Venice. This bourgeois side of the Renaissance, charming enough in the first half of the fifteenth century, sought to make of Christianity a sweet, family affair. Encouraging for others, but surely too facile a humanism in itself to serve felicitously as a first avowal of individual freedom. There was no love of the stone. At a later date Verrocchio himself was well in the business. Death-masks were now the rage, and Orsini Benintendi had divulged to him the secrets of fabricating lifelike wax figures. The Medici Palace must have been overrun with realistic masks and dolls; and the votive offerings which had already begun to overcrowd churches in 1401, now worked to the height of tinsel realism, gave the horrible model for Catholic images which has persisted to our own day. With these new lares and penates, grotesque in their controlled realism and their cold reiteration of a soft, peasant Christianity, the Florentines once more showed themselves to be the older pagans, but without loyalty for the new or for the old, which are cruelly interwoven; and their discovery of Rome but hardened their delight in the frigid, handy tools of ancestor-worship, now sweetened. The sweet, sulky milk of the della Robbia flowed into every Tuscan village. The manufacture of these images spread and spread.

That is one side of the Renaissance in Florence, psychologically of great importance.

CHAPTER THREE

THE MONUMENTAL,
OR SEEDS OF THE BAROQUE

I. *Etruscan Brutality*

THIS TITLE—Etruscan brutality—is no doubt over-picturesque, especially since I have already associated with the Etruscans qualities so diverse as a Japanese imitativeness and, in sculptured figures, a firmness on the ground which the art of Piero della Francesca inherited.

But I cannot forego using the Etruscans again. I suppose their art is felt to be pregnant with so many forms, to be a fount of perpetuation, perhaps because the Etruscans were real modellers as opposed to carvers. Certainly an impregnating with rooted and even dramatic emotions, of the idealized but unspiritual human forms taken in stone from Greece, is a constant impression, if a vague one, gathered from the best Etruscan pieces. Again in the Renaissance, the perfect antique nude was inspirited with varying emotion. It is impossible, though, to identify Renaissance monumentalism (the monumental is always *inspirited*) with any precise Etruscan forerunner.

The purely Etruscan, I have said, is difficult to isolate. But, thinking of those figures that recline bunched up on sarcophagi much too short for any real ease of attitude, I feel they communicate a huge, and otherwise unexpressed animus in the exercise of cruel, impressive emotional reserve. I feel similar animus from the case of Mexican sculptures in the British Museum. Now, Verrocchio in some works, as we shall see, exploited reserve of power to achieve tension; whereas for many Florentine sculptors imbued with northern influence, reserve is but negatively emotional, that is to say it is a coldness, a principle of cold selection. Perhaps Etruscan and Mexican pieces are frightening because sadism is here positive rather than negative.

Our concern now is with Florentines who expressed the monumental grasp latent in Etruscan forms, by a monumental manner that leads on to the Baroque. The Latin as opposed to the Greek, I have suggested, is the modeller as opposed to the carver. And the modeller first, not the carver, seeks out mass in movement, enjoys the scenic and the monumental effect. Etruscan architecture differed from the Greek as did the Roman which followed, being modellers' architecture. Luciano Laurana's fifteenth-century buildings, on the other hand, restore to architecture a static, spatial world. In Quattro Cento sculpture there has been an introjection of the carver's fancy into the modeller's aims, owing to the love of stone.

One notices in connection with modelling the corporeality which Etruscans emphasized in their sculpture, slow and irresistible; one notices that they left untouched the stark marbles[1] of Italy, using grainless volcanic or sand stones: so, like the Indian and Khmer sculptors they got that rough yet cohesive surface, the spongy, charged heaviness of which suggests a momentum. It is unfortunate, perhaps, that owing to love of the antique and owing to the love of stone, particularly marble, abroad in the fifteenth century, and because of their desire to over-compensate still further for the brutality they inherited, the Florentines might not use their *pietra morta* for an Etruscan or Khmer effect.

Undoubtedly the best Etruscan sculpture was of bronze and terra-cotta. They preserved their thought in coarse stone as an animus, but the terra-cotta Apollo from Veii is *informed* through and through. One begins to appreciate and to sympathize with Cato's indignation that the old terra-cottas were

[1]Except for alabaster work from Volterra and the ruins of Luni situated at the beginning of the Carrara range, I can think of no *essentially* Etruscan building nor sculpture in smooth stone.

no longer good enough for the Romans, who now must import the spiritless marbles of Greece. For indeed the Romans were undermining the genius of the land with their love of carved and uncarved marble. Little comfort it would have been for Cato to realize that this new love of stone would culminate, the modeller's art subsumed, in the immediate, timeless mass of Luciano.

Now some sensitive writers on Italian art do tend to introduce the Etruscans, if a little vaguely. Ruskin in *Mornings in Florence* dallies with the race. He describes the huge straw hats[1] of Tuscan *contadini* as pure Etruscan. Adolfo Venturi[2] must begin an account of Jacopo della Quercia with a brief list of Etruscan sculptural symbols alive in popular imagination, and drawn thence into renascent stone. Dante had conjured up beaked Etruscan devils with huge and speaking eyes (Bertoldo transmuted these features into a faun type when he made his Orion statuette), and Jacopo della Quercia and, finally, Michael Angelo —their carving so graphically *informed* with modellers' conception —will always in the end suggest the strong, robustious figures of many an Etruscan group that is slowed up and made voluminous with deep, penetrating emotion —one might say, made sculptural, so often has the achievement of Michael Angelo and of those linked with him before and after, been identified (wrongly of course) with sculpture's essence.

Again, some philologists[3] have induced themselves to suggest that the aspirated *C* of Tuscan pronunciation (hear them saying *harsa* for *casa* in Siena) is an Etruscan survival. Perhaps the same philologists, men of imagination, have pondered the long and harsh and constipated 'ah' with which the Florentine *contadino* encourages his lovely oxen. For in this in-

[1]The famous Certosa *situla* (*circ.* 500 B.C.), which is almost certainly Etruscan and not Villanovan, has figures wearing these straw hats.

[2]See *Storia dell' Arte Italiana*, Vol. VI.

[3]*See* Orioli, *Boll dell' Instit. Archaeol.* 1854. Also, Rise, *Dei tentativi fatti per spiegare le antiche lingue italiane* Milan, 1863.

cident of an emitted vowel amid the groans of the cart's passage, a vowel rocky and long-drawn-out but addressed to a gracious beast, milky-white —I gather an image of the major incident in Florentine art, of graphic or 'musical' asperity driving on docile grace with a monumental goad.[1] Hitherto I have put the cart before the ox. I have put 'finish' and the psychology of the cold statuesque first, and suggested that the monumental endeavour of a Donatello was the reaction. From the angle of the Renaissance alone I feel this arrangement, though artificial, was justified. But for the widest view of art in this region, the view in which the Etruscans are embraced, elegance and the statuesque will not be given precedence. In their place I suggest an anguish, a hardness, which provides a core for good modelling, and in the form of sadistic outbursts as felt in Etruscan art but still more in Etruscan character, explains a reactive emphasis, an old guilty-conscious emphasis on what is calm and on what is sweet (coldly treated as by the suave della Robbia), not raised to a confident art-form for nearly one and a half millennia; and only then by the sympathetic mediation of Christianity.

One feels the Renaissance was a spilling of every kind of racial memory. Was a Luca della Robbia the ancient apology for a Donatello; a Fra Angelico for an Andrea del Castagno? No. For Christianity must first step in. Not until the Renaissance does the western, the Latin, church achieve in art its very own expression. For the sweetness, the human sweetness of the Madonna figure in Renaissance art, and leading out from her, the gentleness of the whole religious hierarchy, is a true and deep expression as well as a mannered one.

Florentine artists show us the antinomy of their heritage. The most emotional may also be the most reserved. Not, however, when the emotions are principally those of love.

[1]Etruscan language has remained a puzzle. Their inscriptions never amount to more than a few words and divulge no general information. They do not appear to have had a literature. Yet they were a musical people and invented several instruments.

Thus the slightly sinister purity of Florentine tenderness. Most Florentine artists manipulated but did not love their materials. So they gained the advantage of facility. But to achieve anything so positive as the Quattro Cento outburst—and who can doubt that the Florentines became pioneers in emulation of the freer Italian character, as yet inarticulate, surrounding them?—they needed the monumental effort which becomes stabilized in the Baroque; they needed sometimes the boldest decorative invention which soon becomes conventionalized as the grotesque; they needed to harness the strength, the deeply charged strength, of Etruscan graphic line hitched on to forcible non-Florentine Gothic line. But the measure they had worked out for two centuries at least, accompanies them yet, the measure which had given them command. Actually, of course, it is misleading to describe any two Florentine artists antithetically. In nearly every case, measure and monumental aim are combined in varying proportions.

The next step is to remark these influences in Brunelleschi's architecture, since architecture was the parent art, and since Brunelleschi was both the pioneer of classical forms and the founder of a school.

II. *Brunelleschi*

Florentines, I have said, felt exuberance as inventiveness and movement; which more than ever confirmed them in the use of line. Thus Brunelleschi, the intelligent copier of classical mouldings, the unrivalled engineer in love with the calm of his native Tuscan Romanesque, invented an architecture which is primarily an abstraction of Gothic line, ordered and speeded up. It is non-emphasis applied to architecture. And, indeed, I might have put Ghiberti's name at the beginning of the Baroque. He too had a monumental aim; but largely in emulation of Brunelleschi. And, in any case, only in architecture can one show how monumental aim combined with non-emphasis, a difficult combination worthy of Florentine genius, must finally break up measure and equal rhythm into contrapuntal inventiveness. There is no pause in Brunelleschi's constructions any more than in Ghiberti's sculpture. But when the demands of the monumental grow more insistent, such smoothly running rhythm becomes fugal. Architectural members themselves are now in flux, architrave and pediment break loose to swell the Ghiberti-Brunelleschi tidy flow, into a swarming river that turns the mill-wheel with striped organ sound. Heavy masses are now used; for 'still waters run deep'.

So we see that the non-emphasis invented to preserve Florentine measure in the face of Roman massiveness and Gothic rampage, entailed a rhythm which monumental aim, also a Florentine heritage, was bound to expand out of all measure. Yet at the beginning of the Renaissance Brunelleschi was able to keep the monumental (excited by Roman remains) subservient to crystalline effects. Remember Florentine Gothic is measured, vertical, dubious as a simple prayer (*Plate VIII*, 1). Brunelleschi revels in horizontal lines which the rounded arch permits; the lines race. But this spirited but calculated turning of the tables, this substitution of invention and resource for exuberance, belongs to the psychology of the Baroque, the psychology, as I shall attempt to show, of nearly all the principal Florentine geniuses. They rapidly developed the Baroque, these the true and faithful followers of Giotto. It was bound to be, and good it was so, when in troubled times the Quattro Cento's immediate possession of the world surviving only in painting, exuberance throttled in the wells of mental anguish—that inventiveness, intellectual high spirits, should already have realized concrete manifestation, should be able to rain upon the abandoned field, so that there should at least be music, the music of fountains as well as of rivers.

To return to the origins of this Baroque. By diverting the massiveness of Rome and of the Gothic vehemence, into the use of multiple thin and rapid lines obedient to the classical orders, Brunelleschi was able not only to secure, but to intensify, Florentine linear bias. The incursion, then, of speed and movement into the Florentine stillness, brings the most extraordinary complications in sculpture-architecture, provoking alike works of genius and efforts which are monsters of contradiction and academic coldness.

Before I attempt to substantiate this, more must be said about Brunelleschi's architecture, so long held to be the purest expression of the Renaissance. Certainly the famous dome of the Cathedral, the Ospedale, the interiors of San Lorenzo and Santo Spirito, the Pazzi Chapel and many works of Brunelleschi's followers, are lovely. But hardly ever before San Gallo, or at any rate Cronaca, is the effect architectural[1]. Swiftness is gained by simple draughtsmanship, slightly strange in an era of expressive sculpture which sought mass, which culminated in Venetian painting of the next century. In most Brunellesque buildings, two colours, white and grey, stucco and *pietra morta* are used like paper and pencil. Pilasters, strips of line, arcs that hurry to their bases, ogival ribs delicate as the legs of a suspended daddy-long-legs vaulting a dome or loggia, are very accurately 'drawn' with grey stone upon the sized canvas of the walls and ceilings. A giant has wielded the pencil, a draughtsman who understands perspective. For this art proceeds from perspective science which was invented to enable fluid effects of speed (*Plates XI*,[2] *XII*, 1, and *XIII*, 1 and 3).

There is spacing, wonderful neatness, delicate carving and adjustment of capitals, uninterrupted flow of skilful line, but no spaciousness. Delicacy, which reaches its height in the interiors of Cronaca's palazzo Horne and Giuliano da San Gal-

[1]Brunelleschi's later work, however, more nearly approaches a mass-effect. Compare the differences between the interiors of San Lorenzo and the later Santo Spirito. L. H. Hegdenreich (see *Spätwerke Brunelleschis*, Jahrbuch der Preuss. Kunstsammlungen, 1931) thinks that this development reflects a visit paid to Rome by Brunelleschi in 1432-34.

[2]I have wanted to choose the loveliest effect of Brunellesque architecture; hence this plate of the Pazzi Chapel interior, though the use of pillars in so confined a space does not make this plate, as an illustration of 'drawing on the wall', altogether happy. But note the thin line of stone on the wall at the corner behind the altar. Compare this with the gap that Luciano left between pillars at the corners of his courtyard (*Plate XXXIV*).

lo's palazzo Gondi, is as sound as the Medici bank—a kind of garlanded celebration of good taste which is most romantic, especially at San Marco where the giant cedar fills Michelozzo's cloister, where the vaulting shoots with such spidery animation from the beautiful cushioned capitals. Michelozzo was very clever in his quiet way. He wanted to give Brunellesque lines a little more weightiness. So in this cloister he has used short pillars raised on cubic bases without the slightest diminution of tidiness. And to invent a library, he simply designed two parallel Brunellesque arcades, and vaulted the intermediate space! But as the Baroque grows, such archly scientific clarities will no longer satisfy. Those who find that the delicacy in spacing of these sound structures outweighs the delicacy of their monotony, should visit Prato and Pistoja, the latter for the sake of Michelozzo (interior of S. M. delle Grazie) and of Ventura Vitoni (Madonna dell' Umiltà), the former for Giuliano da San Gallo's S.M. delle Carceri, the exterior of which, invested with the Prato green and white marble, makes the affinity to the Tuscan Romanesque very easy to apprehend. Design is more professional than in the periods when they built the Baptistery at Florence. But as with the Baptistery, the dry use of the coloured marble is an affront to those who love colour. Later, when the tempo is doubled in the stress of Florentine position, this affront is to become an outrage committed by the more 'advanced' Florentine painters with the premeditated ugliness of their tone. For whatever other kinds of 'ugliness' are permissible to the painter for his effect, I cannot see how brutal coldness of colour can be included, and the whole remain a pleasure—judged as painting.[1]

[1]As tinted design it may well be a pleasure and, indeed, great art; but not strictly as painting of which Piero della Francesca and the Venetians have given us the standard. In their absorption in 'tactile values' which hard colour enhances, the Florentine 'painters' were definitely hostile to perspective as a religion. This is typical of the situation. The Florentines perfected perspective for very particular uses. The chief exception is Uccello whom Donatello, according to Vasari, reproved for his fixation on purely spatial values.

To return to *pietra morta*. How could this grey stone from Fiesole, this stone without heart, be felt as breaking into life, how emulate the concrete apparitions upon the surfaces of Verona marble? Michael Angelo in his disillusioned fury hacked away the marble, searching for apparitions. They came to meet the sun in the Quattro Cento. But before Michael Angelo, no one in Florence but Donatello, Desiderio and Verrocchio, had searched the heart of stone. *Pietra morta* was too sharply carved, and it is idle to argue whether this Florentine stone determined Brunelleschi's style, or whether he casually mounted it for his geometric canter. In any case it must be emphasized that though this stone and this style were capable of considerable grandeur as well as neatness—witness Cronaca's vestibule to the sacristy of Santo Spirito in Florence—however leonine the convolutions of the favourite Corinthian capitals, wonderfully varied in their carving, yet the effect remains one of weak animation.

With the help of pointable *pietra morta* Brunelleschi drilled the timid lines of Florentine Gothic. By rounding off the point of the Gothic arch with a rush of concentric lines, he overcame the pause of the apex, transformed the finality of this vanishing point into a speed that rushed him on to the next arch. If you stand at the entrance wall of San Lorenzo facing the altar, you may experience the release marked by pistol shot that dispatches runners on a hundred yards race. The sport is well governed. Thin bands touch the top of each arch, keep the racing order as do cords that divide runners. For all the pedimented apertures, the grave bevies of pillars and pilasters, aureoles, the Roman mouldings, bead, cavetto, scotia, cyma erecta, cyma reversa, egg and tongue, ovolo, and the bay-leaf garlands that hedge the windows of the Pazzi Chapel as well as the doors to Santo Spirito, Brunelleschi achieved nothing Roman nor Quattro Cento. Classical, yes, classically Florentine.

As for the monumental, monumental indeed are the huge palaces of Florence, the Pitti, the Medici, the Strozzi. Yet there is no silence from the stone. Rhythm is perfectly maintained. The windows of the Strozzi and Medici palaces are slight indentations: there is no recession, but a front used as an etcher's plate. A breaking up of the stone, you will realize, must assist such economical drawing for there to be any suggestion of the monumental. Brunelleschi at the Pitti, was the first to use rustication, that is to say, he was the first to *choose* rock-facing when he could have had the stone dressed. Thus was stone recorded where life of it was absent; and grooved joints, especially in London, remain the dope for those thirsting for architectural conception. One must notch meaningless wall-space (this, then, an academic trick of 'filling up') to multiply 'the features' of a building and to allow of those neat and simple vertical mouldings that look so queenly in the drawn plan when balanced by preponderant horizontal gashes. This is not an attack on rustication *per se*. It is necessarily associated with the monumental.

Some Florentine rustication and channelling were never surpassed. They have perfect neatness. But the running continuity of Brunellesque lines in this palace architecture, the rounded lines of window mouldings as well as string courses, oppose the effect, natural to rustication, of piled-up units. Massiveness is partly smoothed out by delicate and continuous lines. Again, the 'reveals' to the first and second floor windows of the Pitti palace are so shallow that the huge masonry of the wall, in which stones project as much as two feet, appears no more formidable than a weather-beaten skin or the lashes on a stormy tent.

III. *Reckless Tameness*

Bad Victorian neo-Gothic architecture, like other academic art, for all its tameness, can be as shocking as a bad dream or a great work of art. The very tameness is shocking because it is the ornament of a quite inhuman ruthlessness. Such buildings, aping a style whose inspiration was successfully drained into a constructional exuberance, are simply 'constructed' bit by bit. The less appropriateness in such a building, the more deliberate, the more obstinate the architect, the more shameless in his juxtapositions. The heart is steeled to it. A monster thus conceived can be so solid in sleek obstinacy, so reckless in tameness, as to fascinate with horror more strongly than any masterpiece of the grotesque. Here is no formalism, 'classicism', but a purely negative formalization of whatever is essentially informal; this, not by means of abstraction, but by making heterogeneous scraps of done-to-death detail 'suitable'.

I feel the same horror before many a beautifully worked Florentine tomb. The Florentines, out of the coldness of their knowing hearts, invented academicism as we understand it in England. They may even be accused of inventing late Victorian neo-Gothic. I ask anyone who is startled by this statement to search out at Santa Croce, Florence, the corridor which leads from the church to the Medici chapel. There he will find on the left, a window designed, it is said, by Michelozzo about the year 1445 (*Plate VIII*, 2). It is tame, competent, ugly, and, to me, shocking. The whole window-space is framed by a Brunellesque arch between which stretches a base divided into three compartments perforated by three Gothic traceries. Upon the base stand two mullion pillars forming three narrow rounded arches. Above the spandrels are two octofoils. The three arches are intersected at the level of the capitals by a moulding that leaves above it segments like lunettes, and below, oblongs.

One might have thought that in the first zest for classical forms no adaptation would occur to the pure and scientific Florentine mind, however natural to the ignorant with their appealing transitional effects. But the Florentines had a bias that was sincere and even unconscious. They favoured Romanesque forms. Michelozzo made the Brunellesque rounding of the arch a means to introduce the Romanesque mullion window, in this case probably influenced by Alberti's treatment of mullion windows at the Rucellai palace. Here we have a *trifora*. It is not the natural use of classical forms, but 'adaptation' of the Gothic to fit them, that shocks in this window. The Gothic, apparently, no more inherent than the new style, in fact, a case of the shuffling of 'styles', just as with the 'adapted' furniture, nominally Queen Anne may be, from the bourgeois store. These octofoils, so far from being a natural growth, so far from being a Gothic developed to embrace other forms, have been specifically invented by means of a purely literary abstraction, to induce 'that Gothic feeling'. It is not a case of inrooted Gothic tendencies as with the Quattro Cento architects. Gothic and classical, Michelozzo was in this case stone-cold to both. The faith of the Florentine architects was in their Romanesque. In this window we have all the styles, dead. An 'appropriate' window, 'suitable' to the Gothic church, to the environs of religion. Not a transition work, then, but a neo-Gothic. And when anything seen is so *carefully* dead, all gentle gravity becomes unbearable, while the 'daring' variations in these traceries which show how 'clever' as well as inoffensive the design, add boredom to one's recognition of sinister inhumanity.

Now Michelozzo was a great artist, and a great craftsman. There is reason to suppose that he, rather than Alberti, was the first to dissociate himself in part from the Brunellesque conception of mass.[1] Nearby this window at Santa Croce, is Michelozzo's entrance to the Capella del Noviziato, a doorway of deep tympanum.[2] It is a Quattro Cento expression, as

[1]See L. H. Hegdenreich, *Die tribuna der SS. Annunziata in Florenz. Mitteilungen des Kunsthistorischen Institutes in Florenz*, Vol. III, July, 1930, pp. 268-285. The author establishes from documents that the original plan of the Annunziata with nave and two rows of chapels and a circular tribune with chapels, was by Michelozzo. In 1470 Alberti defended the plan against architects invoking Brunelleschi's name. Michelozzo's plan is the prototype for spacious design exploited by Alberti in his churches at Mantua and for the encasement of the Tempio at Rimini.

[2]With this massive deep tympanum doorway, I associate another Quattro Cento doorway which is either the work of Michelozzo or derived from him. This is a side-door on the south wall of the cathedral, Siena. The tympanum holds a beautiful Michelozzian Virgin and child.

is the mantelpiece attributed to him that used to be on sale in the palazzo Davanzati, as also is the severe Virgin and child[1] in a deep shell-encrusted niche enclosed by a square, on the top of which is a tiny compact tympanum. Later on I shall describe a Quattro Cento church façade by Michelozzo, in which Gothic forms are used. I mention this at once in order to reassure the reader. Hereafter he will understand that my purpose is not to give a complete account of Florentine artists; but rather, in classifying some of their works, to isolate several differing tendencies. I shall say unpleasant things in this section, of the work of Benedetto da Majano and of Antonio Rossellino. But later I shall describe Benedetto's Quattro Cento masterpieces. Even the precious Mino da Fiesole had a Quattro Cento spell. I have particularly in mind his Tornabuoni tomb in Santa Maria sopra Minerva, Rome. Again Antonio Rossellino made of the Beata Villana tomb in Santa Maria Novella a Quattro Cento work.

I will even proclaim for these three[2] exquisite carvers, Benedetto, Mino and Antonio, and for their school, an immeasurable sensitiveness to the white marble in which they carved their lovely portrait busts. But this, at least, has been done for me by many writers. In these busts, particularly in those of children, the Florentine genius is happy. Portraiture, we know, was indigenous, and I have admitted how real a manifestation of the Renaissance the Florentine Christian sentiment could be. Sensitiveness to marble is less consistent than a love. Out of such sensitiveness, smaller in range and less impulsive than love, the greatest technical proficiency was evolved, as well as taste. But a reverse side engages my attention, an insensitive frigidity to which these busts are the corollary—must engage me who am a champion of the love of stone.[3]

[1] Recently presented to the Bargello by the Marchese Torrigiani.

[2] I omit the earlier and greater Desiderio da Settignano because he belongs wholly to the Quattro Cento.

[3] Again I feel I must stress the point that I am not suggesting these attitudes were conscious. The question is solely how far sculptor and archi-

I hope the reader will have followed me so far as to understand for himself that the banded, delicate, lines of Brunelleschi's architecture were most unsuited to hint at the Roman triumphal arch; though that was demanded of them. And perhaps the reader will further understand that whereas men of great genius in Florence were able to disentangle the problem, yet among their followers it should not be unexpected to find works which, in that impulsive and passionate age, repel by the coldness of their quiet contradictions, by the unblushing efficiency in half-measures and tasteful makeshift.

I have suggested that nothing could be more shocking than Michelozzo's neo-Gothic window in Santa Croce. But that is exceptional. The inhumanity of which I complain, a slightly sinister, because so deliberate, admixture of Roman triumph, Quattro Cento ebullience and Etruscan staring or suspense, all compounded into the 'sweet tenderness' of *quale visto di ogni canto*, is evident in much of the best known Florentine sculptured monuments, hitherto hailed as the masterpieces of the early Renaissance. And before I can go on to estimate the work of Donatello, Desiderio, Pollaiuolo and Verrocchio, I must analyse that to which they would approximate but for their genius.

In one respect the Florentines achieved their conception of the monumental; in one respect it was exactly suited. I refer to the sepulchral monuments which engross so much of the sculpture of the time and which, therefore, are my best field for examination. One might almost say that the Florentines silenced the cry for the monumental by inventing the vogue for 'monuments', a term which, since their efforts, must always have a mortal implication. Commemorating the dead with their happy thoughts was the action they took to counter the more difficult demand for commemoration of the present, the near and new-found life, a demand that underlay the whole commemorative movement, yet one which rarely found direct expression. But Alfonso built his own triumphal arch at

tect have unconsciously imputed emblem to the materials they use. (*Cf.* the account in next chapter of Donatello's use of the putto.)

Naples, and Sigismondo, commemorating on the conventional lines, so twisted them and bandied them to his will, that in the sepulchre of his love Isotta that he built at Rimini, he celebrated her personal triumph over death: her subsequent triumph, for at that time she was living.

In the fourteenth century, the orthodox and pious plan for a first-rate tomb was in some sort as follows: a sarcophagus supported by weeping Virtues, or other mournful caryatids, and upon the sarcophagus the dead revealed stiff in death by two angels who withdraw the curtains. Above will be represented some apotheosis, the welcoming of the deceased by the Virgin or the heavenly choir. Bernardo Rossellino, who in his Leonardo Bruni monument at Santa Croce established once and for all a new model, withdrew the sorrow and reduced to a quiet and pensive reminder the religious triumphs. In their place grows a light and interminable peace. Within the open cella[1] Leonardo Bruni lies, more asleep than dead. Not even the stillness is profound, though everlasting. Above are angels, playful yet spiritless, sweet yet eternal, with the Madonna and child at the back of the arch. One is reminded of the tender but untiring Florentine lily held toward the blanched Madonna at a thousand Annunciations. Somehow the scent never overpowers, for the lily is equable, cold in the sunlight. As embroidery for this tenacious peace one requires much that is kaleidoscopic, northern, much microscopic raving interest in detail, interest not joy, ornamental and minute industry, much related to the Flemish. And then, as well, there is this Etruscan suspense of the Bruni monument. It is a pleasant work; it does not contain those evident contradictions of which I am about to write in connection with other monuments. It is disturbing, though, to feel that the arch of the cella derives from the Roman triumphal arch. What had these new and sweet Etruscans to do with the concrete Roman triumphs which they parodied with wispy lines?

[1] For this Florentine cella type of monument to which the Bruni monument is the model, *see Plate XVII.*

Florence, Santa Croce. Brunelleschi: Interior of the Pazzi Chapel.

PLATE XI. 'DRAWING ON THE WALL'

1. *Florence, Ospedale degli Innocenti :* Brunelleschi.

2. *Verona, palazzo del Consiglio :* Fra Giocondo.

PLATE XII. A BRUNELLESQUE AND A QUATTRO CENTO
ARCADED BUILDING

Would it have been better if the Florentines had not attempted to embrace Rome nor flamboyant Gothic; if Luca della Robbia and Botticelli, the two 'pure' Florentine artists, had multiplied in the place of the schools of Castagno and Donatello? It would not have been better. For it is difficult to conceive of the Quattro Cento without the example of Donatello, of the Quattro Cento low relief without the three-dimensional perfections of Ghiberti; nor indeed of Luca della Robbia without Brunelleschi's classical measurements. Once again, the situation is infinitely confused both for good and for evil. Yet that is no reason for not regretting that the Roman arch was adapted by the Florentines.

I would instance the entrance to the Capella Carafa built by the Majanos in the Church of Santa Maria sopra Minerva at Rome (*Plate XIV*, 1). Here is an archway which is meant to have a boast in its height and broadened lines, though the space is small. But the revolting quality resides in its 'harmlessness'. One diagnoses that Etruscan suspense has robbed the Brunellesque lines of their pace, and there is revealed the shell of the Florentine vertical Gothic, smiling at its attendant, the harmless wolf of Rome. That elusive Leonardesque smile! This arch uncoils slowly and evenly, describing a gentle arc. There is the usual Brunellesque entablature either side above the pillars, from which the arc rises like hairs bent between the tips of two fingers. Nothing to *engage* the vertical straightnesses thus spanned.

The entrance to the Capella di Santa Fina at the Chiesa Collegiata, San Gemignano, was built by Benedetto da Majano to an effect of even greater wispiness.

His monument of the Bishop San Savino in the cathedral at Faenza provokes the lightest of nightmares, a nightmare of inhumanity in which the horror is absence of ghosts, apparitions; the same nightmare which may visit the contemplator of disused mine shafts (*Plate XIV*, 2). The lower part of the monument is a horizontal oblong of marble on the centre of which are low reliefs flanked by pilasters and candelabra. This lower part is spanned by an arc similar to the one I have described, meaningless, broad, delicate in its sharp edges. Within the niche thus made is the sarcophagus, resting on the architrave which forms the upper long side of the horizontal oblong below. The whole is small, but the diameter of the semi-circle equals the height of the facing beneath. This light-foot, perfect semi-circle, then, as if drawn with one sweep of the compass, though it is broad, makes up half the height of the monument. That would be clumsy merely, and not repellent, if the proportions were not so extraordinarily careful in every detail, if they were not abounding in beautiful workmanship. The carving is exquisite. Why is it that instead of drawing out the life of the stone, the carvings turn the stone to stone? Why should this simple geometry be so monstrous? Because the careful space is mechanical, because the smiling craftsmanship of the reliefs and ornamentals aggravates the preciousness of their symmetry. Because, owing to the whole being made so broad, owing to the lines of the architraves, the most heavy in the monument, owing to the quiet, coldly encircling semi-circle, the design is most agonisingly kept in clockwork rotation; whereas the unadorned vertical lines ending in the ornament on the point of the sarcophagus lid, show that beneath this simpering mask there are the mobile crystalline features of Florentine Gothic. It needed a Brunelleschi or a Donatello to pull these things off; it needed the psychology of the Baroque.

Majano could not always work it, and one resents as monstrous the broadness of this monument, a blind to hide the Gothic, as monstrous the symmetry thus evolved by an artist in this case so cold, so tamely sophisticated. For the rest, I admit the Florentine measure comes out more shining and clear with the evocation that was stirred at the same time as Roman remembrances. I admit the new craft in perfect adjustments. Some of the reliefs of this monument are beautiful. But here again, in the meticulous movements of the figures, in the softish asperity of these scenes which are only distantly

1. *Fiesole, the Abbey.* Brunellesque :
Detail of the library.

2. *Urbino, Ducal palace. Attrib.* Francesco
Laurana : *Window embrasure in the sala
della Jole.*

3. *Florence, pal. Pazzi-Quaratesi :*
Brunellesque-Albertian : *Window.*

4. *Urbino, Ducal palace. Attrib.* Francesco
Laurana : *Exterior of window to sala della Jole.*

PLATE XIII. BRUNELLESQUE COMPARED WITH QUATTRO CENTO

1. *Rome, S. M. sopra Minerva.* Attrib. B. and G. da Majano:
Entrance to Capella Carafa.

2. *Faenza, Cathedral.* B. da Majano: *Monument to bishop
San Savino.*

PLATE XIV. ARCS 'LIKE HAIRS BENT BETWEEN THE TIPS OF TWO FINGERS'

related to the reliefs of Donatello —there is a disproportion. Perfectly wrought agitation is taken up into the Etruscan-suspense-made-sweet of the whole monument; not pleasantly so. For the reliefs, having filled their geometrical function in the general design, either stand out on close examination, or are irrelevant to the whole. They are uncomfortably placed, these symbols of the Quattro Cento, among the smiles of the barren marble. Again the kaleidoscopic, the northern affinity.

They have the awful steadiness of a staring wound, these cold results of exquisite carving, this slow motion rendering of a Baroque design. Antonio Rossellino derives principally from Donatello, Benedetto da Majano from both of them. Nearly everything to which Donatello turned his hand was monumental. Restlessness of his movement overcame the straight courses of Brunelleschi. But Rossellino, and Majano where he followed him, deprived of simple swiftness, incapable of vigour, being at bottom heirs of the slow Florentine vertical Gothic, in their sepulchral monuments sometimes faked restlessness by broken design, which, in conjunction with 'finish', provokes at last a distaste. These bed-fellows are ever weird; at the same time their self-possession refuses to be attainted as grotesque. The Florentine species of mariolatry must be associated with this theme, both as its incentive and its effect. A Virgin and child slowly circulated by a *tondo* set at the top of a niche, will be the steady revolving star in the heavens, while very sculpturesque, by no means expansive angels will float alongside in careful disarray. Here are the elements of a broken design to be carefully wrought without one extravagant gesture (*Plates IX*, 1 and *XV*, 2). The Virgin, may be, will have the enigmatic smile, each gentle curve will indicate tenderness of compassion, this the heart of the new fearless Christianity. The sentiment was real enough. But where this sentiment inspires sepulchral monuments, broken design, in company with avoidance of all *structural* extravagance, appears fundamentally mean. An unusual defect for Italy, you will admit; and therefore slightly sinister: though sweet enough, and rather nun-like, this close-fistedness. The work is good; for the Florentines always had their stout æsthetic behind them. But, however evident are the smiles and prettiness, there exists too a certain coldness, innate, indeed, in the very measured quality of the æsthetic. In the end it is a lack of humanity, this coldness, and for that reason obviously distasteful amid the pretences of humanism, and when associated with the rôle of pioneer. The major sculptors struggled to the greatest heights of the Quattro Cento, all except Luca della Robbia. Yet his case is not a contradiction. For his masterpiece is one in which he reaches an unexampled tensity. The monument of Bishop Federighi in Santa Trinità, alone of his works, is vividly emotional. It is far more serious than the rest. For once feeling is thrown outwards. This is Quattro Cento work. Glamour invests its 'goodness' (*Plate XIX*).

As in the case of the aforementioned Bernardo Rossellino's tomb for Leonardo Bruni, so Antonio Rossellino's tomb for Cardinal di Portogallo in San Miniato is better than the works for which it subsequently served as model. There is something more generous in these flying and kneeling angels. The cella is deep, and I should be sorry not to include in a list of Quattro Cento sculpture the carving on the plinth. Further, the rich use of coloured marble, showing some disposition towards mass-effect, foretells Verrocchio's Medici tomb.

No: postured angels in a broken design, caught and caged Donatellesque putti as well, are best seen in Benedetto da Majano's monument to Filippo Strozzi in Santa Maria Novella, and in his San Bartolo altar for the Augustine church at San Gemignano (*Plates IX*, 1 and *XV*, 2). Above, below and within the *tondo* of each of these works, there are winged cherubs' heads. This cypher I consider objectionably Florentine when used by Rossellino and his kind. It is a shorthand for all the ebullient infants of Donatello, the wings now coming under the chin like cotton wool, the expression of the face anile. Donatello used this shape himself on the choir screen of San Antonio, Padua. But virile heads rise from the jointure of fibrous eagle wings. They are apparitions like the head of a Fury that breasts her way through the bronze of Gattamelata's armour. Further, though intended to have a Donatellesque reference, the winged heads of these monuments are actually derived from Luca della Robbia. This mixture of influences is peculiarly ill-assorted, and in itself serves as well as anything to illustrate the contradiction to which I take exception. For Luca, that unruffled charger of pagan conventions with Christian sentiment, used these angels' heads, as at his beautiful tabernacle in the church of Santa Maria, Peretola, not to any purpose of ebullience and apparition, but simply in the function of antique masks; abstractions, therefore, of pretty tenderness.

This was no mere accordance with the classical. Though no doubt stirred by the revival of learning, Luca reveals himself, as well as being the newest of Christians, an older pagan than the Romans. The fateful spirit of his formalization goes straight back to the beginnings of classical art, to the Greek and Etruscan primitives. Christian interpolation, so strong in him, so perfectly welded with the other source, makes for an art perhaps more singular than any in the world, startling in cold purity, often revolting in muddle. And if this is partly true also of the Florentine sculptors I have condemned, for them there is less excuse. They introduced this deeply-rooted formalization into the furniture of humanism, not only in antithesis to the Christian sentiment by which their native coldness was attracted, but also when handling by themselves the least obdurate and most dangerous emotions. For they formalized the ebullient, Veronese arabesques, they introduced their formal sentimentalism into the cult of the individual. And this they were led to do because Donatello, the greatest Florentine master, stood principally with the Quattro Cento. Luca is a disconcerting product for the age of Humanism and as one of its leaders. But the work of the Rossellinos and Majanos, indeterminate between Donatello and Luca, can shock those who love the thus obscured Quattro Cento. I don't suggest that it was unnatural for them to stand between. If Donatello's overwhelming genius was bound to have repercussion even upon Luca, Luca was the stronger Florentine. He belongs entirely to the tradition.

The winged head as thereafter used by Luca, appears first in a relief of the pulpit of Santa Maria Novella by Buggiano, pupil and adopted son of Brunelleschi. This same relief of the Assumption of the Virgin, shows a *mandorla* in which the Virgin is enthroned, upheld by flying angels. Now it will be understood that when coldest abstraction and Christian temper are not welded as by Luca, there may result a work the quality of which is unfeeling tameness. I associate the *mandorla* shape, or half-walnut shell, with this quality, of which the much-praised Mino da Fiesole is the chief exponent. The *mandorla* had a vogue in Florence at this time because it provided just such a reference to Gothic pointedness as they could manage. For with the assistance of floating angels, they could cause the *mandorla* to appear suspended, as if gravity did not function any more, a trick all too easy to perform with the round *tondo*. This half-shell, too, by framing a Virgin and child or whatnot as its nut, could suggest, with the necessary tameness, the dramatic spirit of Quattro Cento disclosure. See in the sepulchre of Cardinal Forteguerri in Santa Cecilia, Rome, Mino's delightful cracked almond (with little hard studs adding to the symmetry) holding the tender sitter (*Plate XV*, 1).

The strange Mino, whose Lombard followers designed formal arabesques for many a fifteenth-century tomb and doorway in Rome, so that there is little Quattro Cento work there, was excessively mannered in his carvings—though there is no need to connect such preciosity with the Baroque tendencies on the part of those seeking the monumental. But inasmuch as some preciosity of execution is a quality of the slow and delicate structures hitherto discussed, I will take a sepulchre of Mino's to illustrate the difference between the Florentine and the Quattro Cento lunette. Mino, be it said, was a more 'honest' artist than, for instance, Rossellino. That is, Mino's æsthetic conception was less tangled. The ingenuous excesses

1. *Rome, Santa Cecilia.* Mino da Fiesole : *Detail of Forteguerri monument.*

2. *San Gemignano, S. Agostino.* B. da Majano : *Detail of altar in S. Bartolo chapel.*

PLATE XV. SLOW-MOTION POSTURES AND MOUSE-LIKE
PRECIOSITY

1. *Fiesole, Abbey Church.* Mino da Fiesole : *Monument to Count Ugo :
the lunette.*

2. *Venice, Frari.* Antonio Rizzo : *Monument to Doge Niccolo Tron : the lunette.*

PLATE XVI. CONTRAST BETWEEN A FLORENTINE AND A
QUATTRO CENTO LUNETTE

of his bloodless charm convince. He rarely touches the Quattro Cento and as rarely wishes to. Monumentalism would only hinder the delicacy of anile grimaces, anatomy would be futile knowledge for the arch-executor of geometric gestures. If his fellow-artists had similarly intensified their innate preciosity instead of turning it to attempt the 'finish' of the monumental ideal, the development of the Baroque would have been arrested, the influences of Luca della Robbia would have persisted stronger.

To contrast, then, a sepulchre of Mino's with one of Rizzo's, is a just comparison between Florence and Verona, between Florence and Venice. Mino's admitted lack of architectural conception does not invalidate him as champion. On the contrary, he flaunts this Florentine failing by others disguised. The two monuments are Mino's tomb for Count Ugo in the church of the Badia, Fiesole, and Rizzo's tomb for the Doge Niccolo Tron in the Frari, Venice. Later I shall have much more to say about the Tron tomb. For the present I wish to remark only on a difference in lunettes (*Plate XVI*).

In the Mino sepulchre the lunette is the usual enclosure of vertical lines which already have been slowed down by a large entablature and by other horizontal shapes below, principally the sarcophagus and its recumbent effigy. The monument has no pretence to architecture. The stone seems to have been squashed against the wall; particularly the broad band of the lunette suggests pressure and a resultant absence of depth. Otherwise the band is meaningless. A mere tracing would have sufficed to connect the horizontal lines. Why, too, this broad entablature to support the band? Was it a jutting ledge before the occurrence of an overwhelming imprint? Once again this flatness demonstrates an unequalled insensitiveness to space in the pursuit of spacing. No love of space, no love for the medium of the emergent, no love for the science of perspective, for the relationships it can make absolute. *Attention* only for perspective, for its conveniences in clarity and proportion.

The Tron monument is proportionately narrower; but Rizzo was not so conscious of a necessity to harness vertical lines; for the monument inherits a Gothic far different from the Florentine, as a glance at the beautiful Francesco Foscari tomb on the opposite wall of the choir, will show. In neither of these works connected with Rizzo's name are stress and strain apparent. The stone is free, the figures children of the stone. The deep niches of the Tron monument framing their rooted apparitions, promise anew and anew the palpitation of the whole. In contrast with the Florentine mode where it is flat, or nearly flat with the wall, the Venetian lunette-frame projects, so that not only is the space within deep, but the frame is a roof to everything below it. Then, in as much as it does not rise from the extremities of the architrave, the circle is sudden, there is a spread about it, the sudden fan of the peacock's tail or a notched and encrusted shell with shafts of organ sound in its depth, attaining maximum volume in the lunette that crowns the façade of San Zaccaria. A direct inspiration employed the Venetian love of stone. Coducci and Rizzo never forgot the deep bays of St. Mark's, costly eaves fit to reverberate the lion's roar. Quattro Cento artists in Venice strove to gain more light yet equal depth, to gain surprise in the strong spread of the lunette, to reduce the thickness of the trabeation to a minimum, so that the relieving half-circle springs out to demonstrate high spirit in the single, sheltering stone.

Finally, on the subject of Florentine sepulchral art, it may be argued that all the better monuments are conceived in terms of recess, that is to say, those to which the already discussed Leonardo Bruni monument is the model. Granted. But the recess is not of the monument but of the wall to which it is affixed, the wall being scooped out for this purpose so that the sarcophagus lies in a cella. There is still hardly any roof to the lunette whose recess is that of the cella. This model, so wonderfully used by Desiderio, is vulgarized in the skilful hands of Matteo Civitali (*see* tomb of Pietro di Noceto, Lucca, *Plate*

1. Bologna, San Domenico. Francesco di Simone : Tartagni monument.

2. Lucca, Cathedral. Matteo Civitale : Tomb of Pietro di Noceto.

PLATE XVII. UNPLEASANT EXAMPLES OF FLORENTINE 'CELLA' MONUMENTS

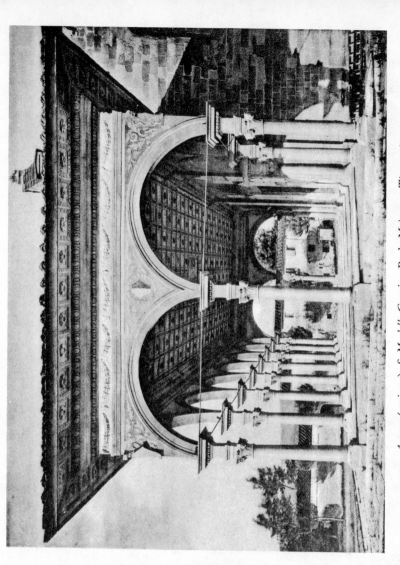

Arezzo (environs), S. M. delle Grazie.   B. da Majano : The portico.

PLATE XVIII. BRUNELLESQUE FORMS ADJUSTED TO A QUATTRO CENTO EFFECT

XVII, 2) and of Francesco di Simone (*see* tomb of Tartagni, San Domenico, Bologna, *Plate XVII*, 1, and of Barbara Manfredi, San Biagio, Forli). The works of the latter artist who commanded fine powers of execution, are particularly repulsive. He introduced a flamboyance inherited from Verrocchio into the Etruscan suspense of Bernardo Rossellino's cella formula.

Let me conclude this section with a reference to two exhibits in the Victoria and Albert. The first is the arch of the altar from the palazzo Ambron, attributed to Benedetto da Majano. The arch begins not at the end of the trabeation but near the end, and turns over hard like a cartwheel performed in a romp. The rich mouldings are magnificent. Inside, the entablature follows round the square of the recess which the arch shelters. The use of black and white marble on the frieze recalls Michelozzo's Crucifixion tabernacle in San Miniato, where he used a similar rolling sheltering arch-form, actually, in this case, the roof of the tabernacle. To Michelozzo, I feel, more than to Donatello, is due the heavy monumental style which this phase of Benedetto's art shows, one that is too compact to suggest any Baroque outcome. On the contrary, I am reminded of the fossil waves and perfect ivory sheerness of Moghul marble construction: still more so by the frozen delicacy of Benedetto's loggia in front of Santa Maria delle Grazie, just outside Arezzo (*Plate XVIII*).

Turn now to the capella Maggiore at the end of the room. The architecture of this chapel is attributed to Cronaca: but it conveys small idea of Brunellesque 'drawing on the wall'. The space is so tiny, and Cronaca used a thicker pencil than did Brunelleschi. He, Cronaca, very wisely concentrated on horizontal lay-out, abandoning altogether the gentle ascensions of the statuesque ideal; with the result that his forms are wider, more nearly at rest. His church of San Salvatore at Florence is beautiful. But notice in this chapel how the apex of the window on top of the entablature so nearly touches the apex of the semi-circle above it, in turn so nearly touched at the apex by the band of moulding at the base of the vault. What is it these spidery, sensitive lines pass on to one another? Responsible for their being there at all, do they flee the imputation of emphasis? Yet excuses in the name of constructional necessity might cover some of their shame. And if they do pass on something one to another, where finally is the message put? Is it passed up top to be circulated round the band at the base of the vault like a hot potato, or is the answer just 'nowhere'? If so, this architecture is, indeed, in perfect taste. For the distinct, as well as the emphatic, are avoided. So too the architectural problem. For, to put the case in an extreme form, how can one pencil stroke be made to cohere?

As for the architecture of the altar, here you may see the anile species of Florentine arch. It is incredible that a curved form could be so drained of all tension. This arch might be a wax horse-shoe just *rested* on the supporting pillars.[1] The tabernacle within the arch, derived, as it is, from Desiderio da Settignano, has a little Quattro Cento import. But oh! for some disintegrating powder to force the angels kneeling circumambient to extend their mouse-like, integrated preciosity into the declaiming attitudes of the Baroque! At the end of the century foreign invasions brought it about.

Outside Florence and Florentine influence one finds plenty of fifteenth-century structures which are badly designed as well as displaying small technical ability in execution. Whereas one is safe with the Florentines for the exhibition of some æsthetic principle, some elegance and refinement. On the other hand, unlike the other Italians, the Florentines, leaders of humanism, experts in artistry, could be inhuman; and the coldness of their art amid the freedom of the early Renaissance can result in a disproportion grotesquely shocking.

[1]*See* also the arch of the tabernacle relief ascribed to Matteo Civitali, next to the Andrea Ferrucci altar-piece in the Victoria and Albert.

CHAPTER FOUR

THE QUATTRO CENTO IN FLORENTINE[1] ART

I. *Donatello*

M Y ACCOUNT of Donatello is inadequate for any but my present purpose. The attainment of Donatello is so immense, I mean the translation of that which moved him into forms of art is so personal, his inventions are so original, so purely artistic, that it gives me some cause for dismay to find that it would be quite irrelevant for me to describe his work from the angle of pure æsthetic value. But the psychological approach is not the nonsense it was some thirty years ago, since, meanwhile, criticism has dilated upon purely æsthetic value. Indeed, there is now the danger that the more literary aspects of art, the aspects in which the co-ordination of art and life are implicit, the only aspects that are fit subject for literature, will be overwhelmed by considerations of pure æsthetic. Is it now time again—for we have learned the anti-Ruskin lesson well—to re-estimate the spirit of the Renaissance, to attempt anew the co-ordination of the spirit of western man with his art; or must we refuse to the Italian subject any consideration which, at present, owing to ignorance and to our distance from African civilization we cannot bestow upon Negro sculpture?

Of course, in the long run, a more psychological approach is not at variance with a more purely æsthetic approach. On

---

[1]The following account of Quattro Cento activity in Florence is by no means complete. Some further reference to it will be made in the next part. I am concerned in this chapter only with the major figures.

the contrary, the former should be indispensable to the latter, and *vice versa*. I have by no means attempted their separation, since neither exists as a pure entity and since only for a partisan purpose does their division seem to exist. But I, too, redress a balance in the appreciation of Italian art. My concern with Donatello is solely in his relation to the Quattro Cento spirit. Indeed the theme of Donatello as artist, as artist in isolation, the theme of the *inventiveness* of his power to transmute the Quattro Cento stimulus into various forms of art, would be one slightly dangerous to my own. For while admitting its necessity to the Quattro Cento, I decry the Florentine power to translate emotions painstakingly into forms of art —of which Donatello's art is the supreme outcome —in favour of an anonymous spirit whose servants are more nearly children of their age, in favour of artists inspired by a patron's personality, whence springs the art entirely emblematic, the art 'twice over',[1] miraculous to us who lack emblem. The Florentine attitude was indispensable to the Quattro Cento, and *vice versa*; their relation mirrors that in art criticism between the more psychological and the more æsthetic approach; and in decrying Florence in favour of the rest of Italy, I seek to redress exactly that same balance as I do in favouring a more psychological approach. But in the case of Florence *versus* the rest of Italy, my partisanship is better founded. For even when an arrogant psychological approach was supreme, indeed, at all times, Florence has won every honour. This badly-founded reverence for Florentine achievement is hard to uproot. For it dates back to the excellent writings of Vasari, the most successful booster in all history. How these Renaissance boosters have got away with it! Pope Pius II, the first redoubtable journalist, is another case in point. I attempt to show him up—for it is not too late, in fact the need is still urgent (see to-day's *Daily Mail*)—in the next volume.

In wandering back from the general to the particular it will

[1] *See* pp. 17 and 45.

Florence, S. Trinità. Luca della Robbia : *Monument to bishop Federighi.*

PLATE XIX. LUCA'S ONLY QUATTRO CENTO WORK

Florence, Cathedral Museum. Donatello's *Singing gallery.*

PLATE XX. 'SWOLLEN WITH VIGOUR THEY ENHANCE RHYTHM BEYOND THE
POWERS OF MUSIC'

be best to lean on this fact; in the first decades of the fifteenth century at Florence, the larger commissions of Donatello, Ghiberti and Luca della Robbia were given to them by the Signoria, the great Guilds and the Cathedral authorities. The vague personalities of public bodies must be flattered by creations that are monumental or profusely dramatic. A greater power of co-ordination will be required of the artist, and a more individual æsthetic than the one which can be so largely imposed upon him from without by the miraculous clarity in the life of a princely patron. The artist who works for impersonal societies hopes to please, not one, but several or many, minds. Esoteric or emblematic significance in his work is likely to lack the tension of projected fantasy that I seek out, unless the society is as real, or more real, than a person. And in fifteenth-century Florence, the great Guilds were breaking up, the Signoria was overshadowed by the leading families, and corporate religious fervour was not at its height.

Now Donatello's works belong largely to the Quattro Cento. He created Quattro Cento emblematic tension though he was generally engaged on the less personal contract, less personal, for instance, than the contract Matteo de' Pasti undertook for Sigismondo Malatesta at Rimini. Naturally enough, Donatello's greater effort, when successful, means a wider achievement. His emblems are more universal. So significant was the putto in his hands that, though no longer emblem, it became essential as a decorative motive to many subsequent arts.

Donatello was in revolt from the statuesque. But he could create Quattro Cento effects only with the material to hand, with the monumental and with rhythm enlarged to an exuberance. Sometimes one sees these two elements imperfectly welded. The Virgin of the Annunciation high relief in Santa Croce is monumental, Junonian—she has even been called Baroque. Ovoids on the frieze are brutally large and plain. On the other hand the rest of the decor shows immense exuberance. In general one can associate exuberance with the relief, while the statuary which soon flourished in Florence, especially the nude statue, could serve to express a monumental plainness.

Although there was waywardness in his tormented savagery, Donatello felt the need for simplification, for a supreme, purely æsthetic *relevance* pervading every atom of humanistic ardour. The painters who followed him, especially in his love of the nude, found that a hard naturalism heightened by hard colour, could provide such a relevance, making of the æsthetic content a brio as abstract as possible, one of anatomical stress and strain. But into such æsthetic realization, and into his unequalled knowledge of the antique,[1] Donatello sent a passion which is altogether Gothic, a revolutionary passion, therefore, here in Florence. Medieval hardihood wins outburst in the sharp and peaked violence of some of his heads. The Umbrian eagle flapping coruscated wings, now no longer lone, is an image that haunts so much of Donatello's triumphant marble. Distraught is the anguish at entombments, but that pain is hammered out into rhythm. The gamin, eagle-sharp, is now no longer lone, and the protestant valour of St. George, he, forerunner of the more intense Christian public-school boy, acknowledges the slum-child shoulders of the St. John, the youthfulness, the pathetic fitness of these shoulders; and the slip of a David wears his locks long, the Greek petasos crowning the slum child.

Donatello's supreme co-ordination of the new sensuousness was a stone-blossom; but not through the simpler fantasies of flower and foliage. He saw the passionate thronging of youthful bodies. The press upon the Pontevecchio, fire behind the eyes pulsating the blood, up out of the low quarters

---

[1] *See* Géza de Francovitch, *Appunti su Donatello e Jacopo della Quercia. Bollettino d'Arte*, 1929. The author reasserts the importance of Donatello's first visit to Rome, and with the aid of confronting photographs makes parallels between Donatello's early sculpture and antique statues, particularly in regard to realistic portraiture.

Prato, cathedral. Donatello and Michelozzo : *Outside pulpit.*
PLATE XXI. 'THE PUTTO MAKES THE AIR MOVE'

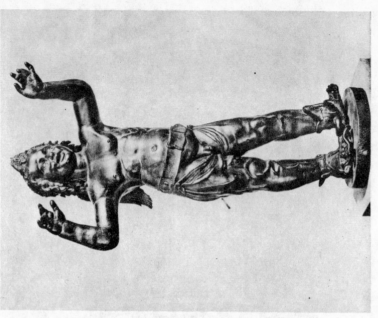

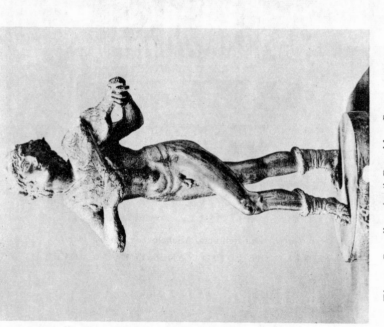

1. *Florence, Bargello. Attrib. Bertoldo: Bronze statuette:*
Orpheus or Orion.

2. *Florence, Bargello. Attrib. Donatello: Bronze putto.*

PLATE XXII. QUATTRO CENTO BRONZE STATUETTES

the quick children he imagines to stretch upon their wildest activities. The gross crowd, sole moisture of these barren streets, human luxuriance that overruns the receptive valleys,— these he disentangles for singleness of energy and of movement. The slum children cannot group about him too long. Their energy drives the air to ventilation. Every child is a newly victorious *amorino*. There is tempered steel in the strain, and no more than any Roman need Donatello be fastidious. Nakedness, however slight the form, achieves an irresistible tension, an irresistible repose, consummate in self-reliance. The fecund slime from which they grew, still clinging, is dried to brittle stone as the putti flash their limbs. Swollen with vigour they enhance rhythm beyond the powers of music. Such a stampede, a thunderous lilt, not heard —as if the ear already deafened, the resourceful eye could store in its depth with one glance a succession of tune which will astound the ear when inaudibility lifts, which will overwhelm the shallow ear again and press down against the sides of the head—such is the rhythm of the putti as they move in their compartments on the pulpit at Prato above the long wrought bronze capital, above the monumental console, such the dance that can never run down, too strong and too subtle for the plodding ear, dance sudden and final in the corridor behind the columns of the encrusted singing gallery at Florence (*Plates XX and XXI*).

In the symbol of the putto, the new ambitions of the body found a wide expression. The animal functions of infants are in themselves symbols to adults of the most profound release. They should have been permitted us: they are symbols of the freedom we cannot win. We relish it that children, when unquestioning in their acts, do not shock. The putto is a pagan emblem to those overburdened by sense of guilt, an emblem that corresponds to so universal a desire for freedom that indecency of putti was indecency to no one. An Agostino di Duccio putto (now hidden, it is true, by a canopy) at Rimini urinates above an altar: even the Catholic Church, mounted as she is on sense of guilt, has turned a blind eye.

Donatello took full advantage of this fact that blithe infants do not shock. His putti are fierce on their pleasures, intense, even precise enough, in their sexual romps. The stone and clay bear sons by the sculptor, not daughters. Out of the hundreds of nude forms attributed to Donatello, two only are female, the bronze figure with cornucopia in the Berlin Museum, and the Eve at Padua. This fact is very significant. What is true of Donatello is true of the early Renaissance as a whole. For no other art, not even the Greek, shows so marked a preference for the male nude, a figure far less easily composed to beauty than the female nude. Such unique choice shows a predominance in sculptural fantasy of a feeling for spatial values alone, of a feeling for mass, for material as being the fruitful female block that will give birth to the most *active* shapes full of prolific sap. From the stone comes a new, fearless energy. And to push this fantasy further, since the architect's building is female, set on the earth like Giorgione's woman by the running stream, the sculptor's attendant statuary are her lovers and sons rather than her daughters or a mere projection of herself. But only sculptors with a passion for the material, stone, will keep so close to this primary fantasy that on their low relief they create for the stone her children in the image of male human infants. And so the marble putti who play along the marble of Donatello's singing gallery, are the most intense manifestation of stone-blossom: also the most humanistic. A certain humanity, as an expression of human love for the near objective world in contrast to the distant, yet relentless, spiritual hierarchy, is attributed to material. Once more stone is not only the medium of humanistic fantasy, but is the near object, object pure and simple, the love for which originates the anti-sense-of-guilt, the humanistic, attitude. Humanism as an intellectual movement is but a pale offshoot of such emotion.

Now Donatello's putto is certainly derived from the pagan *amorino*, and the putto's prankish turn was no doubt evolved from the slightly *genre*, or naturalistic, treatment, already evident at Florence in the fourteenth century, of the Virgin and child group. Donatello's putti are nearly always winged, partly because such crinkled surfaces appealed to his love of incrustation, still more because wings enormously help suggestion of movement, of dynamic passage and of air currents made to whistle. It is as if a dust arose with the dance along the singing gallery; for the putti's wings are set off by a background of black and white mosaic flecks. The putto makes the air move. Indeed he is associated with all the elements. He bursts stone like earth, at Rimini he rides the dolphin, his tempestuous energy kindles a flame that withers tasteful ornamental foliage poor in sap, and heats the luscious growth to a vibrant, tropical bulbosity. The putto is elemental force under the symbol of the infant's animal nature. He is the emblem of Europe. For instead of the generative principle in terms of dark god and fetish or in terms of some cavernous concept of female seclusion, instead of the Indian *yaksi* beautiful though she be, or the jerky satyr who overruns the clear Greek horizon to hairy glades, we of the West have symbolized fecundity by the infant, by the play of infants in whom the primary desires that make the adult world limitless, subterranean, dark, are seen bright and immediate and in their least unsettled state. We in the West believe not only that the child is father to the man, but that the child's intent play in modes hateful and loving, expresses a more real necessity than does the grown god's esoteric power to lure and to destroy. And since the putto is unguarded, without reserve, he symbolizes as well as the necessity, the *ideal* of emotional externalization that I have identified with the Quattro Cento spirit. He symbolizes the process of living, that lies between Life and Death, the translation outwards of the formless flux of passions, to definite, concentrated, objective form. Adult intelligence brings the artistry to living, but only in the child can you discover the material that is worked. The Quattro Cento men uncovered that material in art, always first on the field. And now science as well insists on the sexual life of the child and learns from him. And since we know to-day that the child also is broken by his impotent passions, his cry and his gurgle are likely to remain for us symbols not only of Life, but also of living.

Naturally the Renaissance putto is first of all symbol of joy and freedom. Donatello swells his contours. His putto is a powerful plaything both in muscle and in sex. Donatello is safe-guarded by the 'innocence' which has been so irrationally attributed to the child. The putto is such an infant as every actual infant would like to be, and so with his games. He is a creation of Donatello's, so special, so imbued with unsuspected meaning, so emblematic of an age, that I must insist again that Rococo infants and such-like are not putti[1] at all. In fact any work in which the putto appears, is bound to be not only fifteenth century but Quattro Cento. And here I must distinguish the putto from other and contemporary infants, for instance, the della Robbia kind. As one would expect, Florentine artists were shy of Donatello's putto. Even Desiderio whose work is Quattro Cento for quite different reasons, generally changed putti into children and young boys. Rossellino and Majano followed him. They favoured especially the delicately featured young boy in bust or as guardian of a tomb. Representations of the more youthful saints particularly the San Giovannino or young Baptist and St. Sebastian, belong to this vogue. Pollaiuolo the truculent, avoided both putto and child, both Donatello's avowal and its negation. Verrocchio returned to the putto, but not to the crowd of them. He represents them alone, a little timid, though still bulbous in form. Otherwise, it is outside Florence that Donatello's putto lives, particularly in Eastern Italy. Donatello himself worked for ten years in Padua and planted there the Quattro Cento emblems. Sculptors imitated the putti in San Antonio, but painters, principally Mantegna and, then, Giovanni Bellini, transformed them back into sweet children.

Except for his wings, one might have thought that the

[1]In future I will reserve the name 'putto' for those infants only who conform to the Donatellesque idea.

bronze putto in the Bargello, standing impudent on two snakes, represented the infant Hercules, so robust his shape (*Plate XXII*, 2). He wears soaken workman's trousers looped up on the hips by a huge belt, but fallen down before and behind below the parting of the legs. Other of Donatello's putti wear shirts, but when they have a hand free they often raise the shirts above their stomachs. The thin trousers of this bronze putto serve only to enfatten and to crease his legs like the slickest slime. The belt could easily cover his genitals if the useless trousers were torn away. Instead, debonair belt and fallen trousers frame them. His luminous, bloated form is made swift by tossing hair common to his kind and by wings attractive to a stinging dust. Oh the dust of the studios, the hack hack, pieces flying and stinging, and the secretious putti ruent in this hailstorm! Are they dank leather trousers, made up of an old apron? They will flap pleasantly against the softness. There is a trumpet call again in these textures, leather on vibrant flesh the most delicate, the most alert part of which scatters enclosures just as the tiny sun edges away from itself by radiance, to an enframing margin, the huge and shredded clouds.

Putti mourn on the socle of Gattamelata's statue at Padua. For the strong, plain oval socle represents a tomb. But the games of putti are wild. They make water to trumpet and bronze water-containers to gong. And not only to damps but to the processes of sea-life are they habituated. For Donatello used shell-forms and other incrustation. Witness the magnificent encrusted shell-form under the head of Giovanni Crivelli (*Plate XXIII*, 2), and the twisted enframing posts of the Pecci slab in the cathedral, Siena. For Donatello's twisted posts always express a long-wound notching by millenial currents, as do the sea-tressed tendrils[1] he invented. Again, there are the pairs of dolphins holding between them thick crusty shells along the parapet of the singing gallery in San Lorenzo.

Turning to architecture, such power in rhythm, so deep a

[1]For instance, the ornament on the 'cheeks' of the consoles of the singing gallery in the Opera del Duomo, Florence.

life, will, it is obvious, shake the architectural members. There will be overlapping of marble rolled back by the devices of incrustation, compression that leaves unusual shapes. Donatello came back from his second visit to Rome thoroughly dissatisfied now with the swift regularities of Brunelleschi. The differences of these two artists over the decoration of the sacristy at San Lorenzo is extremely significant. Rhythm still underlies the Florentine art, but Donatello has felt in Rome the instantaneousness of the medieval Cosmati work, has felt the precedence of colour for rhythmic purposes over linear successions. It is now that he works on the pulpit at Prato, now that he introduces Roman tesselation behind the putti on the cathedral singing gallery. Draughtsmanship is taboo. The processes of encrust require the variable colours of crystallization, and the most palpitating rhythm is that of the dizzy flecks which invade with their swarm all the brightest objects of sunlight, the most silent; for they are too quick, too grandiloquent for sound, too continuous as within the beat of the pulsating heart. It was then he designed the magnificent balustrade in the sacristy of San Lorenzo made out of marble shells beneath the slab, and of great shoots of marble oak issuing from their vase to the pattern of volutes (*Plate XLVI*, 2). No doubt Brunelleschi took exception to the coloured marbles and the massive doorways.

But mass *in excelsis*, that complete appearance, arresting as the open face of the rose, a vital steadiness, a forcible concurrence without any throbbing, behind and beyond all rhythm, could hardly be arrived at in Florence. Rhythm swells and breaks here, finally to settle into the fugues of the Baroque. Donatello's second visit to Rome both made the development inevitable, and led him meanwhile to his greater Quattro Cento works. On this visit he carved a beautiful tabernacle now in one of the sacristies of St. Peter's. The rebellious waves of travertine are petrified and encrusted as if by a prolific reproductiveness of the minute life that their seas contain (*Plate XXIV*, 1).

2. *Rome, S. M. in Aracoeli.* Donatello:
   Slab tomb of the bishop Crivelli.

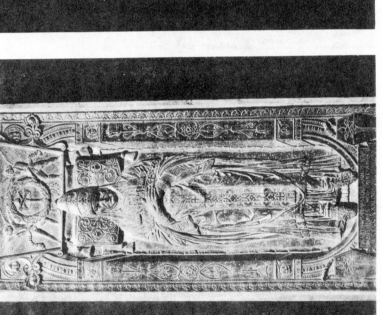

1. *Rome, Lateran. Attrib.* Simone Fiorentino (Donatello's
   companion) : *Slab monument to Pope Martin V.*

PLATE XXIII. QUATTRO CENTO SEA-CRUSTED EFFECT

2. *Florence, piazza della Signoria.* Donatello : *Head of Holofernes : Detail of Judith group.*

1. *Rome, St. Peter's.* Donatello : *Ciborium in sacristy of the Canons.*

PLATE XXIV. TRAVERTINE AND BRONZE.

In the Piazza Signoria, Florence, *haute* is the Renaissance. Cellini's swaggering Perseus holds a baulked Medusa head. For already limbs are stone, compact groups that turn their never-ending cartwheels. Neptune winds his head toward the gleaming David. Satyrs sense their conchs and blow brazen water at the sun. The messenger of the gods proclaims vengeance to a swarthy god. Full-breasted daughters faint, and ripple at the knee. Some gorgeous seam in the fullness of time fills out the anile nudity of old man Neptune, gives him a brassy strength through which the dark tremors of youth never will pass, a warrior's head set to the jaunty fabricating of an old man's gaunt peccadilli. Huge, he presides over the slippery water-sprites. High is the sun of the Renaissance, too hipped with proclamation! These bodies have a cream upon them. Every day the sun warms up tons of blood. Well-practised Perseus has an evil nakedness, though his step be firm. Andromeda's hair flies stiff as though caked with mud. Within the decade Perseus will fatten. A portly Roman, he will finger his toga on his way to the boring baths. For soon the heat of his florid nakedness will have to be stored and clothed between bouts of exhibition.

And then, beneath the enormous pile of the palazzo Vecchio, without shelter, stronger, even in the distance, than the great wall of building, a metal point of lightning amid the circumambient marbles—and you see as you draw close how precious is Donatello's Judith, how emblazoned her underhood and simple robe, how fierce the classical simplicity of their folds (*Plate XXV*). For in this strange manner did Donatello approach the early Greeks, as did the best of the old Gothic sculptors. Embodiment of passion, strict passion, of a tension which must be new (for it cannot last), Judith has raised the sword to strike off the head of Holofernes' sleeping form. But the anger is no longer pure Semitic. Other powers have reinforced the Jews and fallen out with them. Attention wanders to the exquisitely relaxed, the soft anatomy of Holofernes (*Plate XXIV*, 2) over which presides this Helleno-Gothic

Fury, this animus of the lean Umbrian eagle, austere and powerful, peaked. Such was the austerity which lay sometime in the souls of the Roman Fathers, now galvanized by the soft and plastic form of the slumbering pagan tyrant. But new feelings coalesce; it is a miracle, the Renaissance. Judith's scriptural fury shall animate the nude. Upon her triangular pedestal, rich and sharp pedestal, are three bronze reliefs of putti dynamic in game, winged and furious in their natural courses (*Plates XXVI* and *XXXVIII*, 2). Some fly to an embrace; they won't feel the bruise; some tumble about the graven basin. The feet of others trample lightly over the loud and surfeited lord of fountains. One alone is chained. He calls for help, but the others are deafened. Perhaps clear sound of trumpets will organize his slovenly shape, calm his fear, and he will be free with the rest.

II. *Michelozzo*

I want to make only a curt reference to Michelozzo on two points where he touches the Quattro Cento, other than those already mentioned. Michelozzo and Donatello collaborated in several contracts. Discussion has been heated over their respective shares of the work. In view of the new light thrown on Michelozzo in connection with the Annunziata,[1] I feel that the simple, massive design of the John XXIII tomb between two antique pillars in the Baptistery, is primarily his (*Plate XXVII*, 2). And just as Alberti's Roman breadth is saved for the Quattro Cento by the immediate, arresting emblems with which his collaborators emblazoned the Tempio encasement, so Michelozzo's heavy design attains a constriction, a tensity of incrustation from the hands of his collaborators, Donatello and Pagno di Lapo Portigiano, who, though avoiding here much ornament, are probably responsible for such details of the design as the shell-forms in the niches and in the semi-circle above, and for the general notched effect of the carving.

The Naples tomb[2] on which Donatello and Michelozzo col-

[1]*See* note 1, p. 113.   [2]Brancacci monument in Sant' Angelo a Nilo.

138

2. *Detail : Head of Judith.*

1. *Florence, piazza della Signoria.*
Donatello's *Judith (Bronze).*

PLATE XXV. 'HELLENO-GOTHIC FURY, AUSTERE AND POWERFUL, PEAKED'

Florence, piazza della Signoria. Donatello and school :
Bronze reliefs on base of Judith.

PLATE X.XVI. 'PUTTI DYNAMIC IN GAME'

laborated, is not a Quattro Cento work, but a hybrid, a cold adjustment, though some of the sculpture is beautiful. Michelozzo worked with Donatello on the pulpit at Prato (*Plate XXI*). Again, I attribute to Michelozzo the massive console, that heaviness so easily made a means of incrustation by the pictorial powers of Donatello. The lovely bases to Michelozzo's pillars of the Annunziata tabernacle show the power in his developed style to transmute the Brunelleschi line-game into a concourse. Michelozzo has gathered all the runners together and drilled them as one man.

His façade for Sant' Agostino at Montepulciano is one of the few Quattro Cento church façades (*Plate XXVII*, 1). The Gothic shapes are emblematic: altogether different in feeling, then, from the 'neo-Gothic' of the Santa Croce window. Two zones of pilasters treated in a manner that calls to mind the Quattro Cento Cancelleria palace at Rome (*Plate XXXV*, 1), are separated by a zone of deep Gothic niches. In the upper zone, beneath the pediment, there is a deep *occhio* or 'eye' window. The lunette of the door surmounted by Gothic tracery, shelters a sculptured group. There is depth, and from this depth the stone blossoms into straight pilaster, so that the wall-space becomes vital as a nourishing-ground.

III. *Desiderio da Settignano*

Donatello was the prime revolutionary. As with the painter Andrea del Castagno, a brutal animation was the humanistic counter to the cold Florentine æsthetic also in their bones. Donatello is the most profound of Quattro Cento artists. But the monumental aim, I have said, leads quickly to the Baroque where the monumental, with conventionalized complications of rhythm, aspires to approach the enfolding quality of mass, itself without connection with the monumental other than being non-monumental, non-rhythmic. But previous to formalization, while yet every detail is a treasure of dynamic sensibility, the Quattro Cento is created, how richly and with what tension some masterpieces of Desiderio da Settignano, of Antonio Pollaiuolo and of Verrocchio, further demonstrate.

First of all Desiderio. His revolutionary feat is perhaps the most subtle. It would, however, have been impossible without the example of Donatello, though he was away in Padua during the early years of Desiderio's short life. To all three, to Desiderio, Pollaiuolo and Verrocchio, Donatello gave the model for compositions in which balance radically depends on *quality* of movement or emotion, and so less (than in the case of Ghiberti's reliefs for instance) on distribution of shapes. As I have already remarked in connection with Verrocchio's *lavabo*,[1] such *dynamic* design is by no means a Baroque elaboration—though that is what is left when the vital quality diminishes—but the expression of the highest emotional tensity. This dynamic composition was Donatello's answer to the unemphasized homogeneity of Ghiberti's 'finish'. We see such composing best in bronze reliefs, those on the San Lorenzo pulpits or the series at Padua. In the relief there, for instance, representing the discovery of a miser's stone heart, a small group on the left has been entirely dissociated from the main group on the right; but owing to the dramatic or dynamic treatment of the whole, no pause, no sense of distraction ensues from this gap. A still greater design is the Deposition, in which the dead one and the sorrowing are balanced easily, though not in number, by the violent grief of a woman on the right with outstretched arms, and by two other figures. Their shapes alone, apart from the emotion they express, would not make a balance. The composition, of course, coheres in other ways as well, but the one I have isolated, though in relation to the rest, is the most important.

Now I have fully described what I consider to be the stock-in-trade of Florentine artists. So it may perhaps convey something when I assert that Ghiberti's or Luca's amalgam of coldest abstraction with the least obdurate emotionalism or 'finish' — that is to say, measure in movement attained by avoiding em-

[1] *See* Part I, Section IX.

140

phasis, by the cold working of exquisite naturalistic representation—it is this amalgam, foreign to Donatello, with which Desiderio sought to emulate Donatello's dynamic composing, and succeeded. Desiderio was of one mind, and he was warm. He dissociated Luca's sweetness from his coldness. Desiderio is the only genuine case in sculpture of *quale visto di ogni canto*. His charm is genuine, his charming with the playfulness of children. As for workmanship, no one has ever equalled the delicacy of Desiderio's cutting. And in this connection one notices that Vasari described the ornamental friezes of the Marsuppini tomb in Santa Croce as rather dried and gauche (*spinosi*). Vasari accounts for these defects by declaring Desiderio's incomplete knowledge of the antique (in which, it is true, Desiderio shows no more than a general interest); that is, presumably, compared with the sculptors of Vasari's time whose lifeless 'stuck-on' mouldings do certainly reproduce the ornamentals of ancient Rome.

The delicacy of Desiderio was dynamic, his refinement fierce, so that just as Donatello revealed rhythm too profound for the ear, so Desiderio contrived a scentedness not submitted as fumes to the nose, but an ulterior fragrance seized with the eye which takes as immediate, as a revelation, what more gradually intoxicates the other senses. Sensuousness as a revelation, as an eternity of feeling, belongs only to the Quattro Cento. Energy ran loose with such concordance as to permit an appraisal; a flash of the eye, and Space captured the creatures of Time and Growth.

For once, then, for the sake of Desiderio, I concur with the myth of Florence the City of Flowers, a myth cross-grained by the cold and shapely lily, the city's emblem. But it is the smaller wild-flowers, leaves and continual fruit that garland Marsuppini's tomb. Every darkness of the cella is minimized; the sombreness of death flutters away from the winged shell placed at the base of the sarcophagus. Lightness and delicacy initiate a visible conquest over death, no less heroic than the emblazonment upon Isotta's tomb. Two children guard the sensitive foot of the urn, playing at being watchmen. No call for soldiers and funereal genii to guard the breezes of repose, no call to drag at the silky canopy when nothing is hidden, and when nothing is stark or crushed by celestial flames.

This monument has untraversable spaces between guardian children. In the zoning of it, Desiderio displayed not only measure but also great love of space in itself, he alone of Florentine sculptors. The resultant quality, enforced by the panels of coloured marble[1], is not only one of distinctness and of roominess, but also of untraversable positions in a divine interacting; and it is significant that Desiderio's beautiful tabernacle in San Lorenzo has on its face a column-vista carved in perspective (*Plate XXVIII*). To promote such interaction, to emphasize his spacing as quick and alive, and in view of the tepid composure of his traditions, Desiderio used methods the least sombre in the balancing of his compositions. Employing, as he does, the formulae of 'finish', Desiderio must enhance that rhythm by subtle irregularities, by far-fetched correspondence. With Desiderio a very marked degree of sophistication is attained. The composing of the children above and below the Marsuppini tomb reveals neither an instinctive nor an opportunist arrangement. The balance is too complicated. It is the same with the figures about the tabernacle—the two angels at the sides and the putti on the entablature with the infant Christ between them, balanced in benediction upon the lip of the holy chalice.

Desiderio is another revolutionary, another preparer of the Baroque. The Quattro Cento life is in him, but wedding with a Florentine bride means children of violence in the next generation. In what one suspects to be his later work, Desiderio makes particular use of ribbons and streamers for a dynamic purpose. Their correspondence is not simple; their direction must be related to the organization of the whole. The ribbons

[1]Apart from anything else, inasmuch as the coloured marble panels are not reproduced in the cast of this monument at the Victoria and Albert, its effect cannot be gauged in London.

2. Florence, Baptistery. Donatello and Michelozzo:
Monument to Pope John XXIII.

1. Montepulciano, Sant' Agostino : Michelozzo.

PLATE XXVII. MICHELOZZO ACHIEVES QUATTRO CENTO GOTHIC

Florence, San Lorenzo. Desiderio da Settignano : *tabernacle.*

PLATE XXVIII. 'FOR THE SAKE OF DESIDERIO, I CONCUR
WITH THE MYTH OF FLORENCE THE CITY OF FLOWERS'

upon the frieze of the beautiful mantelpiece of *pietra morta* in the Victoria and Albert, attributed to Desiderio, illustrate this point.[1] In the Musée André, Paris, there is a Quattro Cento masterpiece, *Head of a Hero*. With extreme delicacy this strong head comes out of the marble plaque. Last to appear are crinkling ribbons attached to a fillet of bay-leaves. These ribbons spring out behind to mark the distance, one behind the other, one shorter than the other; nor yet as ornament; but they make fall and curl differently their crinkles, so as to suggest variant ambuscades of glory behind the smooth brow, behind the eager, regular features. Never was expression so ebullient while equally sensitive as in this head; recusant, Cæsarian, illuminated, yet toyed by tense delicacy of youthfulness.

Pointed also are the features of Desiderio's Cæsar in the Louvre (*Plate XXIX*). Sensitiveness patrols Gothic eagle faces, blade-sharp now to cull the strongest flower-stem. And tendrils, bay-leaves, shall strap and scent the hair.

Later on, this pointedness was further sensitized for the drawing-room with an outcome in the Faunesque. Thus Bertoldo's beautiful statuette of Orpheus or Orion at the Bargello, the wrapt eyes far apart in the young, angled face (*Plate XXII*, 1). This Quattro Cento statuette is the loveliest I know. It is not a product of 'finish'. Critics mistakenly call it unfinished, because the viol and the bow and Orpheus' chest have not been worked up. Their crude state shows in how rough a form Bertoldo had his models cast. The grinding bow, the rough, compact viol, coin-like with rich sound, particularly the unhewn, clumsy bow, give an enormous solidity to the ecstacy and tenderness of this Orpheus, and to his slight form.

IV. Pollaiuolo and Verrocchio

With a new access of brutality, force, this time essentially forcible, was recovered. We are with Antonio Pollaiuolo, as a

---

[1]*See* also a mantelpiece in this manner at the Museo Bardini, Florence. Verrocchio developed still further this use of ribbons. *See* account of his *lavabo*, Part I, Section IX.

painter one of the principal of the Florentine 'fauves', dead
set on the strains and stresses of anatomical workings at rest
and in movement and in conflict. Quattro Cento exuberance
in Florence now leads quickly to the *terribilità* of Michael
Angelo, and to subsequent formalization in the Baroque[1].
Again the Florentine attempt at mass. It comes out of Donatello's tensity; and meanwhile Pollaiuolo belongs to the Quattro Cento. No one who has seen the bust of the brazen Con-
dottiero in the Bargello can doubt it. The sap runs free and
insolent. The restless, straining balances between the figures of
Sixtus the Fourth's monument (*Plate XXX*, 1) in the museum
of St. Peter's, belong still to the decades of emblazonry; so too
Innocent the Eighth's tomb in St. Peter's. These ambitious
contortions intimate a rich brutality, every nerve tremor of a
once skulking soul passed into terms of vein and bounding
muscle. Pollaiuolo's rebellion against the architectonic of Brunelleschi was truculent, against the limpid cella, against
religion even. Those were the days when they slit your throat
with a diamond, and goldsmiths belaboured the bronze with
minute savagery to ends of anatomical vigour. These tombs
are rich and taut as a result of this expensiveness. But
Verrocchio's Colleoni, conceived with a parallel tensity, will
not be claimed for the Quattro Cento. In this work the Florentine, as did Michael Angelo later on, took the Quattro Cento
exuberance altogether into his own hands. The sternness of
Colleoni is too ripe for our classification, the figure too special,
too conscious. He is a figure-head of the whole Renaissance
as it actually occurred. I leave this architype of *Forza* to the
Fascists.

On the other hand, there are two early works of Verrocchio
which are essentially Quattro Cento, the already described
lavabo and the tomb of Giovanni and Piero di Cosimo de'

[1]Even Pollaiuolo's bronze statuettes of antique subjects such as the
beautiful Hercules in the Pierpont Morgan collection, with one foot on
the head of the bull precariously overlapping the pedestal, show the same
tight broadness of style.

Paris, Louvre. Attrib. Desiderio da Settignano : *Marble relief. Head of
Julius Caesar*

PLATE XXIX.   AND BAY-LEAVES SHALL STRAP AND SCENT
THE HAIR'

1 *Rome, St. Peter's Museum.* Antonio Pollaiuolo : *Monument to Pope Sixtus IV : Detail : Geometry.*

2. *Florence, Cathedral Museum. The silver altar : Relief of John the Baptist's beheading .* Verrocchio.

PLATE XXX. 'HANDS ARE ADROIT TALONS'

Medici.[1] Again the cella has been abandoned, this time for a sarcophagus as precious as a casket, like St. Mark's precious as a cabinet on the table of the Piazza. Such costliness is related to the goldsmiths' art of which Quattro Cento sculpture is so often the development, surviving here to express the Quattro Cento quality of tightness, tensity, the packed dynamic. For that sense of concentration was stimulated, and perhaps indeed often originated, in the handling of jewels or antique cameos. The d'Este and the Medici were in general passionate about jewels; and Sigismondo, as we know from the inventory of his belongings and from his penury, exceeded them all in this love. Further, no religious symbols were carved on this tomb, just as the *lavabo*, though designed for the priests' ablutions, does not have one clerical reference. Pollaiuolo, too, showed distaste for Christian signs. The only other parallel is to the decorations of the Tempio.

Verrocchio's Medici tomb is a sarcophagus of porphyry with medallions of serpentine (*Plate XXXI*, 2). The lid is white Carrara and porphyry. The whole is ornamented with bronze. The base is of white marble resting on four bronze tortoises. The front of the monument is in the sacristy, the back in the chapel of the Madonna, and a bronze grille of twisting cords serves as a partition. Both sarcophagus and grille, on the sacristy side, are framed by a marble band of relief forming an archway. Although the relief is crowded, and even at first sight stiff, formal, it must be resolved into a Quattro Cento expression. But the ardours of Donatello have taken a new turn. By now putti are exhausted in Florence, their revelling can break no further marbles. Driven to new courses of revolution, to new breakages of caskets that seal precious life, Verrocchio discovered a rotation of that sharp vegetable riot which Donatello passed over to goad on the urchins of his neighbourhood. Unique in their strength, spinous are the bronze acanthus leaves on the tomb, and related to the gleam

[1]Also in the old sacristy, San Lorenzo, Florence. This sarcophagus stands on Verrochio's slab tomb for Cosimo de' Medici.

of the shark's spear and tail under the scorching sun, of the dry, crinkling anatomy of the under-sea's most complicated shells. For the fertility of earth is dramatized by images of just such dryness habituated to the swirl of a redundant moisture (*Plate XXXII*).

Conscious, it appears, of the ocean's fruitfulness as conceived by Agostino di Duccio in his sculptures at Rimini, of Venice newly habituated to the lagoon by marbles that match the verdures of flashing fins and scales, Verrocchio confined the exuberance of acanthus blade each end, by two enormous knobbed shells of bronze replete with bronze fruit and cones. These curl below the Medici diamond.

The reliefs of the archway are made up of bunches of corn and ramage, each enclosed by the Medici diamond. Here at last in Florence—and it is this which makes it Quattro Cento —is a work inspired by the costliness of *virtu* and by the drama of significant emblem. Here, as with the *lavabo*, the Medici inspire a Quattro Cento expression, in the person of Piero de' Medici il Gottoso. The only occasion. In both these monuments the Medici diamond incites the artist to make the porphyry more precious, to make the white marble glint and plume, to souse these sharpnesses and brilliant refractions with storms of sensuous scaliness, to offer, as symbols of fertility and flower, the grandest incrustation; since the diamond can part them as through rain or yielding mould. It is highly improbable that the bronze work was gilded, inasmuch as no trace of colour can be found even in the interstices of the metal. These sombre and impressive tones were an antithesis to the bright 'innocent' colouring of the prevalent niche-sepulchral monuments. *Strength Indomitable*, that was the motto of the Medici.

With regard to Verrocchio's development of dynamic design, the subtlety in the arrangement of the bronze foliage should be remarked. This I have already enlarged on in my account of the *lavabo*.

We cannot expect another work like the *lavabo*. The rest of Verrocchio does not concern us. Some of his busts, like the

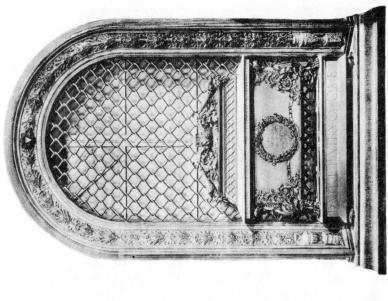

2. *Florence, San Lorenzo : Old sacristy.* Verrocchio: *Tomb of Piero and Giovanni de' Medici.*

1. *Siena, capella di Piazza. Detail of upper part :* Antonio Federighi.

PLATE XXXI. ENCRUSTED EFFECTS

Florence, San Lorenzo : Old sacristy. Verrocchio's Medici tomb : Detail.

PLATE XXXII. 'DRYNESS HABITUATED TO THE SWIRL OF A REDUNDANT MOISTURE'

terra-cotta young woman in the Foulc collection, Paris, though they be beautiful, are so widely separated from Quattro Cento conception as to have a florid, an almost German, look. After Donatello, Verrocchio is the greatest of the Florentine revolutionaries; and it is fortunate for the Quattro Cento that at one time his art was servant to the powers of emblem. He rejected the putto for a dynamism of primitive swarming, and in contrast with Donatello he made great use of foliage, but of a new variety, spinous, prolific, over-growing, which gave the direct lie to the conventional swags and blameless nosegays of the more feeble sculptors. Otherwise, Donatello foretells Verrocchio, sometimes anticipates him. Dolphins, I have remarked, line the entablature of the singing gallery in San Lorenzo, sea-monsters writhe on the pilasters of the 'Miracle of the Ass' relief at Padua, and Donatello's favourite pilasters with spiral grooves, such as frame the base of the Marzocco and the Pecci slab, were developed by Verrocchio into the spines and tendons and fins of monsters.

Now you may find these same images and an equal exuberance expressed in other periods. The point is solely the *intensity*, the *compulsion* of their showing, which keep them altogether distinct from decorated or elaborated effect, and so distinguishes them as unique. I have attempted to show how intimately connected with such compulsion was the feeling for stone. Apart from this, there were many different ways in which that same compulsion was projected in art, and all of them mean Quattro Cento work. I now suggest that Verrocchio exploited Florentine reserve itself as a tension, that the very principle of restraint was exploited as a power, a packed dynamic. Consider, for example, the famous putto with dolphin in the palazzo Vecchio courtyard. His poise is full of active inner force as yet undirected. I have said that no further work of Verrocchio can be connected with the Quattro Cento. This is because my first intention must be to distinguish clearly the Quattro Cento. But should the above sentences be understood, it will be safe to invoke affiliations.

In the unsuccessful effort to obtain trophies for the hero Leonardo, his master Verrocchio has been made to suffer. It is admitted, though, that the equivocal Mona Lisa smile belongs equally to the master.[1] But I suggest that only in the work of Verrocchio does the enigmatic find its proper context, as the foil to violence and yet as the preliminary to all action; the showing, then, of a deeper, still anonymous ferment. The correspondence of this psychological intensity still boundless, dream-like, is with the finite violence born of it. Leonardo stood outside. He would not commit himself. Quattro Cento urgency had slipped away, leaving the fascinating brood of the potentially potential. His, indeed, is the first explicit reverence for the inexhaustible fund of life. The mysterious is an abstraction. But that same boundless fund is *employed* in every work of Verrocchio. He has put Quattro Cento harness on psychological excess. You may see in his silver relief for the altar of San Giovanni, a representation of the saint's beheading (*Plate XXX*, 2). On the right two warriors, preying, combative, beaked, a type which stimulated Leonardo to his grotesques, quarrel about the execution. Their hands are adroit talons, their perfect armour bristles beneath and above their eyes screwed to exorbitant passion. As in the neck of Colleoni, every muscle is a taut string that gets resonance from the shrinking air. Concentration of physiological force, muscular and choleric, is achieved by a goldsmith's precious, articular, care. The executioner swings his blade over the saint luxuriantly kneeling. Behind are three pages; they shrink and elongate holding one another, and slowly sway. The gesture of him on the left is extravagant. Every detail of armour is embossed. His hand waves down a beautiful salver soon to be lifted from the bottom with the torn head upon it. Meanwhile his armour eddies in a stream of life enigmatic, undirected. He is tensile, gracious, withdrawn, impartial, without apprehen-

---

[1] Expression enigmatic also in sorrow, is common in much earlier Florentine sculpture. *See* the figure on the right in Desiderio's *Pietà* below the tabernacle (*Plate XXVIII*).

siveness though murder is enacted. The past is a pool, recipient of gradual night. The future will be an awakened sun that draws to itself lone vapours. Bereft of thong and sinew, as a formlessness made ductile by surrounding exertion, did Verrocchio figure suspense. Leonardo made it isolate, mysterious. But Verrocchio loved compliance as well as power in reserve; and he mingled them. I refer to the St. Thomas group at Or San Michele.

Verrocchio was the first *explicitly* to use Florentine reserve as a reserve of power, and the last. After him, tensity, compulsion goes. The marble is *searched* for forms, the difficulty of their showing increases, though belief in a power within the stone remains for a time. Michael Angelo's matrix from which he rarely frees his sculpture altogether, served for him in just this rôle of a reserve of power. He did not wish to be finally separated from the low relief, from that primitive faith in the stone's animation of which a low relief art is an expression. But actually, little reserve of power is left to the stone, little tension. The stone is spent by Michael Angelo in attaining colossal shapes, joyless, writhing supreme. Hereafter, in the Baroque, there is no tensity of manifestation by stone. The Florentine reserve, exploited by Quattro Cento artists as a reserve of power in the stone, explicitly so by Verrocchio, has been broken down.

If you would measure the difference, with any Baroque monument in eye look at Verrocchio's model for the Forteguerri tomb in the Victoria and Albert. (Said to be a fake, but no matter. If it is, the faker understood his period well enough.) The design of flying angels supporting a *mandorla* with Christ, reaches Baroque dimensions. One would take it for a work of the Seicento, except for the *mandorla*, and except—this is the point—for a certain tightness, a holding in reserve, so that all this extravagance of movement, seemingly uncontrollable, is controlled like that of marionettes by the fingers of their showman. This is an after-thought. But indeed, the simile is even more appropriate to the flying angels of Antonio Rossellino and Benedetto da Majano. In their cases, the string-control is apparent, and, therefore, in shameless but cold conjunction with a white, 'harmless' simplicity—disgusting. For reserve of power is not exploited dramatically, but rather as a denial of tension.

Yet, at the same time, I can now admit what I could not admit while making more subtle distinctions, namely that all fifteenth-century sculpture, particularly the Florentine, shows *some* tension owing to this very reserve of power. For the Quattro Cento spirit had the uniform effect on Florentine reserve, to make that spirit a reserve of power imputed to the materials the Florentine sculptors worked. Even in Ghiberti, inventor of 'finish', of fluency, one perceives a tightness of expression that is lost to the Baroque age and to subsequent ages, though Ghiberti's creations are no less fluent, and a good deal more naturalistic, than those of Bernini. Is it a remnant of primitive stiffness which, though avoided in technique, and even in conception, yet remains somewhere in the whole creative process? Does the supreme charm of fifteenth-century art as a whole reside in those artists' discovery and use of 'modern' technique, 'modern' grace and perspective, to magnify the tension, the non-diffuse accumulated revelation which primitive stiffness expresses but which, in primitive art, is severely confined by that very stiffness?

I have said the Renaissance is an intensification of all forms, of all the primitive art to which it succeeds. In so broad a description I can see the art of the fifteenth century as one. I have found urgent, however, the need to distinguish where the reserve of power engendered by primitive stiffness has been denied its dramatic, revelatory effect, and where, under the title of Quattro Cento art, that tensity, fixed best in stone, has been avowed.

CHAPTER FIVE

IN CONCLUSION

I CONCLUDE THE essay itself with a short account of Luciano Laurana's courtyard at Urbino, with an account of mass-effect, and with a few generalizations, principally upon the union of Florentine and Quattro Cento elements in sixteenth-century architecture and painting.

A reference at this final stage to Luciano is the sufficient make-weight on the side of Verona, on the side of the Quattro Cento, to the only architecture so far discussed, namely the Florentine. Moreover, Luciano's courtyard fixes my issue. For it is the greatest feat in mass-effect known to me. But first I must explain out of what material Luciano constructed a final synthesis.

The surfaces of a Quattro Cento marble relief are smooth, continuous, swelling: for they reveal a growth. But the revelation itself has the tense and immediate quality of primitive art. Such reliefs attain the maximum of spatial objectivization in a primary form. But whereas sculptors of low relief express a directional force out of, or into, the marble[1], the ensuing Quattro Cento architects and painters did not concern themselves with movement. Though contemplating the ebullient life that sculptors had lured to the surface of the stone, they

[1]The Quattro Cento sculptors Francesco Laurana and Isiah da Pisa are typical exceptions. They are to be classed with Piero della Francesca and with Luciano Laurana as expressing a world, a purely spatial world, that is completely revealed. It is not known whether Francesco was related to Luciano. They both came from the neighbourhood of Zara in Dalmatia.

desired to fix —not to perpetuate, since the word suggests a time element—to fix that revelation as an outwardness, complete, unalterable. For the science of perspective had given a miraculous command over disposition in space, and thence at least two painters and one architect conceived the fantasy of a world of space alone in which, unlike among spiritual spheres, all relations were graduated, fixed, a world entirely immediate and revealed, a solid manifestation. Perspective is no longer, as in Florence, the means to art, but the aim of art.

What makes this abstract, mathematical art unique in history, is that it is nevertheless an expression of personal faith. This is true again of Francesco Laurana's sculpture. His busts, conceived geometrically, express an imprint of Quattro Cento finality put upon Quattro Cento emergence-effect. Measurement of bare geometric space, mathematical formulæ, became supremely emblematic; and when used in the treatment of human forms, transmitters of full emotion. So objective a treatment, objective as science itself, could be possible only in an age whose aim, newly discovered, immensely inspired, was to turn subjective matter outwards, to concrete upon the surface of the stone an inner ferment. Thereupon, when all is shown, when each energy is manifest, the whole of this emergent, emblematic matter can be set out, finally objective and so also, finally emblematic, in the pure outwardness of space. No other art equally abstract has been governed by so high a necessity.

Florentine Uccello, be it said, was the first devotee of space. The painting of Piero della Francesca and the architecture of Luciano Laurana, which is allied to that painting, are the ritual of perspective worship, pure and simple, and only thus, in terms of spatial settlement, can the religion as wrapt as any hierarchy be explained. It is a unique religion. For space has never been so significant. Piero synthetized the whole Quattro Cento new detail, new *virtu*, in its most immediate possible form, that is, in two dimensions, and by the manipulation of the immediacy of colour.

Now Luciano's courtyard was built not without defiance of Florentine or Brunellesque architecture. For Federico di Montefeltro, Duke of Urbino, Sigismondo Malatesta's arch-enemy, wrote in the letters of patent he granted Luciano, that he had searched everywhere, particularly in Tuscany, 'the fount of architecture', and found none worthy of his project.[1] No doubt Federico's first wish, himself expert in war, was to build a castle with the most up-to-date store rooms and stables. For this he needed a great engineer, especially in view of the precipitous ground at Urbino. Luciano was an unrivalled engineer, and Federico chose him and chose Francesco di Giorgio after him, because they had already excelled in designing the new kind of fortress invented to withstand artillery. But this concentration, from choice or from necessity, on the machinery of architecture, was intimately bound up (as I shall show in a moment), in the taste of patron and of architect, with concentration on effects of mass that were entirely foreign to Brunellesque design. For owing to the affinities of mathematics and machinery in that age with artistic synthesis, Federico's profession, namely fighting, as it did his rival Sigismondo, must have prejudiced him in favour of the effect of mass. Both of them were exponents of the new 'modern' warfare in which mechanical devices in attack and defence gained a novel importance. The diskiness[2] of some of the ornaments in the Tempio and in the palace at Urbino was not unrelated to the broad and solid roll of the wheels of Malatesta and Montefeltro cannon.

[1]'. . . et havendo noi cercato per tutto, et in Toscana massime dove è la fontana delli Architettori, et non havendo trovato huomo che sia veramente intendente, et ben perito in tal mistiero, ultimamente havendo per fama prima inteso, et poi per esperienza veduto, et conosciuto quanto l'egregio huomo Mastro Lutiano ostensore di questa sia dotto,' etc.

[2]I refer here principally to the medallions on the balustrade to the chapel of San Sigismondo in the Tempio and to bosses between the mouldings of window embrasures in the sala della Jole, the palace, Urbino. In connection with the latter ornament *see* Part III, Section VI, and *Plate XIII*, 2.

Again, Federico had all his life associated with artists whose work expressed finality imposed on Quattro Cento exuberance. The first part of his palace he had built some twenty years before Luciano was summoned to Urbino. These rooms were decorated by a sculptor, probably Francesco Laurana, who, like Isiah da Pisa, expressed in his work what the stone reveals as revealed, final, static in space. I suspect that Piero della Francesca was behind the whole of this phase of Quattro Cento art, behind Francesco Laurana and Luciano Laurana, both of whom he probably met at different periods in Urbino. For intermittently through thirty-five years or so, Federico was sending for Piero to execute his commissions. It is significant that the three panels[1] representing buildings in perspective have been attributed in turn to Piero della Francesca, to Luciano Laurana and to Francesco di Giorgio[2] whom I associate as well with the final phase of Quattro Cento art. Venetian Quattro Cento sculpture and architecture also belong to this phase; and when I come to write of them in the third volume, I shall sometimes use metaphors from machinery.

Luciano's loggia on the west side of the Urbino palace has the distinct beauty of the finest aqueduct, each detail lovely in specific function. It seems now to be certain that Luciano had nothing to do with Alfonso's arch at Naples. Adolfo Venturi's attribution was founded on the arbitary[3] interpretation of a document. The *cedole* or pay-books of the Aragonese kings contain no mention of Luciano before 1472 (when the arch was completed), and then only as an engineer. In any case the Albertian massiveness of Alfonso's triumphal arch, the effects of light and shade, are nearly as much opposed to Luciano's clear art as is Brunellesque continuity.

Imagine the situation when Luciano built his courtyard

[1]One is at Urbino, the others at Berlin and Baltimore.

[2]*See* Part III, Section 2.

[3]*See* Luigi Serra: *Le varie fase costruttive del palazzo ducale di Urbino.* Bollettino d'Arte, 1931. Also G. Pacchioni: *L' opera di Luciano Laurana a Mantova. Bollettino d' Arte,* 1923.

Plate XXXIII). He ignored a technique which seemed unquestionable to nearly all his contemporaries, the Brunellesque arrangement of stone and brick. And Luciano had to use these materials; for Federico could not afford a stone investment, even for the exterior as intended. While, on the other hand, to dispense with stone altogether was unthinkable, at any rate in that part of Italy. Remember the prestige of Florence to which even Sigismondo and Federico thought themselves subservient, remember the prestige of Brunelleschi and the perfect neatness of his architecture, pre-eminently desirable, one would have thought, to him who wished to be civilized in a mountain fastness. And in the circumstances, what other effect than a drawing on the wall could there be when stone was used only for facings, for pillars, pilasters and the moulding of an arch, how else than drawn on the surface of the stucco could the stone appear, especially since Italian climate demanded the long succession of arches in cloister, loggia and courtyard?

But Luciano did not stucco his brick. He left it rough. In the second place his stone is white; pilasters are thin, plain, unfluted, immeasurably straight and smooth. Archivolts have a few deep lines. The stone, then, lies on the brick in low relief, yet stands out simple, distinct, a white magic, *nitidezza*. The unpassable space between window-frame and pilaster along the storey, or the exact framing of a window that lies back on the wall—for the colonnade beneath is broad—give so supreme an individuality to each stone shape, (though every pilaster, for example, except for his place, is the same as the next), that one appears to witness a miraculous concurrence of masterpieces of sculpture, each designed to show the beauties of his neighbour as unique. There is no other traffic among them. Their positions are untraversable, and no hand shall dare to touch two stone forms at a time. They flower from the brick, a Whole made up of Ones each as single as the Whole. What could be more different from Brunellesque running lines, than this sublime fixture of the manifest?

I say with confidence that no carved capitals in the world are beautiful when compared with those in the courtyard at Urbino. Otherwise, there is no ornament except the inscription on the frieze whose Roman lettering is no less significant, no less emblematic, than the most renowned ideographs. Perfect the mass, like a new stratum found packed with distinct columns. Luciano ignored the book axiom of redoubled strength at the corners. They are flanked in each case by a pilaster together with a half-column either side; the actual angle is the space between. Above, the trabeation also breaks for this gap, which would not have been possible had Luciano intended two storeys. But in appearance this space of his between is stronger than fifty columns of another architect (*Plate XXXIV*). His columns are brothers. Nowhere must they irremediably join. They must be apart for concerted strength. No one, except Francesco di Giorgio and his school, has explicitly copied Luciano. For who else has invented the absolute need for capitals as beautiful, and so the means to create them; who else has felt stones as so distinct yet together making mass?

And now I can explain fully what I mean by mass. An effect of mass is one connected with solidity or density of three-dimensional objects. It is, therefore, in part an appeal to the sense of touch though the object be a building and not a piece of sculpture. But solids afford an effect of mass only when they also allow the *immediate*, the instantaneous synthesis that the eye alone of the senses can perform. An undecorated wall, perhaps better than a decorated one, may give a strong impression of mass, but only when there are variations in its surface, mostly of colour or tone, that the eye with one flash discovers coherent, so that perceptions of succession belonging to any estimate of length or height or density, retire in favour of a feeling that here you witness a concatenation, a simultaneity, that the object is *exposed* to you, all of it all at once. And just because stone is solid and fixed and yet has the power in a high degree to reflect light, to accept tone, thus making a purely visual synthesis possible, it is the ideal vehicle of mass-effect and therefore the revealer of the spatial dimension, and so the basic inspirer of the visual arts. And as far as it is possible I would isolate and stress this far more pregnant quality of mass, its appeal to the quickness of the eye, its power to captivate in one second or less. Exploring sense of touch, I admit, introduces a succession, and therefore entails some element of time though it be turned into an instantaneous impression by the quickness of the perceiving eye. But from the point of view of the eye alone, there is no impression of quickness or even of simultaneity, in the objects perceived. Mass reveals an entirety, reveals space, just as music dramatizes succession or time with rhythm. And while admitting that when the eye perceives, other senses are always incited in that very act (for instance, I have inferred an oral appeal in Verona marble), and further, while admitting that visual art is bound to reflect responses of these other senses—for without them things perceived would not be objects—I consider that the *basic* appeal of the art of colour, painting, and of architecture, should be to the eye alone, just as music to the ear.

And what are the values of this rare thing, purely visual art? They are the values of space in the abstract. Just as music can interpret any content in terms of rhythm, so painting can interpret any content in terms of position, of objects related by space. And when the temporal factor, when succession and rhythmic or linear treatment in a visual art are the foremost concern, then it is visual art only in the wider sense that it is perceived with the eyes.[1] For *immediacy* is betrayed, the immediate synthesis that the eye alone can perform and, indeed, does perform on material that incites the other senses, should that material be still conceived as primarily visual, that is to

[1]In any case out of all the visual arts, only from painting and from architecture are purely spatial values to be expected; though one does meet them to some extent in other arts, in the sculpture of Francesco Laurana for instance, where they are translated into a plastic whose point is the isolation or self-sufficiency of each shape.

say, a matter of space, the immediate dimension, of light and colour without all the temporal, rhythmic afterthought that the atmosphere of North and East bestow. What I call purely visual matter is dissociated from noise as well as from silence, from past, present and future. Things stand expressed, exposed, unaltered in the light, in space. Things stand. Some call so immediate an effect dramatic or sudden, for there are no words without temporal association; and in any case, few minds seem to be able to disentangle space from time. This feat belongs almost entirely to the Quattro Cento. Neither Luciano's courtyard nor Piero's painting are in any sense dramatic. The finality revealed is too great in Piero's pictures for any such word, the finality revealed even when, like Uccello, he represents a battle in progress. The disposition of shapes by means of colour and perspective afford a sense of completeness, so that not only is the purely visual aspect of things stressed, but it is enforced to such a degree that happenings, ferment psychological and physical, are subsumed under formulæ of absolute exposure, in terms, that is, of unalterable positions in space. Thus, the highest achievements of visual art not only absorb, but transform, time into terms of space.

It is obvious both why the effect arouses emotion and why that emotion became so conscious as to be projected into the art of the even-lighted South. Objects perceived simply as related in space, encourage the ambition of every man for complete self-expression, for an existence completely externalized. Our love of space is our love of expression. When we complain of lack of light in England, beside the need for the sun's rays we express a lack of spatial effect. Our spaces drift musical, composite. Even the brightest day has abundant 'atmosphere-effects'. We console ourselves for the lapse of the immediacy image as for our own resulting lack of entire expression, with the various rhythm of music, literature and, alas, of the bastard products of the visual arts; since sense of space is well nigh lost, and small the art in which time is turned to space.

Urbino, Ducal palace : Luciano Laurana : The courtyard.

PLATE XXXIII. NON-RHYTHMIC MASS

Urbino, Ducal palace. Luciano Laurana : *The courtyard : Detail.*
PLATE XXXIV. 'WHO ELSE HAS FELT STONES AS SO
DISTINCT YET TOGETHER MAKING MASS?'

Mass, then, is a purely spatial synthesis apparent in a solid and between solids. Now synthesis is only of what is separate, in this case separate because differently disposed in space. Degree of mass-effect in its highest form depends upon the degree of non-temporal synthesis apparent, and the degree of synthesis in turn depends on the nature of the separateness that is synthetized. These separate entities, if their spatial position is to be made emphatic, will otherwise conform to a pattern. Thus the zones of similar columns, etc.—even in architecture avowedly contrapuntal in effect. What I have called scenic or musical mass in connection with buildings, is one in which separateness in space is overborne by so great a stress upon continuity or rhythm, one far more involved than what sense of touch demands, that little non-temporal synthesis is employed, and little effect of space made material or solid, ensues. Instead, the building gains a rhythm, and what is actually an immovable object in space expresses movement or succession.

But inasmuch as we still feel the building is solid, there ensues a partial mass-effect. The *massive* effect, so wrongly identified with mass-effect, is but an enlargement of this rudimentary form and lacks the idealism of purely spatial conception; since the effect, in so far as it is 'piled up', is largely dependent on musical architectonic. A Greek Temple, on the other hand, is certainly a mass without any unnecessary temporal import (except what writers have persistently thrust on to it, encouraged by the ravages of Time). Classic columns, though engaged, are easily seen separate as well as synthetized. But this is not mass in so supreme a form as Luciano's courtyard. It is not enough to banish the time element. A certain stiltedness, a certain gap results. It needs a far greater understanding of the purely spatial to achieve a non-temporal synthesis where arches roll in succession. In Luciano's courtyard there is apparent not so much the detachment of spatial values, but a supreme translation of the successive into spatial effects. This causes it to be an expression far less divorced from the processes of living. It is the greatest triumph of the spirit of man, a greater achievement than Piero's painting because such an effect is realized less hardly within the two dimensions of a picture. To turn subject into object palpable as death the perfect object, to turn time into space without eradicating time as does the incident of death, to show living under the form of the complete, the manifested, was the highest exploit; since it was the final expression of the universal aim, strongest in that time, to show, to objectify; in other words, it alone entirely reflects the process of living carried to conclusion, of object charged with subject. It is an expression as vital as the dance to which it is the opposite, the complement and the end. All the rest of art lies between.

We cannot remain long on this objective or scientific level in art. Rhythm resurges; but the attainment can never be forgotten.

Now the Florentine painters—it is the habitual vital muddle—developed perspective but never worshipped it, with the honourable exception of Uccello and a few others.[1] They 'used' perspective to articulate anatomy and movement. In this, as in all else, they followed Donatello, thus missing the highest rôle of painting at that time. Indeed, the second generation of Florentine painters with their bulky, overwhelming foreground figures, wilfully unlearnt for their major works what Masaccio, Castagno and Domenico Veneziano had taught. Meanwhile from Padua, Mantegna, also inspired by Donatello, spread still wider the cult of muscular strength in movement.

I am justified, then, in giving so much of my attention to sculpture. For both the painting which reflects the Quattro Cento and most of that which does not, must be closely referred to the sculpture of the period. But, as the latest criticism has shown, the influence of Piero was extraordinarily widespread, extending far beyond the bounds of Umbria. So much

[1] For instance, Benozzo Gozzoli, Pesellino, so far as they were cassone painters.

so, that we may visualize the tendencies of fifteenth century painting as finally a conflict between perspective and movement; though each be proper to the other. We may follow out this conflict in the painters of the Ferrarese school, Cosimo Tura, Cossa and Ercole Roberti, until it is finally resolved in Venice by Giovanni Bellini, who, beside having Mantegna for a son-in-law, came later under the influence of Piero through Antonello da Messina, and perhaps directly too, if he saw as his father Jacopo, undoubtedly saw and reflects in his drawings the now lost frescoes of Piero at Ferrara. Only by such influence can we explain a change in Bellini's style.[1]

The religions of perspective and of movement were quickly fused. Painting, by a synthesis at first sight impossible, achieves a height of expression employing every possibility of the medium. Perhaps no art has been so ripe as was painting in the hands of the Venetians. For they managed to subdue to terms of tone a pictorial art which had achieved immense tactile triumphs by definite hostility to tone, by use of harsh colour and by trampling upon the ceremonies of space. Piero's plastic rootedness remains, while dramatic movement is enhanced; so that with the lick, the flower-like, rooted motion of flames, figures dart along and down Venetian canvasses. The flicker of the flame drawn out to an intensity or sullen in the autumn gold, throbs as well in Venetian sculpture. Rizzo had it and the Baroque sculptor Vittoria. The flame passes from Veronese and Tintoretto to Greco, still lives amid the smokes of Magnasco, later to spurt, jewel-like in clarity, from Tiepolo's ceilings.

Somewhat parallel to the fusion of the movement school and the perspective school in Venetian painting, is the fusion of Brunelleschi's style and that of Laurana and of Francesco di Giorgio in the best sixteenth-century non-Baroque architecture. Bramante, born at Urbino and brought up amid examples of Piero della Francesca's art, is the focal point. His own

[1]*See* Roberto Longhi's memorable essay, *Piero dei Franceschi e lo sviluppo della pittura veneziana. L'Arte,* 1914.

courtyard, the cloister of Santa Maria della Pace, Rome, is definitely Quattro Cento. Bramante it was, more than Raphael, who gave to sixteenth-century design something of Luciano's worship for a sublime mathematic, at a time when technical or professional capacity in architecture, as in painting, reached its zenith. Again, Bramante's interior to the cathedral at Pavia shows a sense for mass in the organization of a structural dialectic originally Brunellesque. The manifested with the speedy, the solid with careful, astute delicacy, are co-ordinated in four sixteenth-century masterpieces, which together with the Tempio encasement and Luciano's courtyard are among the greatest buildings of the world. I refer foremost to Antonio di Sangallo the elder's Madonna di Biagio at Montepulciano, then to Vignola's[1] Villa Papa Giulio at Rome, then to the interior of Palladio's church of the Redentore on the Giudecca, Venice, and finally to Santa Maria della Consolazione at Todi, particularly the exterior, begun by Cola di Matteuccio da Caprarola and by Gabriele di Giovanni da Como. The synthesis that Bramante had performed, gave sixteenth-century architecture a grip of non-pictorial yet ample structural design *in three dimensions* that has never been equalled. I stress 'in three dimensions' because Luciano's courtyard, though the mass is perfect within these limits, is, like most Quattro Cento building, essentially a façade architecture.[2]

Meanwhile, particularly in Rome, the Baroque developed apace; whereas in Florence whose art was responsible for the Baroque, they persisted with Brunellesque forms as if inborn refinement had been shocked by the monsters it had produced. Savonarola had left Florence dimmed. Michael Angelo, when building in Tuscany, kept close to Brunelleschi, as did Vasari (*cf.* cupola of S. M. dell' Umiltà, Pisa), as did Giovanni Dosio. So revolt was continually nourished, and genius followed Michael Angelo to Rome leaving behind Buontalenti, Cigoli,

[1]Ammannati and Vasari built the *fonte bassa* in the garden, and Ammannati the loggia and garden wall.

[2]*See* Part III, Section I.

Dosio Santi di Tito and others. We have seen that an entablature above a column and supporting an archivolt is a Brunellesque trait. At Rome they preferred more cohesive forms; they favoured the engaged column, in keeping with Roman architecture and with Luciano's pilasters and with Alberti's three-quarter columns on the Tempio façade already derived from Roman sources.

Now it has not been necessary to describe this or any other employment of classical forms so far noticed, as a 'classical' architecture. Nor is it necessary in relation to Baroque, Palladian, Rococo or Empire architecture or even to the Edwardian Admiralty arch. The term 'classical' is fruitless as a description of an architecture, except to indicate mean-tempered largeness and meticulous barrenness in the employment of classical forms. For what else but classical should one call the cathedrals at Cadiz and Malaga, or the Madeleine and the whole spirit of French building subsequent to the early Renaissance? In Italy the term as applied to a style is practically meaningless, thank goodness, except for the *campi santi*. Where there is no need of music, there will be none of the classical in any of the arts. For the temper of that term, as applied to architecture at any rate, is one native to the concert-room bruised by sound out of content, but not out of shape, to the sombre cloths of the piano's surface, to the correct busts that music encourages, to the chandelier reflected on the piano lid —'la Lune'. The Madeleine is the French sharp repressed guttural anticipation of the Wagner assault. Is there any building less like the Parthenon? And if the Baroque architecture incorporated into stone the elements of music, the classical is the architecture of those harsh ones who fail in this though invaded by music, who have been swept to a refuge of hauteur or snappy academicism by torrents of searching music in art and in life. Good God! Think of Alberti's encasement for the sculpture emblematic of Sigismondo Malatesta's ambition. It is a tight fit, this holding of one man's emblem. Then think of the halls and characterless churches designed, though never a trumpeter enters, to suffer coldly, imperiously, the veils of music. There is not the beginning of a tension. If you want the gist of French Classicism, go to the Symbolist poets. Here you will know the cathedral dome that still is Racine, left cold and immobile after consuming choirs of music; after ding-dong bells have rung—left in the dark. No shape is there, but what death snatches from the silence. Starkness is not a shape. *Les Fleurs du Mal.* A bad Parthenon, not even exotic, only imperious; the *nuances* are blatant, like those shadow judgments mirrors suddenly propound in the concert-room. A musical-box caged in ice, this poetry. Cold as well as heat scorches. What was that delicious pistol shot? A cracking of the ice, or was it the cracked music within, did I hear *Vierge, Filles, La Lune,* and other monosyllabic splutters come crystalline from the lake?

Verona marble has inspired a far-reaching indignation. I have pondered its compact yet luminous substance for every assault. The true reproach of stone is silent and in general unobserved. One needs to pick up pieces and fling them through the more transparent windows.

PART III

OUTLINE OF THE QUATTRO CENTO

AN APPENDIX TO
FLORENCE AND VERONA

OUTLINE OF THE QUATTRO CENTO

THIS APPENDIX outlines aspects of Quattro Cento art which have received so far no more than cursory mention, including some details which would be irrelevant in the succeeding volumes devoted to the Tempio Malatestiano and to Venetian art.

I. Quattro Cento architecture in general

There is no other building to put beside Luciano's courtyard. Complete or final expression of his standard occurred only once in architecture. But there are many buildings which express the Quattro Cento love for stone in a guise more abstract and therefore more intense than sculptors achieved; and these too I call Quattro Cento architecture. Now this attainment of structural expression required at that time a professionalism associated particularly with the use of classical forms, in advance of the professionalism of craftsmanship — required a designer pure and simple, as if abstracted and impersonal. And impersonality was not native to the Quattro Cento spirit. Something extremely Gothic inspired those architects. Alberti,[1] Luciano and Francesco di Giorgio attained so professional a mastery—and it is this that makes their mastery sublime—because the rash as well as the patient loves of the craftsman reinforced abstraction, because subjective and

[1] I remind the reader who thinks I have neglected Alberti that one part of the next volume will be devoted to him.

objective were so nearly one, because mathematic was emblem symbolizing a personal faith. But this genesis of architectural feeling curtailed their choice of forms, as I shall demonstrate. The ideal Quattro Cento structure is itself transitional: for with time, mathematics must inevitably harden its poetry.

One can support the generalization that most fifteenth-century architecture, Quattro Cento and Florentine, is a façade architecture. The single architectural shape to be viewed from many angles and to be enjoyed even from the distance, is rare in the fifteenth century. This kind of completeness required professionalism of temperament as well as of skill, and was attained in the next century amid the triumph of monumental aim. The fifteenth-century architectural effect, on the other hand, needs you close. Like a face it is indistinguishable in the distance. Brunelleschi's dome, of course, is a shape to be recognized anywhere, and perhaps if the Tempio had been completed and rounded off with the dome that Alberti designed, we would have had another fifteenth-century monument of the colossal type. I cannot regret that the Tempio was never completed. Certainly the various modern designs for this completion are hideous one and all.[1] And when one knows the various accidents which reinforced the whole trend of the structure, and which compelled the abandonment of plans not only dissociated by us but repugnant, it is easy to believe that fate interfered once again in the matter of the completion. For the appeal of the Tempio is too personal for me to have welcomed the prospect of a soliloquy directed toward the gleam of it as beheld from the heights of San Marino. One must see the flower from out the stone and the fixation by Alberti's arches of revealed passion. Domes and towers and minarets belong to the embroidery, to the not so intense and particular emotions of high-flown Gothic or Baroque. The Quattro Cento architects possessed something so certain that they had no need to stamp an impression.

[1] See for reproductions of these designs, Corrado Ricci's *Tempio Malatestiano*. Bestetti e Tumminelli, Milan, 1925.

But should an antagonist now retort that I am attempting to make a virtue of fifteenth century architecture's lack of invention, I will hastily mention two Quattro Cento structures, remarking in one case an exterior, in the other an interior, which excel also in mere impression effect. Both are churches by Francesco di Giorgio.

If you look out to the left from the train on the way to Rome, just beyond the station of Cortona, you will see below the town the apparently quadrangular Santa Maria delle Grazie al Calcinajo with a compact cupola rising superb from the midst. This machine with its *pietra morta* fittings, queens it among the grey olive groves, but is ready to desert them for any sphere. Even from such distance of two miles or so, you can engage the vital compactness of the structure, complete for any view-angle. We will not approach to discover how deep is the cutting of the windows, how their pediments shoot out alive. My example of an interior shall be one of uniform colour, whereas the interior of the Calcinajo is a design of *pietra morta* on stucco, though not to the extent of drawing on the wall. The example is the interior of San Bernardino dei Zoccolanti, just across the valley east of Urbino. The impression here is of continuous whiteness, delicate like a blaze; and yet every moulding is distinct; in fact some have read into this building the *divina nudità* of Laurana, have allowed him the attribution. It is unlikely. For the whiteness progresses into the cupola. There you are trapped into a tensile whorl as within the cupola at Cortona. Francesco's magnet exerts its greatest power. The neatness of the attraction as the spectator walks up to beneath the San Bernardino dome, will remain long with him. But what would the diminishing chambers of the cupola attract? No ordinary incrustation, but light itself. The church is planned to the chimney draught of the cupola. There is but one impression on entering.

Yet on the whole, churches as churches were not good game for Quattro Cento expression. The Tempio is a Franciscan church once converted to the uses of paganism. Alberti's two churches at Mantua help, but cannot originate, an understanding of the Quattro Cento. And yet, from the point of view of structural expression, Quattro Cento palaces are rare. Emblematic significance is certainly frequent, but is more often expressed by sculpture, by ornament, by actual symbol, than in purely structural terms. Pre-eminent exceptions are the courtyard at Urbino, the exterior of the Cancelleria palace in Rome (*Plate XXXV*, 1) and that of the palazzo del Consiglio in Verona (*Plate XII*, 2).

This last building, designed by Fra Giocondo, does not express a summing up, a Pieran fixing of that which had already been manifested in sculpture. Fra Giocondo's mass-effect is not the final but the more primitive kind; it is an expression of density in the stone, not rhythmic certainly, but firm, solid, tense, an expression on huge and abstract scale of the love the sculptors showed in carving, the same love that Luciano transposed still further.

And now I can explain why Quattro Cento architecture is essentially a façade architecture. This tense non-rhythmic mass, foreign to other periods, is effected even when no sculptor aids, by presenting a wall-face whose stretches between fenestration and, perhaps, above the blanks of arcading, are seen emblematic, articulate, a joy in themselves though unornamented, because so simply solid and coherent like a lovely garden wall. For fruit trees press the garden wall lovely in tone: viewed from outside, this wall solidly stands, but different and now different in the changing light—solidly stands, a permanent abstraction of the deepening tonalities skins of the fruit amass for tissue through the season.

It sounds as if it were easy to come by this effect in architecture. Just build a wall for a façade and pierce it here and there with windows that show the depth of the wall. But only if wall-space *means* so much, can this Quattro Cento effect be emulated. A hundred elements of design, of materials and of their treatment, go to make wall-space so pregnant. I am not suggesting that this actual effect particularly occupied Fra Gio-

1. *Rome, palazzo della Cancelleria :* Baccio Pontelli ? (*Door on left is later*).

2. *Turin, Cathedral.* Meo da Caprino: *façade.*

PLATE XXXV. QUATTRO CENTO FAÇADES

Pesaro, Sforza palace. Luciano Laurana?

PLATE XXXVI. 'THE STEADFAST FACE OF THE ROSE'

condo's attention. It is impossible as well as entirely irrelevant to attempt to trace the interaction of conscious and unconscious, practical and æsthetic, motives. All one can know in this connection is that certain forms only were possible to architects of that period, for a mixture of practical and æsthetic reasons. One of the possible forms was a structure which appears to us as an articulation of all that a simple wall has meant to our fancies. Perhaps Fra Giocondo was intent on nothing more than combining something Roman with the common plan, dating from the twelfth century, of the Italian municipal building.

The essential point of this Italian medieval form is the building of rooms over an arcade so that there is a certain competition between the wall above and the blanks (betwixt arches) below. In the Doges' palace, Venice, the wall-space is so towering that the shadows between the arches below are overwhelmed. They give one the sense that they do not belong to the building, which, however, is thus made to appear off the ground and ready to fly away.

It is not before the fifteenth century nor before the use of the rounded arch which avoids this particular directional implication of the pointed arch, that competition between blanks and wall-space, always the constant problem of Italian design, is properly harnessed to effects of mass. The palazzo del Consiglio (*Plate XII*, 2) is composed of a storey with mullion windows, above a rounded arch arcade. Pointed arches would have thrust themselves into the storey, have given the effect, not so much of supporting, as of throwing up, the storey. By using the classical decorated pilasters (the centre and corner ones are repeated between, and at the terminations of, the arches below) between the windows, Fra Giocondo broke up the wall-surface so that it appears pregnant with stone-flowers and so that, instead of an uninspiring competition between wall and voids below, positive and negative in battle, wall-space, thus broken up and varied, is *shown off solid* and distinct by those voids. And each pilaster, since its function in design is so relevant, gains a flower-like distinction unknown to any other architecture, past or subsequent.

The Sforza palace at Pesaro (*Plate XXXVI*) is another Quattro Cento masterpiece composed of a storey above an arcade. In this case the competition between voids and solids is transformed into mass-effect without the help of dividing pilasters. There are five windows above six arches, and the very careful irregularity in the arrangement of the windows above the arches breaks up the wall-space successfully; while the vast cornice on top presses the wall down so that it stands in a tension between arcade and roof. Owing to my prejudice against rhythmic or musical effect in architecture, this building appears to me to afford a far greater effect of mass than the huge,[1] beautiful bulk of St. Paul's or the Angkor temples. See the palace front at Pesaro, stucco peeling from brick, forward in the sunlight, steady above the dark recesses of arcade below. Here is use of light and shade without rhythmic effect, nor yet stark. A matter of space alone, each window individual, each ornament and each shadow. With what compare such cohesion but with the steadfast face of the rose?

Non-rhythmic light-and-shade effect, making a perfect coherence of solids, entailed a purely frontal architecture. We see why Quattro Cento architects favoured loggia or arcade, pilaster and engaged column. Brunelleschi, too, employed the loggia form with storey above; and it gives strength to my argument that his Ospedale degli Innocenti affords no impression whatever of a wall made articulate (*Plate XII*, 1). Windows are over the centres of each arch. There has been no attempt to transmute the competition of solids and voids. They are made to approximate by the thinness of vertical lines, by the smallness of the storey and by the lightness of the arcade.

---

[1]Mere size on which monumental aim is nearly always intent, in itself entails rhythm, since when magnitude is too great for immediate perception, the eye must continually follow up and down and along the structure, and will then synthetize largely in terms of rhythm.

Meanwhile bands of horizontal lines keep a race afoot from end to end of the building.

The frontal conception in architecture which reached un-exampled heights in Quattro Cento structures, is inherent in Italy. And after the Quattro Cento achievement, something of Quattro Cento conception was embodied in the façades of later styles. For instance, on many church façades the unsup-ported top zone that English critics have found in such bad taste, is a reminiscence of the feeling for articulation of the simple wall. This chunkiness nearest the sky—and the exact width of the stone is evident—shows a survival of the true feeling for mass, as well as the heroic Italian passion for drama or display, even though it be merely frontal, solidly 'skin-deep'.

II. *Francesco di Giorgio*

To Francesco di Giorgio Martini and to his school we owe the greater amount of Quattro Cento architecture. His paint-ing and sculpture do not concern me at present.

Now Francesco was the universal type of genius with the event of which the Renaissance is so often identified. He ex-celled as engineer, as architect, as draughtsman, as painter, as sculptor, and he wrote an important book about architecture. He was courted throughout Italy. I have already mentioned that Leonardo and Bramante needed to send for him because they could not put the dome on Pavia Cathedral. His name is unknown to the general public. Indeed, before Adolfo Ven-turi[1] wrote his panegyrics, little was known to anyone about Francesco. Yet it is safe to predict, so obvious is the greatness of his achievements, that within a decade or so Francesco's name will become synonymous in popular imagination, like Leonardo's, with the Renaissance itself. The process of cor-recting Vasari's Florentine boost will go on.

Francesco di Giorgio was Siennese. Now Siena and Ferrara

[1] *See* his *Storia dell'Arte Italiana*, Vol. VIII, Part I, and an article on Francesco di Giorgio as sculptor in *L'Arte*, 1923.

have the finest brick buildings in Italy. In Siena this was due to the excellent clay deposits[1] near the city. I think these clay deposits, as much as anything else, caused Siennese æsthetic to differ so largely from the Florentine. For the Siennese loved their clay as a material, and thence their fantasies proceeded to the cast iron, to steel, and to stone in the carving of which they expressed as well their feeling for those other materials. Familiarity with clay can mean not only the triumph of modeller's conception—Michael Angelo studied the grand 'modelling' of Jacopo della Quercia's[2] sculpture at Bologna—but also a predilection for opulent detail in architecture. And yet as their painting shows so well, the Siennese had a greater feeling for delicacy than even the Florentines. But it was a positive, a humanistic, a loving delicacy, and not in part a product of reserve. One feels that the delicacy of carving, for instance, so general in the Renaissance, gained from Siennese workmen a Quattro Cento fire. They had passed on their love for the modeller's clay to iron and steel, in the furnace technique of which a feeling for modelling and a feeling for delicate workmanship can be perfectly wrought together. And then at the Renaissance, to the stone from which originally they had gained their sense of colour, the Siennese returned, endowed it on the brick with all the fantasies they had projected while working the foundry. There results a new kind of tension both in building structure and in ornament. The curve of an arch will display the tensile promptness of a tempered blade, ornamental ribbons will curl back to a heap like filaments in answer to the touchstone (*Plate XXXI*, 1). Thin and sharp architectural forms, so different from the Brunellesque, though sometimes superficially the same, will produce a massed tension.

[1] As for their use of brick, the Siennese are one with the rest of Italy in never engaging in designs of differently coloured bricks. Italians always use thin bricks and avoid vertical joints.

[2] I cannot find a place for the monumental sculpture of Jacopo della Quercia in this volume. My present intention is to discuss him with Venetian art in the third volume.

I shall be speaking more of incrustation than of stone-blossom, though I started the book with the blossom of stone windows on the front of Francesco's palazzo del Commune at Jesi. But my use of these terms, stone-blossom and incrustation, is suggestive rather than precise. In many cases I find the terms are interchangeable. I would not care to decide whether the dolphins above the windows of the Palazzo Letimi (*Plate II*) are swimming out of the brick (stone-blossom) or whether they have been drawn up from the sea to the surface by magnetic power (incrustation). Obviously, as a rule, sea-motives suggest incrustation, while stone-blossom is associated with a seemingly outward growth. The relevance of these expressions is the same; they both indicate, though from different angles, the constancy of life in Quattro Cento stone ornaments existing always in a tense communion with the plane which shows them off. They never give an effect of having been put there, just like that. On the contrary they are integral with the plane, either as a growth it has produced, or as one fetched

· hither from the outside world. They appear to be more than decoration: for through them we witness powers in the wall on which they lie. Again, a façade as a whole, the structural members themselves, may give effect of blossom as we have seen, but not of incrustation. Therefore Siennese Francesco di Giorgio, his imagination fired with the twirl of beaten iron palmettes, is less (but only less) concerned in architecture with the façade conception than were other Quattro Cento builders. We have seen that his Madonna del Calcinajo is to be viewed from all sides. Francesco's tension in structure is of steel bent to symmetry; and whereas a façade itself cannot express incrustation, an enclosed space can at any rate be planned to the attraction of light, as we found to be the case in his San Bernardino dei Zoccolanti.

There is glamour and flame in Francesco's sculpture. His bronze is foam-like, his light and shade effects granular. Perspective drawings by him are no less delicate than his non-perspective paintings. From the drawings particularly one can learn his tenuous, steel-like straight lines. Francesco had a fantastic vein. He saw a mask, a rapid flashing mask at the head of each column. He was faithful to the decorative or 'primitive' Siennese painting. Yet only less than Luciano and Piero did he love the abstractions of space. There is a perspective drawing of houses at Dresden, attributed by Venturi[1] to Francesco. Delicate the alabastrine translucence of his line; but it is strong enough, as if wiry, to fill space with a vista of mass.

Now, Francesco di Giorgio was primarily a military engineer. In his treatise on architecture he tells how he was engaged on a hundred and thirty-six castles for Federico di Montefeltro. Laurana before him was also a military engineer, and in both cases, the abstraction necessary for creating structure is born of their castle building. And indeed, the final Quattro Cento structural ambition realized in Laurana's courtyard, can only be grasped when such castles as those of San Leo and Sassocorvaro have been visited, master engines designed to counter the new artillery. The loveliness of the efficient engine was a sound basis from which to pre-figure finality of brother-columns in a cloister, or the steadfast mount of a stairway. The mass of these castles is organized, disposed, intelligent. No other comparison so well measures the relationship and the difference from the Gothic. And this direct purposiveness of an engine, each tier of niches cranking upon the next to work the eyewindow at the top, will be the language in which I shall describe the superb façade of San Zaccaria in Venice.

Beside the consciousness of stone, I am now asserting a consciousness of metal in some Quattro Cento architecture, evident in arches curled like a bent blade. And although I do not wish thus to interpret the bronzes of that period, steel-consciousness as well as that of stone, appears in many Quattro Cento paintings. The origin is largely Siennese. I have further suggested that only in terms of wiry metallic jointure can the extreme delicacy beloved of the Florentines be a general Quat-

[1]See *L'Arte*, 1925, for a reproduction.

tro Cento expression.[1] Most Florentines completely lacked this feeling. But strong in Siena is the continuous iron: fibrous, sharp the flowering of sown dragons' teeth. Siena at that time was the capital of the wrought-iron industry. Gates woven in iron, and massive encrusted canon, were sent out from this city.

Encrusted; for incrustation is a concomitant of the foundry. The beaten iron cools, air makes holes and bubbles. Though the wind can't wrench out the brazen twirled palmette leaves, dews that settle, fluke and speck the iron. And the iron hoop from out the rock, for some forgotten purpose spans a crevice, joins the rock again, still bent to a tension as hammered in the foundry, a bow reflected in the anemone-pool, flaked and rusty—you know the strength is still there, still elastic to a forgotten purpose, still piercing the rock, still hot to the hand when the temperature is low. So exact this directional energy, that there is now centrifugal motion, or rather, abundance of centripetal attraction, of inflorescence. To the iron bolt shells cling, weeds touch and dry, on that thinness glaucous jelly would paste itself like jewels on a sword hilt. I see just this incrustation of beaten iron in the pictures of Cosimo Tura and of his followers, of Crivelli and of many other painters who work on the littoral south of Venice where the Francesco di Giorgio style of architecture flourished. Dates make it impossible for Francesco di Giorgio to have influenced Tura, for instance. I think the beaten iron in Ferrarese pictures derived from Mantegna, who also had this quality. He, in turn, acquired this feeling from Donatello's immense outlay of bronze relief in Padua; still more from the native Paduan ironwork. But I have already named Ferrara and Siena together for the pre-eminence of their brick. And no doubt a progression similar to the one in Siena occurred in Ferrara, from clay to iron.[2]

[1]'General' as opposed to the delicacy attained by the peculiar genius of Desiderio, for instance.

[2]The cast-iron, russet, splendour of king, queen, and jack in playing

Francesco di Giorgio's architecture sets out before us in abstract concentrated form, the whole application to gold and iron and stone with which *botteghe* rang loud through the century, this lust for materials which in Florence were too much 'used'. But Francesco's paramount remembrance will be of the foundry, the heavier work of tempering the blade or casting the metal wholesale in the furnace, within which the molten mass ejects a shape. Besides, delicacy in structural plan and even in ornament, must, it seems, have a basis in the strength of the wrought iron. Else lines are weak. My greatest difficulty in describing Florentine tendencies was to isolate 'finish' from elegant workmanship in general. For delicacy in some sense is obviously native to the Quattro Cento. In the hands of Francesco it is the instrument of mass-effect. *Una ossatura metallica*. And for incrustation, beads and the sharper acanthus suit.

In the architecture of Federighi, one of Francesco's predecessors in Siena, appear both tension of steel and incrustation. There are Florentine palaces enough in Siena, and at first sight Federighi's Loggia del Papa would seem to be of the same category. But he has employed the Florentine model to a different purpose. These thin arches have a resilience quite foreign to Brunelleschi's style. It would be impossible, though, to mistake for Florentine, Federighi's completion of the capella di Piazza (*Plate XXXI*, 1). Above the fourteenth-century piers, arches spring round like rapiers near snapping. Above again is a wealth of crusted ribbons, not flung to the winds of Verrocchio, but coiling to their heaps near the chopped shields, like filaments answering to the magnet. The frieze is lined with brazen griffins. Monsters, particularly sea-monsters with their shells and armour and their emerald eyes, will pile close to the iron.

The smaller Roman decoratives, bead, bay-leaf, egg and tongue, the tongue-like filament again, the leaf pressed dry

cards probably derives from a Ferrarese source. *Cf.* the playing cards attributed to the painter Galasso in the Malaspina collection at Pavia.

1. *Bergamo, capella Colleoni: Omodeo: Detail of façade.*

2. *Siena, Cathedral. Attrib. Federighi: Base of entrance pilaster in form of altar to S. Giovanni Chapel.*

PLATE XXXVII. STONE-BLOSSOM CONTRASTED WITH INCRUSTATION

1. *Siena, S. M. delle Nevi : attrib*. Francesco di Giorgio : *Detail of façade*.

2. *Florence, piazza della Signoria*. *Relief from base of* Donatello's *Judith*.

PLATE XXXVIII. A QUATTRO CENTO WALL-SPACE AND
A SCULPTURAL EFFECT IT SYNTHESIZES

and spinous, fossilized in the ore, were responsive to incrustation treatment. Let no one think the doorway of the casa Stasi is Florentine, or the doorway of the Certosa cloister.

Efflorescence from stone answers inflorescence. The two superb stone benches in the Loggia di Mercanza[1] are stone-blossom, the one on the right being the work of Federighi, that on the left probably of Urbano da Cortona. Among other masterpieces of Federighi as sculptor is the font in the San Giovanni chapel of the cathedral, and the entrance pillars to this chapel (*Plate XXXVII*, 2).

The stone crystallized, not crystalline, not indifferent. That is another departure from Brunelleschi celebrated by the façade of Santa Maria delle Nevi (*Plate XXXVIII. 1*). The church, probably an early work of Francesco di Giorgio, is one of the most important of Quattro Cento structures. From the Quattro Cento point of view it is the most important sight in Siena.[2] Nothing could be more delicate; yet it is strong. The *ossatura metallica* conveys a freshness, the sweet springing freshness of the Tuscan new year acquired by stone from steel. And after my carping at the beauties of the Tuscan landscape, it is a relief to admit here a Quattro Cento transvaluation of that crystal delicacy. *Limpidezza* has been won to us in the lines and decoration of the frieze, of the doorway and the window. But there is apparent also efflorescence, stone-blossom. The bare, steep frontage of stones, as on the façade of the Tempio, will shove out well any symbol of growth. If the ornament of the deep *occhio* window be inflorescent, the shields in garlands either side are shallow and tender like a navel (*Plate XXXVIII*, 1). So, a wall-space sheer and smooth, a blank preparedness, can attain the immediacy of final revelation from a few archi-

---

[1] Now the Circolo degli Uniti.

[2] I do not think it is necessary for me to comment on the fact that Francesco was largely copying Roman design. (This façade suggests the now restored temple of Augustus at Pola.) The same forms were used intentionally or unintentionally—the latter is more probable—to altogether different effects.

tectural features thus knit. The wall shows off its active progeny. What the matrix held is shown. No other generation knew it to this degree. Or one might say that since the wall was made smooth, the stones of it cut square, roughness so far from being lost, is martialled to show as flowering and incrustation upon the prepared surface. It is the heart of the stone that shows. This is the exact opposite to the statuary of Michael Angelo, for which the usual background of unhewn stone is intended as a reserve of power.

A perusal of the Codice Strozziano in the Biblioteca Magliabechiana at Florence, where one may see Francesco's architectural drawings, prepares one for the synthesis of workshop activity performed in his architecture. He carried his sublime sense of craft into the most abstract engineering calculations. Thus an exquisite plan for the mining of a walled town gives cause to regret that the stables full of labour-saving devices that he says he built for Federico di Montefeltro no longer exist: because neatness and efficiency were once expressions of humanism. To Francesco they were forms of beauty, of architectural *nitidezza*. In contrast with Alberti's high-flown generalizations, Francesco's book on architecture is severely practical. Questions of drainage construction, water-supply, etc., are for him the primary considerations of such a treatise; and yet in all planning and design, reference to the proportions of the human anatomy show how complete was his amalgam of science and art, of the abstract and the human.

If Alberti in designing the Tempio encasement and in refusing to superintend the building operations, made clear the distinction between builder and designer, Francesco di Giorgio with his practical ability at one with his power of design, was the first and the ideal embodiment of the professional architect. For Alberti, though efficient, was by choice dilettante. One suspects of Francesco a hostility against the amateur, the first of these hostilities. He avoids mention of Alberti's book on architecture in his own. And since Alberti's book had immense standing and was the only precedent for such literature in modern times, the omission must have been deliberate.

For a time Luciano was Francesco's master. When Francesco came to Urbino he found the architecture which was Federico's choice. Francesco learned some of the 'Urbino style', and it remains in doubt whether such Lauranesque fragments as the palazzo Passionei are by the master or his pupil. There is the same difficulty of attribution in the Ducal palace.[1] But I do not think that Federico employed Francesco much at court; nothing can with certainty be attributed to him save the frieze (now fragmentary) of emblems of war, and a share in some of the intarsia. Certain other ornamentation, though, particularly acanthus decoration in the sala del Magnifico, suggest Francesco's influence. Again, Lauranesque window embrasures and doorways and mantelpieces to be found in various parts of the palace, in a few instances may have been designed by Laurana himself and subsequently ornamented, or they may nearly all be the work of his followers. The point is not important, except as showing how often one connects Francesco with Laurana's name. Indeed, the general impression gained from the palace's interior is of a Laurana framework decorated with Siennese incrustation motives imperfectly executed[2] and often imperfectly designed. Florentine and Venetian design are here also, but do not predominate. I treat of the unique sala della Jole wing in another section.[3]

We know so little about Luciano Laurana that it is impossible to limit or to extend his activities with certainty. But the Lauranesque is a precise enough conception. It is simpler, so

[1] The traveller is warned that no windows or doorways on the outside of the palace have any connection with Laurana. Within, probably only the courtyard and the staircases to the towers are more or less untouched Laurana, and the vaulting of some of the rooms, particularly the wonderful sala Maggiore.

[2] A great part of the ornament belongs to the next century and has an unrelieved 'stuck-on' effect.

[3] *See* Section VI.

far as Francesco exhibited a Lauranesque style, to make him follower rather than pioneer. The Castle of San Leo is the work of master or of pupil; at any rate it is Lauranesque. One of the finest characteristics of Francesco's later building is a rectangular doorway decorated or undecorated, derived from Luciano (*Plate XXXIX*). To Luciano's thinly graduated lines of a sharpness and accuracy more associated with wood mouldings than with stone, Francesco di Giorgio added a plated yet delicate tension that is altogether Siennese. You may see unornamented doorways of this kind in the palace at Gubbio.[1] One of the finest examples is the doorway to the casa di Con-

[1] I am not referring to the ones with 'stuck-on' arabesques, some of which are now in the Victoria and Albert Museum. This effect of superimposed ornament is bound to result from ornamental carving of *pietra morta*, a stone not unsuitable, however, to the plainly moulded, iron doorways of which I write. These are, of course, an adaptation of the ordinary classical architrave moulding carried down the sides. There are only slight changes of plane from one edge to the other. The lines are few, and thus a central raised line along the beam and down the sides appears isolated and constant, giving a beaded effect. Both Luciano's doorways, and the windows and the arches in his courtyard have this beautiful moulding which Francesco di Giorgio adopted (*Plate XXXIX*). The same lines generally square the bottom of such a door or window where it is not treated with pilasters. So do the architrave mouldings of Brunellesque architecture; in fact, this mode, deriving from Brunelleschi, is a Renaissance *cliché*. But in Brunellesque construction, owing to the thickness of the outer moulding (*see*, for instance, the door of the Pazzi chapel), and owing to the fact that the inward change of plane is sharp, such squaring at the base gives much the same effect as a block. Brunelleschi's treatment is the heavier; and squaring appealed to him for the continuity it allowed. Nothing grows straight there or encrusts steel-like. But Luciano employed this mode to gain a sublime distinctness.

Alberti's adaptation of architrave moulding (at San Sebastiano, Mantua, for instance), is one of beading, rather than of planes swiftly cut away inwards as in the case of the common classical moulding. But Alberti misses the incomparably clear Laurana effect by an over-elaboration of lines which do not allow of a central distinct line. The door to the camera degli Sposi in the castle at Mantua, probably by Luca Fancelli, Alberti's follower, has its mouldings squared at the base, but suffers from the same shortcoming.

Urbino, Ducal palace. Luciano Laurana : *A doorway.*

PLATE XXXIX. LUCIANO LAURANA

1. Ancona, Palazzo degli Anziani : Francesco di Giorgio :
Archway from courtyard.

2. Idem : Courtyard colonnade : Detail : Columned pier.

PLATE XL. 'FULL-WOUND THE JEWEL-LIKE TENSION'

cia just by the Madonna del Calcinajo at Cortona. Francesco often added encrusting ornament, particularly a course of small, hard beads, changing the Lauranesque form from a flower upon the brick to a sinuous, seductive iron (*Plate III*, 1). Deft fantasies about the wrought-iron strand were stimulated by the achievements of Luciano's severe mathematic. The Siennese, for their part, had already evolved on doorways the squaring of raised lines to the effect of armoured incrustation. Examples at Siena are the doorway to the palazzo Costantino and Federighi's doorway to the casa Stasi and the entrance to Santa Maria delle Nevi which Francesco probably designed before he went to Urbino. Later on Francesco spread the Laurano-Siennese type of moulding throughout the Marches where it remained a convention far into the sixteenth century.

As for structural plan, although Francesco gained a clearness in construction from Luciano, he did not carry outside Urbino what Adolfo Venturi calls the *divina nudità* of Laurana's style. The courtyard of the palace at Gubbio, while showing features derived from the courtyard at Urbino, sacrifices a purely static quality in favour of a delicate emphasis upon function, which must entail a feeling of progression. Thus for Laurana's window architrave continued round the whole rectangular frame, Francesco substituted an entablature supported by pilasters.[1] On the other hand, where some emphasis upon progression exists in Francesco's architecture it is not to be compared with Brunelleschi's aims. Francesco's deftness and neatness, we have realized, have a far different origin. And in spite of the fact that the Gubbio courtyard is built of *pietra morta* on brick, it is in no way Brunellesque.

The mouldings of Francesco's palazzo degli Anziani at Ancona are far preferable to those at Gubbio (*Plate III*, 2). The superb archway to the courtyard is a good structure in which to study the difference from Brunelleschi (*Plate XL*, 1). For superficially the lines of the arch are comparable to his, and

---

[1] There are windows of this kind at the Ducal palace, Urbino, on the façade where one enters the courtyard.

the three-quarter pillars with their lower thirds cabled and the upper portions fluted, call to mind Michelozzo's columns to a doorway in the cloister of Santa Croce, Florence. But the Ancona arch is braided, full-wound the jewel-like tension. Once more there is mass without movement though the forms be delicate. There is not a trace of the Roman triumphal arch. Quattro Cento architecture here proves itself independent. I recommend first this palace at Ancona, and next the one at Jesi, to those wishing an introduction to Francesco's work. The traveller must not miss at Ancona the colonnade of the courtyard where Francesco adapted the Gothic to *nitidezza* (*Plate XL*, 2). If you have not seen this, you cannot know that even a pointed arch colonnade can be made to approach the Lauranesque ideal, and yet be Gothic, a style which carried well the iron effect.

Particularly beautiful is the smaller side door (the main door is sixteenth century) of the palazzo del Commune at Jesi. A blade-like arch goes humping over within the oblong. One expects sparks from the touching of the transverse lines above with the long apex of the arch. The flash is perpetuated by impetuous stone. Incrustation is manifold upon the side door with pilasters (*Plate III*, 1). Dolphins naturally figure; two of them, like fireworks flaring through water, sear troughs in opposite directions away from the rampant lion of Jesi. Dolphins in similar motion above doorways and windows are found often in the Marches, and even sometimes in Romagna (*Plate II*). The swags curling away from shields over the superb windows of the Sforza palace at Pesaro (*Plate XXXVI*) are a variant of the same idea.

III. *Quattro Cento architecture in Rome*

I have linked the name of Francesco di Giorgio with architectural lines attracting incrustation. He stressed the *functions* of architectural members so that he could show the stone resilient like steel. His windows with pilasters and entablature, or as at Cortona, with pediment, passed to Rome. Quattro Cento Roman buildings display a fusion of Florentine traits with Francesco's style. The first floor windows of the Cancelleria palace show the manner of this fusion (*Plate XXXV*, 1). The influence of Francesco is predominant. These windows are brazen on the stone walls, are encrusted there and arranged between pilasters with a more than Albertian distinctness.[1] Besides the sixteenth-century palazzo Giraud, there are remains all over Rome, belonging to the late fifteenth and early sixteenth centuries, of palaces with similar brassy windows[2] piercing hard on ashlar walls and seemingly made fast by disks at the spandrels: alternatively, these windows appear as mineral wealth incompletely extracted from stone-ore.

A similar mineral compactness served even the go-ahead architects in the first decade or so of the sixteenth century. Bramante inherits something from Francesco di Giorgio as well as from Luciano. But Siennese Peruzzi was Francesco's direct heir. The tight low roll of the street front of Peruzzi's palazzo Massime alle Colonne shows an almost Quattro Cento tension; so too the compressed delicacy, the smallness of Antonio da San Gallo's palazzo Linotte, though entirely renovated.

The San Gallo family was of course Florentine. The earlier Giuliano, if it were he who built the façade at Rome of Santa

---

[1]A reference to Alberti's use of pilasters on the façade of his Rucellai palace in Florence.

[2]These semi-circular windows enclosed in rectangular mouldings and with disks at the spandrels, may originally be an Albertian invention: though the Francesco di Giorgionesque door of the *Domus Verronum* at Jesi, except for pilasters at the sides, is the same form. But as for windows, the casa di Baldo degli Ubaldi at Perugia has several lovely examples of this kind which are probably some twenty years older than the Cancelleria windows. Now Agostino di Duccio carried to Perugia from Rimini several Albertian forms, perhaps this among them; though it does not appear in Alberti's existing architecture. Or perhaps it is Agostino's own adaptation of Alberti, or an adaptation of Agostino's Albertian San Pietro gateway by some Perugian follower.

Maria dell' Anima, created at least one Quattro Cento work. It is certainly the design of a follower of Brunelleschi with some Albertian sympathy; and yet—take the *occhio* or eye-orifice at the top—there is a depth that gives mass. Particularly Quattro Cento is the effect of the unsupported top zone chunk whose thickness you can gauge at once.

The architect of the Cancelleria palace (only the magnificent façade is Quattro Cento) has not been identified. The attribution is sometimes given to Bramante. I suggest once more the name of Baccio Pontelli, not because any known work of his affords a key to this particular palace, but because he is the one architect from whose circumstances one might expect a design incorporating Siennese, Florentine, Albertian and Lauranesque elements. On the one hand, structures attributed with less doubt to Baccio Pontelli reflect the style of Florentine Bernardo Rossellino who had built extensively in Rome for Pope Innocent V, often with the advice or under the direction of Alberti. Vasari states that Baccio Pontelli was Sixtus IV's architect and engineer. He was also at Innocent VIII's court. On the other hand, in the year 1481,[1] Baccio Pontelli sent Lorenzo de' Medici a plan of the Ducal palace at Urbino. Like Luciano and like Francesco di Giorgio, Baccio Pontelli was at one time in charge of fortifications. He may be underrated as an artist for the reason that some of his best effects have been destroyed.[2]

The façades of Santa Maria del Popolo and of Sant' Agostino, from time to time attributed to Baccio Pontelli, show a mixture of Siennese with Albertian style. Whether Baccio Pontelli is an important figure or not, it is certain that the main streams of fifteenth century building, all except the Venetian, met in Rome at the end of the century. At least two Quattro Cento masterpieces resulted, the façades of the Cancelleria palace and of Sant' Agostino (*Plate XLII, 2*) whose Quattro Cento effect has survived Baroque adjustments, even the

[1] *See* Gaye, *Carteggio degli Artisti*, pp. 274-277.
[2] *See* Emilio Lavagnino, *L' Architetto di Sisto IV* (*L' Arte*, 1924), where the author writes of cheaply built palaces in Rome of that time.

scrolls. As for the ornamentation contemporary with these designs, it is generally of the post-Francesco di Giorgio-Siennese style,[1] that is to say, without merit. For instance, the decoration to the doorways of Santa Maria sopra Minerva and of San Giacomo degli Spagnuoli, connected with Baccio Pontelli's name, are 'stuck-on' in effect. Carving at Rome is rarely Quattro Cento; but there are two doorways belonging probably to the fourteen-seventies, which both in design and in carving are completely Quattro Cento. And the first one is unlike any other work. These doorways are those of the palazzo Venezia at Rome, the first one (*Plate XLI*, 1) on the piazza Venezia, the second (*Plate XLI*, 2) on the Via del Plebiscito. Adolfo Venturi attributes them to the Dalmatian sculptor Giovanni da Trau whom, on his first arrival in Rome, he considers to have worked for Bernardo Rossellino. Certainly the piazza Venezia doorway presents an Albertian bulk, and the brackets to the cornice will be called Albertian. But otherwise the doorway cannot at present be put under the name of any school. The carrying on down the jambs of the same knobbed embossments that line the frieze, is apparently unique, and may be expressed in terms of the categories I have used, only as an unique casting back into a static sculpture[2] of Luciano's architectural lines for window and door frames.

The other door shows Florentine influence, but remains intensely Quattro Cento. On the other hand, when Giovanni collaborated with Mino for several tombs, he lost his style.

I have mentioned that Quattro Cento carving is rare in Rome. In all the centres of art, however, after 1480 if not be-

[1] *See* Section XII.

[2] What I mean by 'static' Quattro Cento sculpture will become clearer further on (*see* Section V). It is the sculpture I have already connected with the name of Francesco Laurana. Venetian sculpture in general is also of this kind, and perhaps in the third volume we may arrive at some wider conception to cover the Lauranas, both architect and sculptor; also we may find some parallel to this doorway by Giovanni da Trau. For the art of Dalmatia belongs to the Venetian subject.

fore, decorative carving became increasingly ornamental and less emblematic. After 1480 no new Quattro Cento motives were evolved, except perhaps in Umbria and the Marches where Francesco di Giorgio and his followers were working. On the other hand, Luciano was building at Urbino from 1465-72. Quattro Cento architectural expression now develops. For previous to 1460 or so, a developed Quattro Cento building did not exist, except for the Tempio Malatestiano and for Alfonso's triumphal arch at Naples. The change, then, from sculptural to architectural expression, from the act of revealing to the presentation of the revealed, can be suitably expressed by dates. Indeed, throughout the examination of sculptors and of architects I have been able to follow roughly their temporal order. But I must now go back within the century and describe the two pre-Laurana Quattro Cento buildings.

IV. The Tempio Malatestiano

Sigismondo's Tempio and Alfonso's arch cannot for any purpose be dissociated from those princes. Their emblematic fury needed room. They wrote their names in overflowing sculpture, but were soon led to find building to contain it, and thus reveal the heart of that primitive fury which carving cannot by itself expose.

Luciano's courtyard expresses Luciano's ideal for his period and for his prince. Sigismondo's Tempio expresses Sigismondo. There he is, projected directly into stone, not as a succession or a story, but as something immediate. It is an effect impossible to other generations. All the fifteenth-century genius for emblem, for outwardness, centred in Sigismondo. The impetus of all times to art was, without disguise in that age, the impetus as well to civilized living. Artists needed little abstraction to project Sigismondo into stone. Each characteristic passed easily into a form of art, non-musical, tense.

So the second volume will entail a considerable excursus into the life of Sigismondo and into fifteenth-century history.

I give now a few details concerning the origin of the Tempio so that the reader may gather some impression of this subject. Also, the Tempio has become fairly well known of recent years. But no English nor French book contains the correct facts, nor even correct dates. Meanwhile Corrado Ricci's important researches[1] have settled most of the problems previously outstanding.

The circumstances (in short) of the Tempio's origin are these:

On the 31st October, 1447, the first stone was laid for a chapel in the thirteenth-century church of San Francesco at Rimini. Sigismondo Malatesta, the lord of Rimini, wished to build the chapel in honour of his patron saint, St. Sigismund, an honour which should reflect also on himself, the reigning Malatesta, who not only shared his Christian name with the saint, but also a military and amorous disposition. Such was the beginning of the Tempio, a certain embellishment of a Gothic church. And San Francesco was already associated with the Malatesta family. It was their burial ground, the church, the cloister and the surrounding meadow. Giovanni Malatesta, Dante's 'Il Mastin vecchio da Verucchio' who in the course of his hundred-years life established his stock in Rimini, was buried here in Franciscan habit, that is if the desire expressed in his will materialized. This Verucchio Malatesta was father of Paolo il Bello, protagonist of the Paolo and Francesca story. The families of several Malatesta despots who had held Rimini, were buried in and about the same church. Moreover, the Malatesta had built at least two chapels. Thus in 1364 Malatesta Antico, self-styled 'Guastafamiglia', built a chapel, and barely eight years later Malatesta Ungaro left ten thousand ducats to provide another.

Sigismondo, then, made no departure with the chapel for his patron saint in San Francesco. Strictly not *in* San Francesco, because the chapel was built out beyond the line of the pre-

[1] Embodied in his *Il Tempio Malatestiano*. Bestetti e Tumminelli, 1925, limited to 600 copies.

existing church wall; as we know from a bull of Nicholas V referring to the chapel before its consecration as 'partim in prophano et partim in sacro locis'. By May, 1448, Sigismondo planned another chapel next to that of St. Sigismund. Already so closely had he associated his own name and personality with his love, Isotta, as well as with the saint, that while proposals for the chapel of St. Sigismund become more and more personal to Sigismondo, another and contiguous chapel must be built to reflect his love. We know that the walls of these two chapels were finished by the spring of 1449, because there is extant a letter of Sigismondo to Giovanni de' Medici, asking him to send along the painter immediately though the mortar is not yet dry. Sigismondo will give him some other employ meanwhile, and, indeed, would like him to come and settle in Rimini and to have every provision made for him there

> 'so that he can work as he likes,
> Or waste his time as he likes
> (affatigandose per suo piacere o non
> non gli manchera la provixione mai),
> never lacking provision.'[1]

This painter was possibly Filippo Lippi. Whoever he was, he never frescoed the chapels. Perhaps Sigismondo changed his mind, perhaps he alone realized the powers of sculpture in that age as emblem of personal release. One painter is associated with the Tempio, the master of the only painting which belongs to the Quattro Cento, Piero della Francesca. His fresco is still on the wall of the cella delle Reliquie. And to Rimini he returned in his old age (1482). All the same, though Piero did come to Rimini to paint the fresco in 1451, and though he in his old age—Sigismondo had been dead fourteen years—came to live in Rimini, I cannot identify the painter to which the letter refers, with Piero della Francesca; just because his

[1]From Ezra Pound's *Cantos*. Three Mountains Press, Paris. *See* also XXX *Cantos*. Hours Press, Paris, 1930. The Malatesta Cantos only were printed in the *Criterion* for July, 1923. In the next volume I will be referring constantly to this great poem.

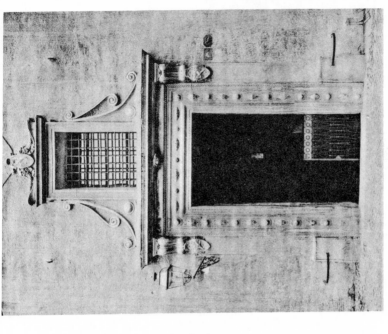

1. *Rome, Palazzo Venezia. Attrib. Giovanni da Trau:*
Doorway on piazza Venezia.

2. *Idem : Doorway on via del Plebiscito.*

PLATE XLI. QUATTRO CENTO DOORWAYS

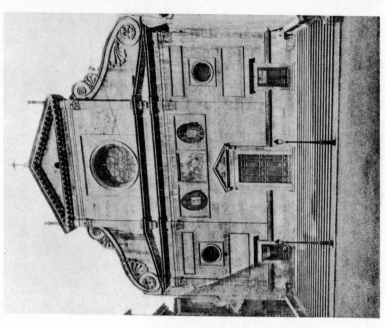

1. *Pienza, Cathedral :* Bernardo Rossellino.　　2. *Rome, Sant' Agostino :* Baccio Pontelli ?

PLATE XLII. QUATTRO CENTO FACADES RELATED TO THE TEMPIO

painting was ignored in Florence, and, as far as we know, he had no patronage from the Medici or from any other Florentines after he left Florence in 1440 or thereabouts.

Probably it was when Sigismondo had despaired of getting his painter, had determined upon sculpture, that he first conceived the investment with stone of San Francesco which held the bones of his ancestors, to the honour of his love for Isotta. Other chapels were built in keeping with the two already made, which, in turn, conformed to the Gothic church. In this process the old San Francesco was almost entirely pulled down, for inasmuch as the chapels extended beyond the walls, those walls disappeared except, in some cases, between the chapels. The outside walls, then, of the chapels, and their Gothic windows, were built by Sigismondo and conformed to the plan adopted for his first chapel while the old church still existed. Before Ricci made his researches, these outside walls were considered to belong to the old structure.[1] Around the Gothic chapels which Sigismondo had been induced to complete by the unambitious start of his project, Alberti built a white encasement (*Plate XLIII*). Great arches, making deep niches to the brick walls, roll down the flanks. Light comes into the Tempio conducted through the arches behind which are the Gothic windows of the chapels. But on the façade, it is largely the bricks of the old San Francesco that press the encasement. This majestic encasement of the Gothic packed with emblem, these double walls upon the public and secret glories of Isotta, give as no other planning could have done the sense of a casket with contents so precious, relics so alive, that not only superb embossment breaks forth, but also a divine adjustment and strength in this exterior, which alone will contain them and give them their finality. So, ever rich, the four engaged columns and the deep doorway press back strong on the blind façade; and superabundant pressure turns at the corners to reinforce the roll of arches down the flanks.

[1] *See*, for instance, Yriarte's *Un condottiere au XVième siècle* (Paris, 1882), the book on which English authors have drawn.

Everywhere Sigismondo compelled death to serve life; and as if to boast his unequalled success in outwardness, in the compelling of death to purpose of life, Isotta is celebrated within the Tempio by her tomb built when she is at the height of her youth, and embossed with the magic date of 1446, the year in which Sigismondo first possessed her. From that year Sigismondo wants the finality that death alone procures. He insists upon Isotta embalmed as well as alive. He feigns Isotta dead in poems, and crowds her empty tomb with his own heraldic elephants. Her roses spring fresh from the thousand marbles. The bones of all the ancestors, uprooted from their resting places, were pressed into one triumphal sarcophagus. Their monuments and memorial tablets were used to build Alberti's encasement. The meadow, stiff with tomb-stones motionless like trees standing upon the dead end of the year, was rifled for the same glory. So too the dying marbles of the ancient San Apollinare in Classe. The dead were disturbed, the multitudinous corpses of the Black Death a hundred years before: this the catastrophe which gave the new generations their chance.

Inscriptions discovered by Ricci in 1912 prove that Veronese Matteo de' Pasti was the architect of the chapels, and Agostino di Duccio their chief sculptor; while letters to Sigismondo in the archives at Siena show that Pasti superintended also the execution of Alberti's design for the encasement.

The Tempio's influence was widespread. We find echoes of it throughout Italy, particularly in Venice. Two free adaptations (from entirely different angles) of this façade will be noticed here. They are both important Quattro Cento structures though the carving at Turin is by no means Quattro Cento. These fronts are the one to the cathedral at Turin by Meo da Caprino (*Plate XXXV*, 2), and the one to the cathedral at Pienza by Bernardo Rossellino (*Plate XLII*, 1). The resemblance between them and the Tempio façade is of the same equilibrium, the same flowering quality, though attained by entirely different structural method. Rossellino worked with Alberti at

Rome. His achievement at Pienza is all the more remarkàble since he employed several Brunellesque formulæ. But they stand absorbed. To see the perfect Quattro Cento façade at Pienza is worth the trainless journey. But let no traveller forget that the original name for Pienza is Corsignano, and that he comes here to honour Sigismondo, not Pius II who had this his native village renamed, not after his own suitable patronymic, Piccolomini, but after the journalese-wistful title he assumed as Pope —Æneas Sylvius Piccolomini becomes Pope Pius II; Pius Æneas II, you see. Æneas as a pious but gouty Pope was the man who ruined Sigismondo, and you come to Corsignano to honour Sigismondo because invariably Sigismondo's enemies had to fight him on his own ground. To counter him at all, they needed to enure themselves with subtle doses of his own spirit; or perhaps I should say they needed to confirm themselves in their own ways with a liveliness to match Sigismondo's. Otherwise he was a monster beyond their pale. Both Federico of Urbino and his friend Pius learnt from their deadly enemy; and both at Urbino and at Pienza[1] we now seek out the Quattro Cento. These places sheltered the huntsmen of the Malatesta elephant, and when we come to them, we should remember him.

The palace at Pienza has no Quattro Cento significance.

Mention must here be made of work at Fano and Cesena by Matteo Nuti, an assistant architect to Pasti. Until Sigismondo's ruin, the former town belonged to him, while at Cesena his brother, Novello, was the lord. There is an archway ascribed to Nuti leading out of the piazza at Fano, which is definitely Quattro Cento; while at Cesena, Nuti built Novello's library, a work that should not be missed by any Quattro Cento enthusiast though it has now been entirely renovated.

---

[1]Pio issued a bull threatening excommunication to any one who altered his cathedral. Alterations started less than forty years after he died, and have gone on ever since. For in 1503 the foundations began to sink. *See* Alfredo Barbacci, *L'edificazione e il decadimento del Duomo di Pienza. Bollettino d'Arte*, 1931.

One item about the Tempio I shall mention here and no-where else, namely Sigismondo's tomb. The first intention to display the tombs of the ancestors and of Sigismondo on the façade had to be abandoned owing to constructional difficulties. Not many years later Sigismondo was ruined, and shortly afterwards he died, probably without having made provision for burial. No doubt some remaining workmen in Rimini, among them certainly a Florentine of the school of Francesco di Simone, were commissioned by the impoverished Isotta to make a cheap tomb.

V. Alfonso's arch and static sculpture

This archway, erected principally between 1452 and 1458, celebrates King Alfonso of Aragon's triumphal entry into Naples in 1442 when he supplanted the Angevin dynasty. The archway is the entrance to the Castel Novo extended a few years previously in magnificent Catalan Gothic by the Spanish architect Guglielmo Sagrera.[1] The archway presses between two bastions of this castle (*Plate XLIV*). Inside the castle, the great hall has a lovely Quattro Cento doorway, one side of which was only uncovered after the recent fire.

The Plate shows well enough that the archway overlaid with sculpture is the epitome of stone-blossom. And in this context I want to introduce a subject to which so far I have made only cursory reference, the subject of a 'static' kind of Quattro Cento sculpture which is in contrast with the 'dynamic' or Donatellesque Quattro Cento school; or perhaps I should merely say, concurrent with the Donatellesque; since the static sculpture is a commentary upon the dynamic. This static sculpture, when it can be entirely isolated, has no *other* connection with Florence. I cannot stress the fact sufficiently strongly. Here is a field of Quattro Cento sculpture whose intrinsic style does not owe a preliminary debt to Florence.

[1]*See* Conte Riccardo di Candida, *L'Architetto della Reggia Aragonese di Napoli. L'Arte*, 1928.

And now that my argument is finished and the ground is cleared, I will use the next two volumes for this subject, since both the Tempio sculpture and Venetian sculpture are largely of the static kind. So it is for purposes of outline only that I here make some mention of static qualities in Quattro Cento sculpture. Moreover, Piero della Francesca in painting and Luciano Laurana in architecture have already figured as static artists.

The most easily defined connection of static sculpture is with them. The deep life does not course in the men and women of Piero's frescoes. Their deep life stands revealed as if they are pools, millions of drops run together into a still shape. These types are the necessities of Piero's spatial conception. Francesco Laurana, the static sculptor *par excellence*, translated this feat into marble. Characteristics are run together completely into a plastic shape as in a T'ang figure. But, unlike the Chinese, the process of his art is not so much an abstraction as a concretion; which is true also of Piero's painting. Laurana busts are characterized by their severely frontal presentation, by cylindrical necks and by heads tilted slightly back, in general, by a *rigore geometrico* of what is yet Renaissance modelling. There are also Pieran characteristics, the closed mouth, pupils down, eyelashes well marked under which the glance is steady. But plastic conception of pure sculptor is very different from spatial conception of pure painter. Francesco showed no interest in spatial relations. Each of his shapes are self-sufficient; there is a stress upon their self-sufficiency. His groups are like an untended border of perfect flowers.

Now the serenity of this plastic should probably be connected with the classic serenity of the greatest Gothic sculpture. But this does not imply that there was a re-introduction of decorative or non-naturalistic concept in the middle of the fifteenth century. Francesco's busts are not fundamentally decorative nor abstract, no more than is Piero's painting, no more than Uccello's and Antonello da Messina's painting. The style, I repeat, shows a concretion rather than abstraction, as far as one can judge only possible in that time when the emotions released by Donatello and his followers had already run out as into a pool, when the compulsion to make manifest was still bearing fruit, when all that is vital appeared quite simply as vital. Francesco's serenity is not employed on the side of life nearer death, but on putti, on all the emblems and symbols of the Quattro Cento fire.

Francesco probably met Piero at Urbino. Agostino di Duccio, too, whose art displays equal proportions of Pieran and Donatellesque qualities, was doubtless influenced directly by Piero. In terms of the joint influences of Piero, Francesco and Agostino upon a local style, we can analyze beautiful examples of static sculpture, mostly in wood, that are to be found scattered in Umbria and the Marches.[1] But when one realizes that some Lombard Renaissance sculpture displays static qualities, and that nearly the whole of Venetian sculpture and decoration belongs to this kind, then, great as was Piero's influence, it cannot be considered the root of the phenomenon. Luciano and Francesco Laurana came from Dalmatia. Their roots were in the local art and in Venetian art. Agostino spent a year or two in Venice before he appeared in Rimini. Critics have insisted (for quite different purposes) that the lavish calm of the old Pisan Gothic survived the fourteenth century in Venice. So, it will be finally in Dalmatia and the Veneto that we shall seek out the origins of Quattro Cento static sculpture.

Now it is often denied that there is any Venetian *style* in the early Renaissance sculpture at Venice. Italian critics concentrate upon 'allocating' Lombard and Florentine work. In the subsequent period, Giovanni and Bartolommeo Bon are denied an important sphere of influence, or are reinstated. There results a major confusion. Artistic personalities cannot be defined. Attributions change from month to month. At the moment, Agostino's little stay in Venice is still a cause of dissen-

[1] *See* the extremely able article by Géza de Francovitch, *Un gruppo di scultura in legno. Umbro-Marchigiana. Bollettino d'Arte*, 1928.

Rimini, exterior of Tempio Malatestiano : Alberti.

PLATE XLIII. TOMB-STONES RIFLED FOR LIVING EMBLEM

Naples, Castel Novo. Triumphal archway of Alfonso of Aragon.
PLATE XLIV. 'EPITOME OF STONE-BLOSSOM'

sion; while the subject of Pietro Lombardo has led to some notable rudeness from German expert to Italian professor. The Germans, Planiscig in particular, have shown great ingenuity on the subject of Venetian sculpture. The results are inconclusive, the wider question avoided. We know the relation between Bartolommeo Bon and Giorgio di Sebenico, but what of a wider conception that should cover artists so different, yet in a fundamental way similar, as Bon and Laurana and Rizzo and Agostino and Giorgio di Sebenico, and even Isiah da Pisa, all in part static sculptors? And even if there were no important Venetian sculptors in Venice from the death of the last dalle Masegne in 1403 until the advent of Giovanni Bon about 1420, at any rate there was Venice. What happens to the Tuscan sculptor there? He is set to work to produce a Venetian idea, to steady the sky-line with statues grown from their plinths. And is that Venetian idea really Lombard? Only partly. Stone over a flood, even in cases when architect or sculptor have sought dynamic effect, is always still and substantial. Such water at once bestows mass, an effect of the revealed, the concentrated.

Francesco Laurana has generally been regarded as a sculptor apart, wrongly I think. Sometimes, though, the connections made for him are even more misleading. For the serene qualities of his art have no connection with the cold and reserved and abstracted art of Luca della Robbia. Lionello Venturi in his 1914 *Studii sul palazzo Ducale di Urbino*[1] mapped out a distinction to which I am indebted, between the Donatellesque dynamic sculpture and static sculpture. But he associates together Francesco Laurana, Luca della Robbia and Ghiberti, under the static name, as well as Venetian sculpture, and even the Greek. Thereupon the step was easily taken to identify in fundamentals Venetian with non-Donatellesque Florentine art. Actually, nothing could be more distinct than the art of Luca della Robbia on the one hand, and that of Laurana or of Venetian sculpture on the other. Luca's serenity is withdrawn

[1] *L'Arte*, 1914.

and sentimental, abstract because cold.[1] Laurana's serenity is that of the perfectly banked fire. At its zenith it is a finality imposed on Donatellesque exuberance, not a withdrawal from that exuberance. Grace and elegance are not essential to this Quattro Cento sculpture. Laurana's more famous busts are perfectly wrought, it is true, but 'graceful' is not the word for them, whereas of Ghiberti's work we know grace to be the fundamental quality (*Plate XLVIII*, 2). In some groups attributed to Laurana, the self-sufficiency and squatness of the figures are even rude. For instance, entirely Lauranesque is the sculptured group of soldiers with Alfonso wearing a helmet, under the arch at Naples (*Plate XLV*, 1). Much fierceness stands collected, just as the storm-drops are calm together but undiminished in the pool. One notices Francesco's distaste for *genre*. These soldiers are without the Italian swagger. A dog reposes watchful and half-heraldic. On the opposite wall is a slightly more Donatellesque relief of the same subject (*Plate XLV*, 2). Here there is some grace and attitudinizing. The dog sniffs at a helmet held in the hand.

But I admit that in the negative sense of static forms, that is, as displaying no emphasis upon representation of movement, Luca della Robbia and Francesco Laurana, contrasted with Donatello, had common ground; though in a more fundamental way they are poles apart. So it happened sometimes that a static sculptor (in the sense in which I use that term) was disposed to reflect some della Robbian feeling. In any case, all influences were mixed together. I have already mentioned that Agostino was no less Donatellesque than static. Domenico Rosselli made a similar fusion of styles; and it is from such overlaying of fertile traditions that the greatest art is born: the art most difficult to analyze.

---

[1]At the same time I am ready to admit that Luca's Federighi tomb (*Plate XIX*) is the only Florentine Quattro Cento monument that is in no sense dynamic. In this one work, then, Luca *does* approach the Laurana static conception and, moreover, attains the sole Quattro Cento concretion of religious sentiment.

2. *Idem : Alfonso and soldiers : Relief to left.*

1. *Naples, Castel Novo. Alfonso and soldiers : Marble relief to right under archway : Francesco Lauranesque.*

PLATE XLV. QUATTRO CENTO STATIC SCULPTURE AND THE LESS STATIC

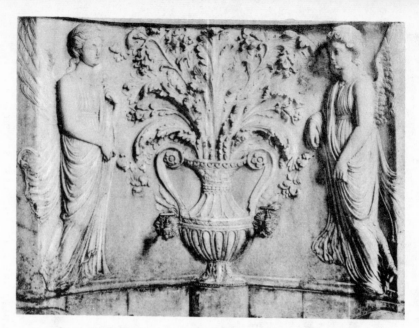

1. *Rome, S. M. Maggiore : Sacristy.* *Attrib.* Isiah da Pisa : *Marble lavabo.*

2. *Florence, San Lorenzo : Old sacristy.* Donatello . *Marble balustrade.*

PLATE XLVI. REVEALED EFFECT AND REVELATION EFFECT

There are plenty of Donatellesque characteristics about the sculpture of Alfonso's arch, though the Laurana feeling predominates. Isiah da Pisa worked on the arch. His tombs in Rome are now unfortunately in fragments[1] as is also the tabernacle in Viterbo attributed to him. One gathers the impression that Isiah was a great sculptor of the Laurana static kind, even if from his Tuscan days he had inherited a few quiet and graceful prepossessions from della Robbian art. Possibly Isiah's static quality is entirely derived from contemplation of antique sarcophagi, thence put in rapport with the Donatellesque forms he used (*Plate XLVI*, 1). For outside Florence, far more than in Florence, such Donatellesque stone-blossom motives as the putto, were used extensively by static and dynamic sculptors alike. This is confusing. But let me explain.

The arabesques Pasti employed so plentifully in the Tempio (I call them Pasti's because they are a Veronese Gothic form, and Pasti was Veronese) were adopted by Francesco Laurana for the Mastrantonio chapel,[2] one of his few works to which one can attach a document. The bulbous shapes of this foliage were suited to Francesco's art and also to that of Dalmatian Giorgio di Sebenico. And if I were to employ the expressions stone-blossom and incrustation with exactitude, I would confine stone-blossom to indicate the more static carving, and incrustation—when it is not a question of figures, particularly putti—to indicate the more dynamic; though the two be combined in the same piece. There is, of course, emergent and exuberant effect in such stone-blossom. I call it static in opposition, not so much to Donatello's dynamic, as to his Florentine monumentalism. That is the real point about this static sculpture. It is a Quattro Cento sculpture which, unlike the Florentine, does not carry seeds of the Baroque. In non-Florentine Quattro Cento carving, in the Veronese decoration along the stylobate of the Tempio, for instance, the stone blooms peacefully and

[1] While the Eugenius IV tomb in San Salvatore in Lauro was removed to this church and there reconstituted.

[2] San Francesco, Palermo.

richly. On the other hand, without the *example* of Donatello's dynamic it would have been ornamental rather than emblematic. Indeed, if isolated from emergent effect (but in Venice the statuary *grows* out of the buildings) static sculpture is by no means Quattro Cento. Often it is only 'primitive'. On the other hand, a less pictorial approach meant a purer plastic. Static sculpture realized many free-standing forms which yet retain, because they embody, the Quattro Cento stone-blossom effect.

I have outlined this subject in a most cursory way. But additional generalizations would make it no more precise. The beginning of the next section, however, deals with some decoration at Urbino attributed with reason to Francesco Laurana.

VI. *The Palace at Urbino*

Urbino is among the mountains behind Rimini. Federico's palace is a renovation and extension of an older structure. Clementini,[1] writing of the Tempio, says: 'Nel qual tempo anco fu prencipiato il Regio Palagio d'Urbino da Federico, correndo voce, che queste due fabbriche insigni erano a competenza erette.'[2] It is improbable, though, that either Federico at Urbino or Pio at Pienza started to compete extensively with Sigismondo in building before they had him on the run round about the year 1460. Luciano Laurana did not arrive in Urbino before 1465. But at least two rooms on the façade facing San Domenico had been decorated before he arrived. These are the sala della Jole and the room adjoining, probably decorated by Francesco Laurana in the years 1459 and 1460, after his work at Naples and before he went to France.

Nowhere is Francesco's predilection for clear shapes more evident. I would instance particularly the shell door of the sala della Jole (*Plate LI*, 1) where disky concave shells line the

[1] *Raccolto istorico della fondazione di Rimino e dell' origine e vite de' Malatesti.* Rimini, 1617.

[2] Roughly: in those days Federico started work on his palace at Urbino. And they said he built in competition with the Tempio.

Urbino, Ducal palace. Attrib. Francesco Laurana : *Sala della Jole : Mantelpiece.*

PLATE XLVII. THE QUATTRO CENTO BREADTH

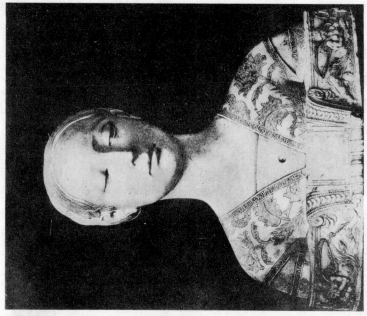

2. *Berlin, Kaiser Friedrich Museum. Francesco Laurana:
Marble bust of Beatrice of Aragon.*

1. *Urbino, Ducal palace. Room adjoining sala della Jole:
attrib. Francesco Laurana: Mantelpiece.*

PLATE XLVIII. LATCHKEY AND CYLINDRICAL SHAPES; 'CONCRETION NOT ABSTRACTION'

extreme edge of the beam so that they cut upon air. The up-raised palm of a hand conveys well the arrest it would command. But the gesture is preliminary, and so, evanescent, like a peacock's fan; whereas the firmness of grooved shells cut by Francesco are the complete repository for every delight in suspension of the rush of time. Not mysterious like the appearance of a hieroglyphic, not peremptory. The suspension evoked has long been dormant. It is now large with the one-piece stability of dreamlessness, here in the light. Thus firm is an ordinary latch-key, the disk solid at the end of a carefully carved shaft; and within the arches that frame the window seats in the sala della Jole, you will see this shape, long grooved bundles of foliage ended by concave discs sometimes with a head, sometimes with carefully ribbed shells (*Plate XIII*, 2). The same formula is used in convex form for the decoration of the windows themselves.[1] No other single decoration achieves so well the steadfast bossiness which is the final impression of Quattro Cento stone-blossom (*Plate XIII*, 4). On the face of the window-seat arches, Laurana has employed, as in the Capella Mastrantonio, the Veronese arabesques used by Pasti in the Tempio (*Plate XIII*, 2).

The superb mantelpiece in the adjoining room again suggests the sturdiness of latchkey shape, this time in terms of putti and strong flowers (*Plate XLVIII*, 1). As for the mantelpiece of the sala della Jole (*Plate XLVII*) it has been blamed for the clumsiness of its double frieze. But this amplitude, which is picked out by the animation of the small figures carved there, is the means to a Quattro Cento breadth shared by Matteo Nuti's beautiful door to the library at Cesena. In the case of the mantelpiece, the Hercules and Jole statues, from the beauty of their fixture, from the firm enunciation of their anatomy, go far to explain the double frieze. Two long lines

[1]Budinich has remarked that the decoration of these windows calls to mind Lombard terra-cotta ornament, and it is suggested that the windows are of earlier date than the interior decoration. This seems to me possible but unlikely.

of drama are spread between, yet they cannot overtop the settlement below of Hercules and Jole. For when both friezes are taken together, their incidents, being diverse, make a spectacle; whereas a putti-dance along one frieze only, would covet all emphasis for an irresistible processional. Compare the resulting bossy effect of this mantelpiece, the staring-rose effect, with the rampage along Donatello's singing gallery (*Plate XX*), and you will perhaps grasp the difference in the management of similar Quattro Cento motives between the static and dynamic Quattro Cento sculpture. Putti ride pigs and fish on the frieze of the sala della Jole main door. The pilaster capitals are made up out of flowers between dolphins. But the effect is not of incrustation, but of bossiness. Most lovely of all in this manner are the already mentioned mantelpiece in the adjoining room, and the three heads in the tympanum of the door there (*Plate XLIX*).

The next period at Urbino was constructionally the most extensive. I refer to building by Luciano. He never held the conception 'decorative', and everything intrinsically ornamental at Urbino belongs to a later period when Federico blossomed out as a Duke and as a Knight of the Garter. Then occurred the change in workmanship from a Quattro Cento abundance to a sixteenth-century adornment. For Federico's palace, as does his career, reflects, and in part created, the passage from the Quattro Cento to the *haute* Renaissance so tediously described in art-manuals. Some six years after Sigismondo's death in 1468, Federico stops competing in Quattro Cento forms. Youth is passed, so too his enemy and the tension. Federico is ripe, the Renaissance is ripe. The infant Raphael will soon be tottering round the courtyard.

Yet, simultaneously, another art takes up the Quattro Cento rôle. I have mentioned that Francesco di Giorgio probably supplied designs at the palace for intarsia or the inlay of wood. Some earlier intarsia there, and also some later, are of the Florentine variety and without Quattro Cento significance. But other pieces, particularly those of Federico's study, were

*Urbino, Ducal palace. Room adjoining sala della Jole : attrib. Francesco Laurana :
Tympanum of door.*

PLATE XLIX. THE STATIC, THE REVEALED

1. Urbino, Ducal palace. *Sala degli Angeli: attrib.* Domenico Rosselli: *Mantelpiece.*

2. Urbino, Ducal Palace. *Sala degli Angeli: attrib.* Domenico Rosselli.

PLATE L. THE FINEST QUATTRO CENTO ROOM

founded in the Laurana-Pieran æsthetic which had so long centred in Urbino. The home of intarsia was Siena; and at Urbino this process of inlaying wood was developed largely to represent perspective subjects (*Plate LII*, 1) and those subjects known to us as 'still-life'. This surely is significant, that the laborious and ingenious processes of mosaic should in that time be put to the service of object-arrangement pure and simple. There are compositions in intarsia at Urbino, particularly those representing musical instruments (*Plate LI*, 2), that at once suggest a Severini, or even some cubist painting. The warping propensities of wood, so far from ruining the design, often give the subject. Thus we see a book represented as having been left out in the sun. For the binding will not shut, and almost every page must be laid in separate by a minute strip of wood. It is significant, too, that the stillness associated with wood since the eras of primeval forest, suggested to the Quattro Cento mind simply and solely the arrangement of objects in space, set down, positioned, all the more intensively from the slow ardour necessary to this technique. Perspective illusion, gained so very decisively by this difficult form of inlay, is, of course, a constant trick in Italy for seizing the imagination. Even a feigned shutter colouring a house-wall transports one immediately into the world of spatial values. The analogy of intarsia to the colour successions on wooden panels employed by cassone painters is obvious. Cassone painting is a Quattro Cento art, even in Florence. But Florentine intarsia workers often avoided a 'spatial' subject, preferring to transcribe the work of important painters. An early instance is Giuliano da Majano's Annunciation[1] and other pieces founded on the designs of Alessio Baldovinetti.

My point is that Florentine intarsia, though used ornamentally as a method of spacing, was rarely employed to construct perspective or realistic illusion. At Verona we can take our fill of such wonders in Santa Maria in Organo where Fra Giovanni worked out his patient exuberance.

[1]In the new sacristy of the cathedral, Florence.

In Federico's study at Urbino we have both figure and still-life intarsia. We see represented Federico entering between drawn curtains, we see a loggia set still over Umbrian mountains, a furtive squirrel with a nut, and leaves crushed in a basket of pomegranates; we see represented a careful disarray of books within a chest, its lid so deceptively ajar that you go to touch it for reality—you can read the names, Seneca, Virgil, Tully. The ducal emblems shine from here and there, the eye fixes on an hour-glass, on a parrot in a cage, on the scores of music, on the new-looking twang-less instruments of sound.

I cannot linger now in Federico's study as I shall certainly do in the next part of this book, and again when concerned with Piero della Francesca. But I must point to the northern, even Dutch, affinity that suggests itself at all times in relation to Federico. It is not only that the whole country house civilization develops softly from this hill palace at Urbino. The precision, the *genre* precision of those intarsia pieces, their homely anecdotes, actually suggest such outcome. But note a vast difference. In the landscape pieces, distance is brought near along the bright wood. Nothing forlorn about the open cupboard of books. The intimacy is set once and for all, apparent, immediate: it will not grow on you nor glimmer with the seasons: and note the ever-present music pieces, rotund viols without mist between the strings. The silences associated with wood make them instant, they have just ceased upon the air. This is Italian *genre*, innocent of *arrière-pensée*, of the distended reflectiveness dear to the North. These symbols and figures are the codex of the Renaissance man. And is it not for such articulation of cultural intimacy all mosaicked on the tiny walls, that they pined, even those who later fitted their houses with stout panelling, upon which surface they could but expose the high portraits of ancestors who watch yet do not make the afternoons?

There is one other Quattro Cento part of the palace, namely the sala degli Angeli (*Plate L*, 2), the finest of Quattro Cen-

1. Urbino, Ducal palace. *Sala della Jole : attrib.* Francesco
Laurana : *Door with shells.*

2. Urbino, Ducal palace. *Sala degli Angeli : attrib.* Domenico
Rosselli : *Door with lunette.*

PLATE LI. TWO QUATTRO CENTO DOORS AT URBINO

1. *Urbino, Ducal palace.   Intarsia : Perspective view on door.*

2. *Ferrara, Schifanoja palace.   Terra-cotta decoration on upper wall of a room.*
Probably designed by Cosimo Tura *and executed by* Domenico di Paris.

PLATE LII. QUATTRO CENTO USES OF WOOD AND CLAY

to rooms. Probably Domenico Rosselli was the decorator.[1] He, likewise Florentine by birth, shows a fusion similar to that performed by Agostino di Duccio, of dynamic and static style. Domenico is often accounted to be purely a follower of Donatello. Yet some of his sculpture, the altar-piece in the cathedral at Fossombrone, for instance, exhibits a prepossession with cylindrical shape common to Francesco Laurana and to a multitude of Venetian painters and sculptors. Domenico was also a fine cassone painter.[2]

In the sala degli Angeli there are two magnificent doors with lunettes cupping shells (*Plate LI*, 2). Dolphins and fruit baskets encrust the ceiling. As in the Tempio, the prevalent colours are blue and gold. These are the Quattro Cento colours for sea, land, and sky, vast nurseries of the bright putti. The sun is on the sea in the solid council chamber upon the hill top: sea-scape distraught down in Rimini, is here cupped in silence and closed to the mountain winds; so that the ear aches for the relaxing sigh of the pines.

The wonderful chimney-piece is Quattro Cento (*Plate L*, 1). On the chimney is an encircled eagle, Montefeltrine emblem sustained by two swarming putti. The putti that dance along the frieze lack the monumental fury of those upon the singing gallery at Florence. All the better for council and living room that their ebullience is slightly anonymous, even dainty, though without a hint of della Robbia's mode. For these putti have welled from the stone, marble dust upon their eye-lids still. Perfect the design, so that their movement goes incessant though lacking monumental gesture. It is the work of a Donatello who had no need to react from paucity of emphasis, from the unemphasized movement of Ghiberti's perfect 'finish'.

In Rosselli's work I think I can detect an unusual love of stone; all the more easily since, though he was born Tuscan,

[1]*See* Serra, *op. cit.*

[2]*Cf.* 'The Triumph of Chastity' at the Royal Gallery, Turin. This panel, attributed to Rosselli, was in the 1930 Italian exhibition at Burlington House.

he is not claimed as an ornament to Florentine art. The fact of the matter is that he spent childhood at play among the Rovezzano quarries. It probably was he who sculpted the decoration to the Sforza palace windows at Pesaro, and many other Quattro Cento windows that derive their composition from Francesco di Giorgio, in Umbria and the Marches.

This closes the account of Quattro Cento work in the palace. The traveller is therefore warned that beyond Luciano Laurana's structure where it is still apparent, beyond Francesco Laurana's two rooms, beyond some of the intarsia and the sala degli Angeli, there is no further Quattro Cento work. The rest of the ornament approximate in date was executed by Ambrogio Barocci, by Francesco di Simone (*see* p. 125), and by Cristoforo Romano and others. Ambrogio Barocci, who is responsible for decoration on the piazza façade, for the main staircase and for the coloured marble chapel named *del Perdono*, shows himself a disciple of Pietro Lombardo, though he had worked for the Quattro Cento artist Mauro Coducci at San Michele. A Venetian note intrudes itself, which makes the palace all the more comprehensive of the contemporary styles. But Pietro Lombardo will be, in part, the villain and the Florentine when I come to write of Venetian sculpture.

VII. *Lombard architecture and sculpture*

Lombard Renaissance architecture and sculpture is disappointing. For the carvers enjoyed exuberant effects, and on the whole they were hostile to Florentine influence.[1] Their skill, too, was considerable; yet they rarely achieved Quattro Cento effects. Lombard Gothic is a more fruitful subject. I write of

[1]*'Perchè noi siamo fiorentino'*, writes Filarete to Piero de' Medici, *'loro ci fanno ripulsa.'* Filarete was working on the hospital in Milan. But owing to the opposition of his masons he had to retire from the contract. Castiglione d'Olona (famous for the Masolino frescoes) is exceptional. There, Brunellesque forms were established at a very early date. The only objects of Quattro Cento interest at Castiglione d'Olona belong to the Venetian subject.

it in connection with Venice. In the building of the cathedral at Milan, a good deal of interesting friction between the original foreign architects, French, German, Swedish, Belgian, and their Italian masons, resulted in the reinforcement of an Italian idea. Over and over again foreign designs for the cathedral structure were modified to the ends of unity, of something 'classical', and away from the swept flying laceworks of the North, away from the confusion of ropes and buttresses that were ship-shape enough in northern skies, but which would have been grotesque if anchored over fair Lombardy flats. Subsequent developments both in sculpture and architecture make it doubtful whether without some such triumph in a dramatic conflict, the Lombards would have proved themselves so Italian in the early fifteenth century. They had not developed their Romanesque during the fourteenth century, nor fully embraced the Gothic. But in the fifteenth century they attained Quattro Cento expression in this foreign style with the inducement to modify it according to the new feeling for stone.

The kindred feeling for space, however, was weak; and later, the use of classical or semi-classical forms made this imperfection glaring, particularly in structures by members of the Solari family; since they lacked a Brunelleschi's genius to transform borrowed material to a novel purpose. But Lombard builders would not relinquish their desire for mass-effect although they were confined for the most part to the use of brick and terra-cotta. They sought to mitigate their poverty of conception by introducing those foreign elements they had combatted when building in stone at the cathedral. I refer now to the greater and more hideous parts of the Certosa near Pavia, to such Milanese churches as the Incoronata and Santa Maria Podone by Pietro Solari, and Santa Maria delle Grazie by Guiniforte Solari. In these structures there is a tiresome mixture of altogether arid spaces with distinctly fussy and therefore French (though in no way actually derived from France) dwarfish Gothic terra-cotta decorations, and with stumpy little arcades or roofed-in loggias that twist and turn and give a pagoda effect to many a Milanese edifice, including the Sforza castle. These arcades were, of course, a derivation from Lombard Romanesque. But only in the Renaissance do they appear so Chinese. For similarly, the flimsy Chinese pagoda or umbrella roof, a thoroughly 'oriental' elaboration of Buddha's sunshade, uproots the meagre spaces that it shields (*Plate LIII*).

This lack of scale in Lombardy I put down to French influence. Much of the detail at Milan cathedral is far more closely foreign, yet for the longer view it is more Italian, since an Italian proportion and scale are evident. I imply no condemnation of French Gothic. The borrowing is here fortunate and there unfortunate. Anyone who has seen such Piedmont church façades as that of the cathedral at Chivasso or of San Antonio at Ranverso, will understand what I mean about French Gothic in Italy. The slowness and 'smallness' of the giant ogival arches on these façades confuse Italianate design, showing just how grotesquely Italians may express a form that is foreign to them, if the appropriation be undigested. On the other hand the façade of Pinerolo cathedral is beautiful.

Bramante was not free of the storeyed pagoda when he worked in Lombardy. Witness the huddled roofs and grotto-like interior of San Satiro. In short, the patched-up quarrel between northern fussiness and Italian feeling for mass was celebrated by a wedding-cake of year-in-year-out proportions when they built the cathedral at Milan. But the Solari vaunting in brick of would-be Italian space, causes the couple to become ill-assorted. Now we have pendulous terra-cotta decoration nullifying the thrust of a deep *occhio* window.[1]

Most disappointing of all are the post-Gothic Lombard

[1]This is not true, of course, of later and more generously conceived palaces such as the Cancelleria-like palazzo Raimondi at Cremona. By 'Cancelleria-like' I intend a common feeling rather than an actual imitation. Whereas the ground floor and first storey of the palazzo Tabarelli at Trentino do closely reproduce the Cancelleria façade.

Pavia, Certosa : View of church from smaller cloister.

PLATE LIII. ARID SPACES, FUSSY DECORATION AND STOREYED-PAGODA EFFECT

1. *Isola Bella, chapel of the villa Borromeo : Monument to Giovanni Borromeo.*

2. *Bergamo, Capella Colleoni : Omodeo.*

PLATE LIV. LOMBARD WEDDING-CAKES

sculptors, Omodeo and his school — that is from the Quattro Cento angle. For Gothic intensity was still the source of an unrivalled luxuriance, while as yet there was little striving after the purely classic. Reliefs and monuments disclose plenty of freedom, of the non-correspondence in ornament that I have associated particularly with Verrocchio's designs, but there is no *broadness*, nothing really large. Similarly, the extravagance in representation of movement and even in design, hardly ever suggest a Baroque outcome, as is the case with works by the great Florentines who belong to the Quattro Cento. For the truth is, Lombard freedom is largely so much elaboration; the scale is small. The same psychology is apparent as the one rejoicing in huddled roofs. Exuberance was elaborated, often laboriously in northern fashion, though here in response to Quattro Cento aim. In many of the finely worked reliefs by Omodeo and his school, all minutiæ are exaggerated, enriched—maybe veins of an ecstatic hand—not to Ghiberti's ends of perfect 'finish', it is true; but no bonds are broken nor a new domain brought in. Again this smallness is the result of French influence, which in its native form could stir little Quattro Cento fire. One misses the quick and hooded types of Donatello. The Lombard type has a drawn or tense look, but the face is also sullen, and even contradictorily rounded. There were also German influences working on the Lombard sculptor. A ruggedness and a violence that remind one of German wood-engraving provoke a noisy or 'musical' effect. One associates yelling with the prominent stomachs and indented backs of Lombard anatomy. These characteristics often confuse the Quattro Cento quality, where it exists.

Lombards excelled as modellers. The same 'yelling' quality helped them to gauge the clay to most vivid effects. The modelled *Pietà* in San Satiro, Milan, attributed to Omodeo, is far more satisfactory than any Lombard carving, though in cutting they were also expert. But unlike Quattro Cento carvers, they rarely joined a modeller's plastic with an appreciation of stone. On the whole, stone ornament is more luscious than exuberant, like the intricate and slow terra-cotta swags. As carvers they relied entirely upon modelling for vivid effect. Thus the Lombard *cliché* of cutting heads sharply away from their background in stone-relief groups.

In the case of stone arabesque decoration, the Lombards evolved a technique with less dependence on modelling. Still, this technique reflects too literally the processes of another art, the goldsmith's. Now we call very low and intricate relief in Spanish Renaissance decoration 'plateresque', because it suggests, and was suggested by, the engraving of metal. This analogy of a certain kind of stone ornament to the chasing of silver, is not confined to very low relief. Lowness of relief is not the essential point: even high relief is occasionally best described as plateresque. For the deeper analogy of this sculpture to chasing, lies in a certain uniformity. There is an effect of the whole surface being patterned. Pattern *is* the surface, it seems; thus, although stone-ornament projects from a background, the effect is almost the same as if the pattern were engraved there. More truly sculptural ornament, on the other hand, cannot for one moment be confused with its background plane on which it appears to be stuck or from which it appears to emerge, and so on. Actually, ornament may not cover its surface, the background may be clear in parts, free of carving, and yet the ornament is plateresque if no directional relationship between background and relief is apparent.

There is a definite Mohammedan affinity in this type of stone ornament. The very low relief decoration of the entrance to the Loggia, Brescia, is plateresque, also the entrance to the Madonna dei Miracoli in the same town[1] (*Plate LVI, 3*). These instances are sixteenth century and are not without connection with the ornamental patterns of Raphaelesque painters who, following Raphael closely in such work, displayed an almost Mohammedan conception of decor, though the themes are Roman and grotesque. Such was the change from

[1] Perhaps the best instance of such plateresque carving is to be seen on the sixteenth-century balustrades to the chancel steps in Siena cathedral.

Bergamo, capella Colleoni : Omodeo : *Marble reliefs on pilasters to presbytery.*

PLATE LV. LOMBARD QUATTRO CENTO CARVING

1. *Rome, S. M. del Popolo.* Florentine-Lombard : *Monument to Cardinal Cristoforo Rovere.*

2. *Rome, S. M. del Popolo.* Lombard : *Monument to bishop Gomiel.*

3. *Brescia, S. M. dei Miracoli : Decoration over entrance : Detail.*

4. *Siena, Cathedral.* Lorenzo Marrina : *Entrance to Piccolomini library : Detail.*

PLATE LVI. 'STUCK-ON' AND 'PLATERESQUE' ORNAMENT

the early to the high Renaissance in the expressing of exuberance.

But Omodeo's decorations belonging to this category, on the pillars of Colleoni's tomb at Bergamo, were executed before 1476. An almost damascene-like pattern now appears in the carving of the candelabra shape which was used architecturally at the Colleoni chapel and on the façade of the Certosa and elsewhere. The bulge of the candlestick shape will carry such damascene well, every inch will appear chased, subdued, without tension. At Ferrara, too, one recognizes not only Lombard use of terra-cotta, but also this Lombard candelabra engraving of stone. An instance is the Schifanoja's doorway attributed to the design of the painter, Francesco del Cossa. Unfortunately Ferrarese carvers did not impute the deeper fantasies of metal to the stone, fantasies that were rife in that town.

The case of Venetian fifteenth-century ornamentals is not essentially different. True, the relief is always high and daringly cut away. The arabesque may be most sinuous, yet conception remains plateresque as defined above. Arabesques decorating the pilasters of the Miracoli, Venice, do not give the impression of having been stuck on as do many sixteenth-century ornamentals. These pilasters reflect unimpaired images of the goldsmith's art, images that govern the stone, unlike Verrocchio's goldsmith's images which he put at the service of the stone. In speaking of Quattro Cento effects it would be contradictory to introduce the ugly noun 'ornamentals', since it expresses a dissociation from the stone. Venice is full of ornamentals. But fifteenth-century statuary there is often Quattro Cento.

When the transposition from metal to stone is facile—that is to say, reflecting no deep satisfaction, no image that is profound—carving will lack tensity. Still worse if there be an oral connection that is superficial. The fierce richness of Lombard monuments rarely attains a form more intense than tiers upon tiers of the wedding-cake airiness already noticed in relation to Milan cathedral. Again the French *chic*. Giovanni Galeazzo

Sforza's tomb in the Certosa is a wedding-cake, also the Giovanni Borromeo[1] monument sometimes associated with Omodeo's name (*Plate LIV*, 1). Certainly the same effect is experienced in the Colleoni chapel, not only on account of the tier architecture of the tombs, but because one feels that *every* surface has been sweetened, whether it be the embroidery on Medea Colleoni recumbent above her tomb, or the varied eatable-looking crystallizations on the cruelly smooth marbles of the façade[2] (*Plate LIV*, 2). Here is an icing that will defeat the stamper on a tiled floor. You won't break off one pagoda. I mention tiles because the alternating diamonds of black and white marble on the front of the chapel immediately suggest them.

A Quattro Cento effect comes when the stone, or a Quattro Cento motive, leads the sculptor. Thus the putti climbing about candelabra on the entrance pilasters of the presbytery (*Plate LV*), and the balustrade pillars in front of Colleoni's tomb. There is so delicate a bubbling in the colour of this marble that the pattern appears luminous and potent.

VIII. *A Quattro Cento use of terra-cotta*

Michelozzo could supply a breadth to Lombard sculptors so fertile in small things. Their collaboration was happy in the capella Portinari.[3] The terra-cotta dance of angels with bells round the drum of the vault is beautiful, particularly in colour. Even at the Certosa, terra-cotta ornamentation in the cloisters

[1] In the capella della Villa Borromeo, Isola Bella.

[2] Marble is not a plaything. Lombards thought it crystal like sugar. No doubt the extreme hardness, both in texture and in the light they reflect, of some Brescian and lake marbles explains this attitude, so common also in other countries.

[3] In Sant' Eustorgio, Milan. Also Quattro Cento at Milan is the Medici bank door designed by Michelozzo but decorated by local masons. This door is now in the Sforza castle. The traveller there should also inspect the so-called portico dell' Elefante, the entrance to the Ducal chapel in the castle. These rich Lombard doors have their Quattro Cento significance, at any rate the first time they are seen. Another fine door is the one in the Louvre from the palazzo Stanga at Cremona.

is more nearly Quattro Cento than Omodeo's famous marble door that leads from the smaller cloister to the church, though this door is crowded with Quattro Cento motives. But they are profuse, treated richly but niggardly; and the double jambs, so emblematic as used by Francesco Laurana at Urbino[1] are here the means of elaboration.

I have stressed the point that love of any material in the fifteenth century could result in Quattro Cento effect. The best instances of a Quattro Cento use of terra-cotta are found in Bologna and Ferrara. For the Aemilian plain lacks stone. Ferrara was none the less a Quattro Cento nucleus. The ruling d'Este figure in Quattro Cento history both as patrons and as characters. Niccolo d'Este and after him and Leonello, Borso d'Este who built the Schifanoja, were Sigismondo's friends. They had the Quattro Cento temperament. Geographically they were close to Romagna, politically they were always in contact with Venice. Many of our heroes were at one time or another at Ferrara: Pisanello, Alberti, Matteo de' Pasti, Piero. Ferrara is the first planned city in the modern world. Borso's architect, Biagio Rossetti, was largely responsible. His neat churches which show a fine use of brick, cannot be claimed for the Quattro Cento; while the summer palaces he built for the d'Este are destroyed. The unfinished palace, however, begun for Ludovico Sforza, has a Quattro Cento import drawn from Venetian architecture.

Biagio Rossetti's use of terra-cotta was harmonious, unlike his sixteenth-century followers who decorated the palazzo Roverella. But it is not with Rossetti that I find the tense or Quattro Cento use of terra-cotta in this town.

I have mentioned (*see* p. 177) that the Ferrarese painters Tura and Cossa reflect an appreciation of the iron and the harried bronzes up at Padua. In addition, Tura was despot of a fantasy-realm that lay on the Aemilian littoral. Were the whales

---

[1]For the main entrance to the sala della Jole. These double jambs like the double frieze of the mantelpiece (*Plate XLVII*) help to create a static quality.

and acrobatic monsters left high and dry on these long sands with which the Po has silted the sea, does this shore serve up as on a plate the larger animals of the Adriatic? No longer do they scintillate, no longer does the sun catch a fin. Every sharpness has multiplied thorny, like coral. Turn over the bleached skeleton of a dolphin. It creaks. Is anything so dry as these bones that once fed from the salt sea? Teeth alone gleam. You cannot make these powderous bones slippery. They won't surrender one image of incrustation, and stone cannot represent a desiccated explosion into thorns and powder, nor reptiles dried by the sun to barking tatters, even by moonlight unfloated. One material may give an image worthy of desiccation. Without a dampness the terra-cotta jar will hold liquid a thousand years. An expanse of water will die before its container. After several thousand years terra-cotta utensils will be turned up mawkish, light, unchanged, in percolated tombs. Only grinning bones are so deceptive in their lack of weight as of gravity. Not that the fantasies of Cosimo Tura are macabre. He expressed a power. For a heap of skeletons are their own dolmen, and sinews of the crashed aeroplane in a field are more expressive of power than the engine in full blast through the sky. Moreover, Cosimo used the spiny horn as cornucopia for fruit, exotic fruit. His imagination rioted with dryness, jewels and fecundity, with the dry shore and the fertile Aemilian flats, with light arthritic figures and their heavy eatables, with the whole deceptive weight of materials and their interaction. As a painter he greatly excites the tactile sense. But coloured terra-cotta, always unexpected in its lack of density, can realize these fantasies in a direct form. In the Schifanoja palace, above the frescoes on the walls of the antechamber, you may see projected in their greatest liveliness the potent images of thorniness and fruit. Here are the terra-cotta decorations executed by Domenico di Paris. No further description is relevant for these Virtues, these putti and the huge crackling festoons, for the liquid music the putti blow, for the shells and brittle horns tossed among the apples (*Plate LII*, 2).

Dryness of coral, though not Ferrarese translation of Gothic energy into prickly points, worked the imagination of Sperandio, the medallist, who lived long at the d'Este court. Sperandio possessed bravura. He achieved quickly, adaptable to each material, at one time in the pay of Federico Manfredi, lord of Faenza, for commissions *'de bronzio, de marmoro, di terra, di designi, di piombo, di picture, di orfesarie'.* The façade of the chiesa della Santa at Bologna is attributed to Sperandio[1] (*Plate LVII*, 1). Here is a Quattro Cento façade of brick and terra-cotta alone. The square, brick pilasters with the doorway in the centre, give a strong feeling of emergence and of depth in ways entirely suited to these dry materials. Yet here also is the Tura alternation of aridity and lusciousness expressed by rounded shapes. For Sperandio owned a vaunt of nobility and fierceness which led him to posture wide the shell in the lunette of the door, and to cut it deep. The use of terra-cotta for this fan-like shape and for the round blind window-frames above, lying so rich on the mortar-divided brick, in conjunction with the pilaster decoration and the inlaid coats of arms, provide an enormous effect of fertility however dry. The three-lobe decoration that surmounts the façade is a Venetian reminiscence.[2] In San Francesco is the monument for Pope Alexander V attributed to Sperandio (*Plate LVII*, 2). This lovely composition is expressive by its very design of Quattro Cento energies; rich, compact, suffused, yet fierce in the sway of figures. On top two hippocentaurs support a vase on which stands the Virgin holding her child.

The technique of terra-cotta ornamentation, the casting from moulds founded upon designs often furnished by painters, did not make for the development of an architectural school. In the beautiful city of Bologna one notices a certain mechanical variation in the buildings of the late fifteenth cen-

[1]At any rate, it is thought he had a hand in it, collaborating with Marchione di Faenza and Bartolommeo di Dozza.

[2]The other Quattro Cento façade in Bologna, that of the Madonna di Galleria, belongs to the Venetian subject.

tury. Unusual is the sixteenth-century-looking Municipio, related to Alberti and his work at Mantua. The palazzo Malvezzi-Campeggi, on which the terra-cotta was used emblematically, has some Quattro Cento significance. More to my taste is the compact palazzo del Podestà at Forli where brick, terracotta and stone are together at a tension. The Malatesta once held Forli.

IX. *Quattro Cento works by Florentine artists*

In this section I enumerate several so far unmentioned Quattro Cento works by Florentine artists. Most of them were created outside Florence and reflect local influence.

The reader may recall the blame heaped upon Benedetto da Majano in connection with the San Savino monument at Faenza (*see* p. 117). Benedetto later worked at Siena on a ciborium for the high altar of San Domenico. This work is a Quattro Cento masterpiece. For now Benedetto's cold artisanship, unrivalled in delicacy except by Desiderio and by Antonio Rossellino, is under the influence of Federighi's passion for encrusted effect, the Siennese passion for the iron. Benedetto uses his Florentine heritage to express incrustation as whiteness upon whiteness, as delicate forms emblazoning delicate forms.

At Arezzo, in the conventual church of Sante Fiora e Lucilla, there is a tabernacle attributed to Benedetto, based upon Desiderio's tabernacle in San Lorenzo, Florence. The Arezzo piece also is Quattro Cento, principally in view of the link with Desiderio.[1]

The Majanos, Giuliano and Benedetto, were constantly working together near the Adriatic littoral. Perhaps this explains an occasional Venetian element in Benedetto's designs. The San Domenico pyx is topped by a statue of the Redeemer. This statue is not ornament, it is the crux of the design. And

[1]Another beautiful tabernacle of this kind is the one in the cathedral at Cortona.

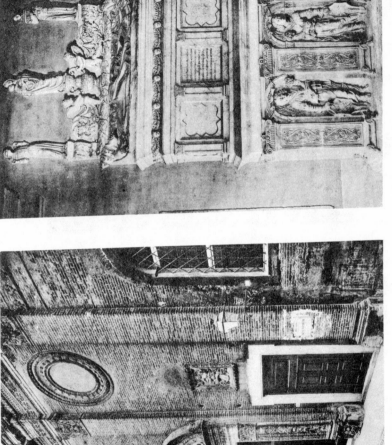

1. *Bologna, chiesa della Santa.* Attrib. Sperandio: *façade.* 2. *Bologna, San Francesco.* Attrib. Sperandio: *Monument to Pope Alexander V.*

PLATE LVII. QUATTRO CENTO USE OF BRICK AND TERRA-COTTA

1. *Genoa, palazzo Gnecco. Giovanni Gaggini : Entrance.*   2. *Florence, palazzo Vecchio. B. and G. da Majano : Sala d' Udienza : Door.*

PLATE LVIII. TWO QUATTRO CENTO DOORS

when design appears founded on the emergence of statuary on top, as if the construction existed to supply this birth from humanistic marble, there has been a reference to Venice and to Venetian art. Again, on the cornice of the door in the sala dell' Orologio of the palazzo Vecchio, Florence, Benedetto placed a statue of John the Baptist, and at the edges of the cornice putti clinging to candelabra. Benedetto's experience in Siena of incrustation was reinforced. The red marble inside the lunette shows the influence of Verrocchio. On the frieze are marine centaurs, chimaera and other brittle sliders through the sea. Between the volutes of the capitals there are shells cupping the slippery Virtues.

In spite of the monumental massiveness in this doorway of cornice and of pilaster construction, a massiveness which both Giuliano and Benedetto took over from Michelozzo (*see* p. 125), one is at once reminded of the doors with lunettes in the sala degli Angeli at Urbino. The Majano door's other side (*Plate LVIII*, 2) in the sala d'Udienza, suggests Urbino even more strongly. For here there is apparent an attempt to give a Michelozzian version of Luciano's beaded moulding that is squared at the base (*see* p. 182n). But the resemblance is not so much to Luciano's work as to the adaptation of Luciano's work in the sala degli Angeli lunette doorways (*Plate LI*, 2). Who has influenced whom? We know from the Baccio Pontelli letter (*see* p. 186) that Giuliano da Majano who collaborated with his brother for the palazzo Vecchio doorways, passed through Urbino in 1481. But documents[1] show they were working on the doors between 1476 and 1481. Was the sala degli Angeli decorated before 1476? If so, Adolfo Venturi[2] who attributes the designs to Francesco di Giorgio, is certainly wrong, because Francesco did not arrive in Urbino before 1477. Domenico Rosselli, on the other hand, was working at Pesaro for Costanzo Sforza in 1472 or 1473. Did

[1]*See* Alfredo Lensi. *Il palazzo Vecchio*. Bestetti e Tumminelli. Milan, 1930.

[2]*See* Venturi, *op. cit.*, Vol. VIII, I, p. 758.

Federico summon him from nearby Pesaro to decorate this room lavishly as soon as he, Federico, had blossomed into a Duke in 1474?

The relation between these doorways can hardly be the other way about. The Urbino doorways can hardly be derived from those at the palazzo Vecchio, since it makes their construction uncomfortably late for their style. And apart from the question of the non-Florentine lunettes in the palazzo Vecchio doorways, the mouldings of the sala d'Udienza door contain a definite reference to Luciano's mouldings.[1] It remains, however, possible but unlikely that the Majanos took something from Luciano's work only at Urbino, and that Domenico Rosselli later took something from the Majanos and made it more Lucianesque for his decoration at Urbino. At any rate it is extremely gratifying to find two Quattro Cento doorways in Florence. Next to the sala degli Angeli, the sala dell' Orologio is the finest of Quattro Cento rooms; while Benedetto's coffered ceilings for the salone degli Ottone and for the sala d' Udienza are equalled in Quattro Cento richness only by some of the early sixteenth-century ceilings at Sabbioneta, the Gonzagas'[2] model township.

When working afterwards at Loreto, the Majanos repeated Urbinesque forms. An instance is Giuliano da Majano's doorway to the Santa Casa. But the effect of the Quattro Cento lunette is slowed down and destroyed by the heaviness of its mouldings in relation to its span, and also by the heaviness of a Michelozzian cornice below. For the Majanos were faithful to a monumental cornice which tends to take the spring out of a lunette.[3] On the other hand, Benedetto's

[1] Further, this door has intarsia panels of perspective subjects. The subject of doors ajar is to be seen on the sala degli Angeli door (*Plate LI*, 2). It appears to me more likely that this theme came from Urbino to Florence than *vice versa*.

[2] The ruling family at Mantua.

[3] Compare the Venetian use of cornice and lunette (*Plate XVI*, 2 and p. 123).

beautiful *lavabo* in the Basilica has some Quattro Cento significance.

In Rome, an early Donatellesque Quattro Cento work of note is the bronze slab monument in the Lateran of Pope Martin V (*Plate XXIII*, 1). It is attributed to Donatello's companion, known as Simone Fiorentino,[1] whom Vasari, in referring to this monument, confuses with Donatello's brother. I must also mention the fantast, Filarete, who was responsible for the bronze doors of St. Peter's. He was a Florentine goldsmith with a boast quicker than Cellini's. Come to Rome, he introduced pagan figures on the doors of Europe's premier church (so he thought it), by no means echoes of the antique on which he considered himself an expert, but exuberant crudities that belonged to his own early day, but hardly to the academic generation among whom he passed at Florence. The reliefs are laughable; but the squat richness of the surrounding arabesque (*Plate LXIII*) interspersed with figures and animals, is a unique Quattro Cento expression of exuberance from a Florentine; because there is not the slightest suggestion of the Baroque psychology. Saints and Roman soldiers— Filarete might represent only with the utmost crudity. His bronze altar-piece[2] of Virgin and child shows a similar clanging inconsequence, which in combination with the richness of detail, affords an unusual, if slight, Quattro Cento effect.

Apart from the palace, there is at Urbino a Quattro Cento work of the greatest importance. This is Maso di Bartolommeo's doorway to San Domenico (*Plate LIX*, 1) opposite the Ducal palace (*Plate XIII*, 2). Maso was Florentine and had worked with Luca della Robbia and with Michelozzo. He is at Rimini in 1448 making bronze gates for the San Sigismondo chapel in the Tempio. These were destroyed by a populace. Now the San Domenico doorway, which belongs to the year 1452, is not only the earliest Quattro Cento achievement in Urbino, but

[1] *Cf.* A. Venturi, *op. cit.*, VI, p. 372*n.*   [2] In the Louvre.

the earliest Quattro Cento doorway anywhere. In the lunette there is a beautiful terra-cotta group by Luca della Robbia, harmonious with the Quattro Cento qualities of the structure. This doorway, then, because of its early date, and because it contains a successful fusion of Quattro Cento and Florentine character, is the best frontispiece to the period as a whole.

If a slight excess of superstructure appears in this doorway,[1] it is the result of Maso's resolution to convey as well as Florentine grace, the Quattro Cento solidity he had seen in Matteo de' Pasti's decoration for the chapel of San Sigismondo, where magisterial if miniature pilasters line the wall with swags between them. But in the doorway, Florentine and Quattro Cento are not merely side by side. They are welded by a bronze worker of genius; and even if the lunette does shoot slowly with della Robbian roll of leaf—encumbered, as it were, by a dragging sweet measure—yet by means of the pilasters and frieze and pediment above, the design remains firm, remains stalwart. The deepness of the lunette and of the pediment, the lovely proportion of the columns upon their high consoles,[2] show that Maso had felt to his uttermost the glories they found in stone at Rimini. The carving of the frieze and of the capitals is exquisite. But it is as if fibrous iron tautened their fragility, in anticipation of Francesco di Giorgio. We imagine shells barnacled upon delicately lashed rocks, and flower from strong earths, to discover as receptacle for such riches the two empty circles in the spandrels of the lunette, flanked by the small pilasters from the Tempio. No doubt these voids were prepared for coloured marble disks such as those with which Alberti buttoned up the Tempio encasement; or possibly for della Robbian terra-cotta medallions which Maso, perhaps, quite properly refused when trying their effect.

[1] Far less in actuality than in the photograph.

[2] The beautiful Quattro Cento door of the casa Buonaparte at Ascoli Piceno, has pilasters upon high consoles derived from the San Domenico doorway. Also a double beam—that reflects Francesco Laurana's influence—beneath a Venetian lunette.

The tympanum of the doorway projects over the deep *occhio* windows above. Such inconsequent overlaying of depth over depth—and no doubt a nicely adjusted Gothic portal was pulled down by the monks when they commissioned Maso for one in a new style—is not only clumsiness of estimate, corresponding as it does to a feeling for the compact, crowded tension which animates one kind of Quattro Cento spirit. For the deep eye of the rose-window contiguous allows the doorway a greater projection and a higher density.

I suggest that the fusion, evident in this doorway, of an exquisiteness with an effect of stolid and emblazoned mass, had wide appeal to the artists who came to this town. Maso was primarily a worker in bronze as was Francesco di Giorgio after him. Particularly close to Francesco's decorative style are the acanthus on the frieze.[1] Probably when Francesco arrived in Urbino some twenty-five years later he studied Maso's work. But further, the door mouldings have small changes of surface. The lines approximate to the beaded effect Laurana was soon to invent. Did the doorway inspire Francesco di Giorgio, and have we discovered something to which even the sublime Luciano was indebted? Or did Piero guide Maso, Piero or his patron, the constant factors in Urbino?

X. *Other aspects of Lombard sculpture*

The traveller to Italy who visits only the Riviera will see little that is Quattro Cento unless he should read into the Genoese panorama the images that Genoa has evoked (*see* pp. 40ff.). Quattro Cento sculpture is sparse on this coast. The Gaggini family of sculptors who came to Genoa from lake Lugano, sometimes deserve attention. Giovanni, the elder among them, was responsible for the model of slate doorways surmounted by a relief of St. George[2] and the dragon. Two such

[1] As evident already on the frieze of Santa Maria delle Nevi (*Plate XXXVIII*, 1).

[2] St. George is a patron saint of Genoa.

reliefs are in the Victoria and Albert. These doorways and their variants are common in Genoa (perhaps the best is the entrance to the Palazzo Gnecco — *Plate LVIII*, 1), and are found along the coast at Rapallo and Sestri Levante; for the same models were exploited far into the sixteenth century. The type shows a certain Quattro Cento compactness, a stability which refers to Giovanni's Venetian training; for in his youth he worked in Venice. Some of the St. George reliefs have the manifested and static quality that I have identified in sculpture with the name of Francesco Laurana.

The work of Elia and Domenico Gaggini is less sympathetic. The San Giovanni chapel erected by them in Genoa cathedral, affords nothing Quattro Cento except the balustrade. All the rest of the decoration is a kind of disease, alternatively, a clothing, an ornament, nothing but ornament common also in one early phase of the sixteenth century—pillars ridiculously buskined with hardy threads of marble far above the knee.

Domenico Gaggini, however, later worked at Alfonso's archway and in Sicily. Although he kept his own thinness of form, he developed a predilection for Lauranesque fixity. One feels besides that he was invigorated by the Gothic he found at Palermo, and by the many Levantine forms. Certainly the side door attributed to him for Sant'Agostino at Palermo, is Quattro Cento (*Plate LX*, 1). It is a curious work. The decoration is of a most spidery Gothic that knits strongly the low and crowded lunette. An unusual tension results, the distributed packing of sharp but curling fragility. Another redaction of Spanish Gothic motives to Renaissance, though not in this case to Quattro Cento terms, is the doorway of Santa Margherita at Sciacca, attributed to Domenico. As for the holy-water basin in Palermo cathedral (*Plate LX*, 2), it appears to me to have more connection with Francesco Laurana than with Domenico. The solid superstructure, like some primeval engine of unknown power, suggests again an image associated with statuary in Venice, namely, the mechanistic reproduction of marble from marble.

1. *Urbino, San Domenico.* Maso di Bartolomeo : *The portal.*   2. *Verona, San Fermo.* Il Rosso : *Brenzoni monument.*

PLATE LIX. TWO EARLY QUATTRO CENTO WORKS BY FLORENTINES OUTSIDE FLORENCE

2. *Palermo, Cathedral.* School of Francesco Laurana: *Stoup.*

1. *Palermo, Sant' Agostino.* Attrib. Domenico Gaggini: *Side door.*

PLATE LX. 'THE MECHANISTIC REPRODUCTION OF MARBLE FROM MARBLE'

There are hundreds of fifteenth-century tombs in Rome. I particularly warn the traveller that none of these are Quattro Cento beyond the monuments already described as such. Lombard sculptors flocked to Rome in the second half of the fifteenth century. In contact with the Florentine sculptors, and influenced by the stunted carving on Roman-Christian sarcophagi lying about the city, they tempered their native exuberance with a certain primness that results in unceasing ornament. The tier conception of sepulchral design was not relinquished (Pio's tomb has four tiers), even when accompanied with Florentine forms (*Plate LVI*, 1).[1] While to counteract the reduplication of horizontal lines, the Lombards often introduced some broken shape instead of a lunette. The example I reproduce of such a tomb on Plate LVI, fig. 2, is sixteenth-century, and was chosen in the first place to illustrate sixteenth-century 'stuck on' ornament. But it represents fairly enough the common fifteenth-century type of monument in Rome.

XI. *Quattro Cento Gothic in Palermo*

At the outset of the essay, I made cursory mention of a tense fifteenth-century Gothic in the South (*see* p. 84). I had in mind doorway arches depressed from their points by the upper horizontal of a rectangular frame-work. A fine example is the main door of the palazzo Bonifacio in the via Portanova at Naples. Such new tension of Gothic form will give the traveller at Naples a far better idea of the Quattro Cento spirit than will the famous 'Renaissance' monuments by Antonio Rossellino and Benedetto da Majano in Monteoliveto.

The same arch, depressed from its point, was elaborated in Palermo. Towards the end of the fifteenth century Palermo produced a great architect, Matteo Carnelevari. He blunted the bent-blade arch with reduplications of concave moulding. He wanted a wider tension, a mass effect. One's delight is the

[1]The Virgin and child in the lunette are probably the work of Mino da Fiesole.

more poignant since Carnelevari's mass has not descended from the blue or from Urbino, but consummates Sicilian medieval styles: upon the long-drawn-out Saracenic lace-work was the imposition. His palazzo Aiutamicristo is much renewed, particularly the front; but the lambent *loggiati* of the courtyard show how he made generous the Saracenic psychology of scimitar. To Carnelevari, bluntness and breadth were symbols of constriction to reveal, to open out the minor tangles of the soul. The palazzo Abbatelli is particularly beautiful. The main door (*Plate LXI*, 2) suggests that now the scimitar is a pipe, a conduit shape, not in the northern sense of Gothic shrieking organ shafts, but sensitive, elastic as rope, close-knit as that fibre. Carnelevari's masterpiece is the church of Santa Maria della Catena (*Plate LXI*, 1). The Quattro Cento appeal of it is blank, impersonal, because the traditions here embodied were hardly those in which Quattro Cento expression can be voluble; yet only as Quattro Cento should such mass be reckoned. It is curious to witness Saracenic lace-work figuring in effects of instant depth. Features of the interior are the sharply cut angles of the pillar's high pedestals along the aisle, the strange cuneiform projections with which those of the chancel are reinforced, and the tortoise-feet of the pillar shafts.

XII. *Some carving at Siena*

The derided[1] sculptor Urbano da Cortona who worked for Donatello at Padua, belongs to the Quattro Cento. At Siena he adapted Federighi's incrustation to virulent motions learned from Donatello. Urbano's tomb in San Francesco for Cristoforo Felici shows this double richness (*Plate IV*). Recumbent and close the effigy, but the legs of the flying putti upon the frieze go wide as if in water. Rich garlands and their masks hedge the commotion, while above are fan-like shells each set in an undulation. The cella for the effigy has an exaggerated

[1]Venturi always writes of Urbano as a 'povero tagliapietra', as an inept and god-forsaken stone-mason.

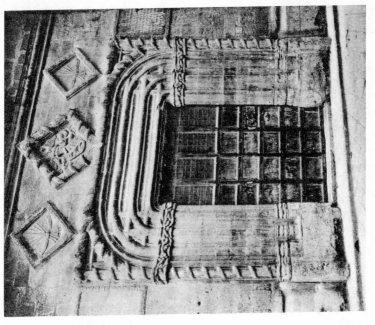

1. *Palermo, S. M. della Catena*: Matteo Carnelevari.   2. *Palermo, palazzo Abbatelli*: Matteo Carnelevari: *Doorway.*

PLATE LXI. 'UPON SARACENIC LACE-WORK WAS THE IMPOSITION'
A QUATTRO CENTO GOTHIC STYLE IN PALERMO

2. Brescia, chiesa del Carmine : Entrance : Detail.

1. Brescia, San Pietro : Doorway.

PLATE LXII. LITTLE KNOWN QUATTRO CENTO DOORWAYS

perspective. Over this forcing of depth the putti emerge rampant. Effect of mass comes from so compendious an order of sentiment.

So we will regret the destruction of Urbano's Madonna delle Grazie chapel in the cathedral.[1] I have mentioned that the stone bench on the left in the loggia della Mercanza is attributed to Urbano;[2] to which may be added the Quattro Cento Madonna and child plaque in San Francesco.

Giacomo Cozzarelli and others spread Francesco di Giorgio's architecture in Siena.[3] Sculpture, though, loses all tension. Magnetism fails. Ornament is 'stuck on', crowded and large; complicated but no longer exuberant. Neroccio Landi and Giovanni di Stefano fail as sculptors. Giuliano Turapilli, the so-called Siennese Pollaiuolo, created nothing precious. In spite of Baroque ingenuity his work is dull. Equally dull is the work of Lorenzo di Mariano (Il Marrina). His entrance decoration to the Piccolomini library in the cathedral, where each ingenious ornament appears 'stuck on' (*Plate LVI*, 4), should be compared unfavourably with Federighi's holy-water basin close by, or with his entrance further along to the San Giovanni chapel (*Plate XXXVII*, 2), or with the font within—all works in which incrustation is rife.

XIII. *At Brescia*

The Quattro Cento enthusiast will visit Brescia. He will seek out San Pietro on the castle hill for its doorway of Veronese-Brescian marble (*Plate LXII*, 1). Another fine Quattro

[1] A few remains of the chapel are in the Opera del Duomo.

[2] *See* Paul Schubring, *Urbano da Cortona*. Strassbourg, 1903. Also *Die Plastik Sienas im Quattrocento*. Berlin, 1907. Schubring attributes the beautiful marble Virgin and child within an *edicoletta*, at the Ducal palace, Urbino, to Giovanni di Stefano. Because of the static and bossy reduplication in the architecture of this piece, I feel that Adolfo Venturi's attribution to Francesco Laurana is nearer the mark.

[3] *See*, for instance, the palazzo del Magnifico and doorways at the Osservanza convent.

Cento doorway in a rougher style, squat with the compactness of flower tension, is the doorway of Santa Maria del Carmine (*Plate LXII*, 2). The putti are big, non-precious, the arabesques figuring birds pecking from lily-cups, transitional from Gothic. The Church of Santo Cristo has a Quattro Cento doorway; but not so Santa Maria delle Grazie, the Amadeoesque medallions of which should be contrasted with the large and ropy virility of the transitional decoration at the Carmine. In the Duomo Vecchio, in the wall as you mount the stairs on the right, there's a Quattro Cento tomb dated 1478. The Monte di Pietà in the piazza della Loggia belongs to Venetian Quattro Cento.

XIV. *At Verona*

The structure of Verona marble, when sculpted, entails round forms. When the stone is used in blocks for building, it suggests the resilience of bamboo. Any archway in this stone seems to possess something Gothic or plumed, because the resilient spring of such an arch evokes the Veronese twisted cables that are so common a Gothic decoration in Venice. Glance at the sixteenth-century plain oblong doorway in the cathedral piazza, Verona, or at the classical arch (1810) of the third altar on the left in San Tomaso. You will experience an ulterior sensation of Gothic in circumstances the most inappropriate. Jointures of the stone are not visible, curve of the arch suggests a snapping point. Incidentally, Verona was famous through the fifteenth century for its workers in wood led by the Giolfino clan. The continuity of grain in Verona marble always suggests the live shoot. And it is because such fantasies of blossom attend one in Verona that I have headed the essay with her name.

I admit that Verona was poor in native sculptors during the fifteenth century. On the other hand, large and helmetted Gothic, the forms that Verona marble always suggest, inspired Pasti's elephantine shapes at the Tempio. The cry of Florence for elegance in the fifteenth century no doubt confused the Veronese sculptors. The Scala had lost their city. Verona was in pawn, nor yet accustomed to Venetian rule. But Verona Gothic was still a power. The Florentine Nanni di Bartolo came to Verona in the'twenties of the fifteenth century and made two monuments[1] in which he shows he succumbed to the native Gothic, though retaining a Florentine sense of design, of a problem and its solution, possible only among Florentines at so early a date. The monuments are that of the Brenzoni family in San Fermo (*Plate LIX*, 2) and Cortesia Sarego's tomb in Sant' Anastasia. The rollicking foliage about the latter, a development of the Cavalli chapel decoration of the previous century, appears also in the Tempio.

The Brenzoni monument[2] was accomplished by a Florentine command in design clarifying a Veneto style. But so fractious were these together that the design approaches the extreme compulsions exercised by a Baroque ruling. At any rate the clarity attained, the open arrest of so much rough style, causes surprise. For here is a pause in the complications of transitional style, of the passing from Gothic to full Renaissance: a Quattro Cento intensity opened out for us.

Later Il Rosso (so he was called) probably went on to Venice. Another and later Florentine, pupil of Donatello, who threw in his lot with Venice, was Niccolo Fiorentino. He worked chiefly in Dalmatia. These and other Florentines, of course, were the means by which the Florentine æsthetic grasp was spread in northern Italy, an influence that was so essential to the development of Quattro Cento aim. In this respect the Florentine sculptor Niccolo Baroncelli, who was working in Padua between 1434 and 1442, is particularly important.[3] Yet

[1]The second cannot be attributed to Nanni di Bartolo with any certainty.

[2]An Annunciation painted by Pisanello is seen in the spandrels.

[3]*Cf*. the newly discovered documents showing how extensive were the activities of Florentine artists in the early fifteenth century at Padua. E. Rigoni published these documents in *Archivio Veneto*, Vol. VI, 1929. Baroncelli also worked frequently in Ferrara.

the Quattro Cento decoration attributed to him on the Eremitani side door reflects the art which he encountered in the Veneto.

At Verona, the Gothic door of San Lorenzo is the most Quattro Cento. It was built some time between 1460 and 1476 when Ermolao Barbaro was episcopal vicar. The sculptors of doorways with arabesques of which there are a great number, were Lombards, such as Pietro da Porlezza, Domenico da Lugo, Matteo and Bernardino Panteo. Their relief is generally hard and crowded, often with trophies that are cut away in sixteenth century style. Many of the reliefs, those the more inert, do indeed date from the sixteenth century. The best, the most Quattro Cento, are the two displayed in the museum. In the streets, the most attractive is the doorway surmounted by dolphins of the Albergo Accademia in the via Mazzini. The Church of Sant'Anastasia has three vivid arabesque archways at the entrance to the first three chapels on the right, and again in the cathedral the first three chapels on the right have similar archways, though the second and third ones belong to the first decade of the sixteenth century.

Gothic overshadows in Verona. Even Roman archways have a Gothic fierceness: and decorations on the Roman Porta dei Borsari has been the model for these arabesques.

I have reserved until the end the finest of all Quattro Cento incrustation effects. In the church of Sant' Anastasia, on the inside of the entrance arch to the small chapel on the right, just before the transept (capella del Crocefisso or del Jesù), there are sculpted two candelabra reliefs, the one figuring sea-horses, the other sea-bulls (*Plate LXIV*). They have been little noticed. The Victoria and Albert museum possesses a Victorian photograph of one of the reliefs the date of which is given as 1585. They are at least a hundred years older. Archives show that the decorating of this chapel[1] was ordered by the will of

---

[1]Cipolla in *Ricerche storiche intorno alla chiesa di Sant' Anastasia* (*see* L'Arte, 1913 and 1914) suggests that this chapel was originally the nucleus of an Arian church.

Rome, St. Peter's. Filarete : *Detail of bronze doors.*

PLATE LXIII. QUATTRO CENTO BRONZE ARABESQUE

Verona, Sant' Anastasia. Pietro da Porlezza?: *Decoration on entrance
to the capella del Jesù.*

PLATE LXIV. A QUATTRO CENTO MARBLE ARABESQUE

Francesco Pellegrini in 1458. Probably Pietro da Porlezza was the sculptor. Like many other Lombard sculptors he came from the shore of Lake Como. The Lombard technique of undercutting—notice how the fins which overlap a rim of the candelabra, and the flukes, are cut away razor-sharp—here serves Quattro Cento feeling.

At the end of so much analysis of Quattro Cento effect I find it unnecessary to describe the relief and the intricacy of its composition; although the only work known to me in any way parallel is decoration on the fragments of the Tarchetta *edicola* in the archeological museum at Milan.[1]

But I would end this book speaking of marble. For once more, nature of the stone is the key to the understanding of the Sant'Anastasia achievement. The reliefs are of the same ivory-grey Verona marble that was procured for the Tempio with such difficulty, and upon which Agostino di Duccio carved his greatest reliefs, those of the planets. This Verona is hard, can be cut to a fine point. It is neither bright nor dull. No other marble is as luminous. Forms sculpted there are distinct yet suffused. The parallel is to objects seen in moonlight and to the curious magnetism of the moon mingling sea and earth.

Even pavements in Verona are marble, not this ivory-grey but the common fiery kind. But now the shapeless alps shoot up. . . . London pavements lie barren, or glistening dead in rain.

Was it an insult to show that in the South stone is life-giving? I am ready to apologize. For even the lovely Gloucestershire limestones can appear barren and sinister, even in that county of beautiful stone-construction. You will need to look over hills at one level and among shapely evergreen, to dis-

[1]There is another possible parallel. This is the extraordinary Quattro Cento carving on the door to the tower of San Niccolo at Collescopoli (a village on a hill near Narni). I hope to reproduce a photograph of this door in the second volume.

cover a world of space alone. To the eye trained in Italy, perspective of the English scene appears distorted. Some things loom, others glitter. This is true of all lights and of every object-arrangement. And since perspective science grew up in the South, I feel I can give my impression which can only be conveyed by saying that in England and in the North and East generally, no proper perspective is ever apparent.

I have written, not only for unfortunate northerners who love the South, but also for those who love the North passionately, so that they might know the essence that is foreign and dangerous to their art. Or do we all need light in place of lighting . . . must we always turn South?

GENERAL INDEX

Works mentioned in the text as 'Quattro Cento' are not in most cases included in the general index—they will be found indexed separately under place names, in the 'Index of Architecture and Sculpture described in the book as ' Quattro Cento ' '.

INDEX OF ARCHITECTURE AND SCULPTURE
DESCRIBED IN THE BOOK AS 'QUATTRO CENTO'

Entries will be found under place names.